D1565294

BY THESE WORDS

BY THESE WORDS

Great Documents of American Liberty, Selected and Placed in Their Contemporary Settings

By PAUL M. ANGLE

Illustrated by Edward A. Wilson

RAND McNALLY & COMPANY
NEW YORK CHICAGO SAN FRANCISCO

PRINTED IN THE UNITED STATES OF AMERICA

Acknowledgments

To Willard L. King and John S. Miller, both of the Chicago bar, and to Richard W. Leopold and Clarence Ver Steeg, both professors of history, Northwestern University, for invaluable criticism; to Miss Margaret Scriven, Librarian of the Chicago Historical Society, for a typist's performance that included incisive comments as to style; and to Miss Winifred Vernooy and the staff of the University of Chicago Library for the kind of library service that arouses one's lasting gratitude.

To Harper & Brothers for the quotation on page 16, from *Colonial Self-Government*, by C. M. Andrews, 1904.

To Little, Brown & Company for the quotation on page 227, from *Supreme Court in United States History*, by Charles Warren, 1922.

To John C. Winston Company for the quotation on page 227, from "Roger B. Taney," in *Great Lawyers*, IV, 1905.

To Samuel Klaus for the quotation on page 278, from his book *The Milligan Case*, published by Alfred A. Knopf, Incorporated, 1929.

To Charles Scribner's Sons for the quotation on page 305, from the *Dictionary of American History*, edited by James Truslow Adams, 1940; and for the quotation on page 344, from *Mr. Justice Holmes*, by Francis Biddle, 1942.

To Doubleday & Company, Inc., for the quotation on page 331, from *Woodrow Wilson: Life and Letters*, by Ray Stannard Baker, 1927.

To Houghton Mifflin Company for the quotation on pages 383–84, from *The Second World War*, Vol. III: *The Grand Alliance*, by Winston Churchill, 1950.

P.M.A.

A Note to the Reader

The documents in this book cover more than three centuries. In that period spelling, punctuation, and paragraphing have changed greatly. In many instances the retention of the original form would have raised a barrier between reader and text without serving any useful purpose. Therefore, spelling and capitalization have been made to conform to modern practice, and punctuation has been revised where necessary to achieve clarity and readability.

The reader interested in an exact transcript of the document, faithful in every comma and archaic spelling, and in the complete text of all those that have been shortened, is referred to the sources listed on pages 409–414.

CONTENTS

---

*The asterisk indicates that the complete text of the document is given here.

INTRODUCTION

The word "document" has many meanings. It may stand for papers in an old desk drawer—a canceled mortgage, deeds long since recorded, an ancient military commission or discharge. It may, in fact, mean almost any piece of paper. It may represent the published proceedings of governmental bodies ranging from a village school board to the Houses of Congress. And it may signify the charters, compacts, proclamations, and pronouncements that have marked almost every step in the progress of the American people from the beginning of their history to the present. It is in this last sense that the word is used on the title page of this book.

So defined, the document has no isolated existence. It is both result and cause. The Constitution, for example, sprang from experience under the Articles of Confederation, and the Constitution has determined the course of the nation ever since its adoption.

Let us admit that the document is often something less than

exciting reading. But what about the situation that gave rise to it? The Mayflower Compact should be read in the light of the events that led up to it—the perilous voyage across the Atlantic, the failure of the Pilgrims to reach their expected destination, their consternation at the irrelevance of the charter with which they had equipped themselves. The Ordinance of 1787 is a noble statute, but unless a reader has some notion of the vast territory to which it was intended to apply, and some notion, also, of the ambitions of the men who hoped to occupy that territory, it remains little more than words. Taney's opinion in the Merryman case has not come down in history as a literary classic, but one who can relive that gray day in the spring of 1861, and see the aged Chief Justice risk, as he thought, his own freedom in defense of a greater freedom, may find that dry legalities can make high drama.

In this book an attempt has been made to portray the settings of certain great American documents in such a way that the documents themselves will have more meaning for a reader than they would if they were offered with only the customary factual introductions. Such an effort takes space, and therefore limits the number that can be presented. The choice, in this instance, has fallen upon those that exemplify two themes that have distinguished American history from the beginning: the growth of democratic government, and the evolution and defense of individual liberty.

Even here selection has been necessary, for to have printed all American documents bearing on these twin trends would have been to expand this book beyond reasonable limit. In this profusion of material an American can take pride, yet the mere fact that documents of this kind exist in such numbers warns, with Goethe, that

> The last result of wisdom stamps it true:
> He only earns his freedom and existence,
> Who daily conquers them anew.

One further limitation should be noted: the choice has been restricted to official documents and those which, like John Brown's last speech, originated in an official context.

P.M.A.

BY THESE WORDS

By these words a people established a nation, maintained a republic, and demonstrated to the world that men could govern themselves . . . in dignity, harmony, freedom.

THE PILGRIMS SAIL
FROM DELFSHAVEN

THE PILGRIMS DECIDE TO GOVERN THEMSELVES

1620

The tide was right, the wind fair. The departure of the ship the English Pilgrims hoped would take them to a permanent haven in the New World could not be delayed. For eleven years, unwelcome in their own land, they had lived among the friendly Dutch of Leiden. Now they were sailing from the nearby port of Delfshaven. Not all could go, so those who were to remain gathered on the deck to say farewell. Kneeling, their cheeks wet with tears, the Englishmen heard their pastor ask God's blessing. As they embraced each other, many for the last time, the stolid Hollanders who looked on in curiosity found their own eyes dim. But, in the words of William Bradford, one of their leaders, "they knew they were pilgrimes, and looked not much on those things, but lift up their eyes to the heavens, their dearest countrie, and quieted their spirits."

Thus began the journey that was to end off the coast of Cape Cod on a gray fall day in 1620. The Pilgrims had left Delfshaven in a small ship, the *Speedwell.* At Plymouth, England, where they took into their group a number of Londoners more concerned with finding fortune than the peace of God, the *Speedwell* was joined by the *Mayflower*, a three-masted, double-decked merchant ship of

180 tons. Soon after heading into the Atlantic, the *Speedwell* proved unseaworthy, and turned back. The larger ship continued alone.

The *Mayflower's* destination was Virginia, but when her master hove to, on the ninth day of November, off a bleak and sandy shore, he knew that he had made land hundreds of miles too far north. Although the season was far advanced, he pointed the ship's bow to the south. Along the shore, waves foamed in angry breakers, while at what should have been a safe distance, he found one treacherous shoal after another. The next day, with the consent of his passengers, he turned back. On the eleventh the *Mayflower* dropped anchor in what is now the harbor of Provincetown. New England, rather than Virginia, would be the home of the Pilgrim colony.

Before leaving the Old World the Pilgrim leaders had obtained a patent that gave them the power to establish their own government. The patent, however, had no standing outside the limits of Virginia. Some of the Londoners, aware of that fact, now boasted that when they went ashore, they would do as they pleased, or, as William Bradford put it, "they would use their own libertie, for none had power to command them." Knowing that only chaos and disaster could result from the lack of rules for the common good, the Pilgrim leaders determined that no one should leave the ship until some basis of government had been decided upon.

One can imagine the scene as they gathered in the cabin of the *Mayflower*, smoky and rank from the flickering wick of its fish-oil lamp. In the dim light sat William Brewster, spiritual leader of the Plymouth brethren; John Carver, soon to become the first governor of the colony; William Bradford, wise beyond his thirty-one years; Miles Standish the soldier, plump, sturdy, as short in temper as in stature; John Alden, the tall, blond, blue-eyed cooper—all sober, godly men, well aware that in this uninhabited land, thousands of miles from their mother country, they could rely on none but themselves. Many of them knew the covenants by which their congregations—"independent" of the Church of England—were regulated. These they took as their model. The document they drew up we call the Mayflower Compact.

The Mayflower Compact

November 11, 1620

In the name of God, Amen. We, whose names are underwritten, the loyal subjects of our dread Sovereign Lord King James, by the grace of God, of Great Britain, France, and Ireland, King, Defender of the Faith, etc., having undertaken, for the glory of God, and advancement of the Christian faith, and honor of our King and country, a voyage to plant the first colony in the northern parts of Virginia, do by these presents, solemnly and mutually in the presence of God, and of one another, covenant and combine ourselves together into a civil body politic, for our better ordering and preservation and furtherance of the ends aforesaid; and by virtue hereof to enact, constitute, and frame such just and equal laws, ordinances, acts, constitutions, and offices, from time to time, as shall be thought most meet and convenient for the general good of the colony, unto which we promise all due submission and obedience.

In witness whereof we have hereunto subscribed our names at Cape Cod the eleventh of November, in the reign of our Sovereign Lord, King James of England, France, and Ireland the eighteenth, and of Scotland the fifty-fourth. *Anno Domini*, 1620.

John Carver
William Bradford
Edward Winslow
William Brewster
Isaac Allerton
Miles Standish
John Alden
John Turner
Francis Eaton
Stephen Hopkins
Digery Priest
Thomas Williams
Gilbert Winslow
Edmund Margesson
Peter Brown
Richard Bitteridge
George Soule
Edward Tilly
James Chilton
John Craxton
John Billington

Joses Fletcher
John Goodman
Samuel Fuller
Christopher Martin
William Mullins
William White
Richard Warren
John Howland
John Tilly
Francis Cooke
Thomas Rogers
Thomas Tinker
John Ridgdale
Edward Fuller
Richard Clark
Richard Gardiner
Mr. John Allerton
Thomas English
Edward Doten
Edward Liester

THE CONNECTICUT TOWNS ADOPT DEMOCRACY

1639

Each infant settlement on the Atlantic seaboard quickly became a magnet to discontented Englishmen. Despite the dangers of the long voyage, regardless of the hardships that they would certainly encounter, they migrated to New England by the thousands. Plymouth —the settlement of the Pilgrims—and the larger colony of Massachusetts Bay to the west and north, became crowded. To the westward, the fertile valley of the Connecticut River extended a beguiling invitation. In 1635 and 1636 three venturesome groups, spurred principally, in their own quaint words, by "the strong bent of their spirits to remove thither," broke the bounds of the older colonies and founded the towns of Windsor, Hartford, and Wethersfield.

In the beginning, the Connecticut settlers lived under a loose government established by agreement with Massachusetts, but after a year or two they decided to take control of their own affairs. The leader in the movement for self-government was Thomas

Hooker, Cambridge graduate and Puritan clergyman who had emigrated from England to Massachusetts in 1633.

A stanch democrat, Hooker had been repelled by the autocratic atmosphere that already marked Massachusetts, and determined that all the people, rather than the elect of the Congregational churches, should rule in the Connecticut towns. In the spring of 1638, while there was much talk of the form of government to be adopted, he preached a sermon in which he laid down basic principles. "The choice of public magistrates," he asserted, "belongs unto the people by God's own allowance. . . . . They who have the power to appoint officers and magistrates" also have the power "to set the bounds of the power and place unto which they call them."

The Fundamental Orders of Connecticut, adopted by the freemen of the three towns in January, 1639, rest on Hooker's principles of democracy. The Orders include specific provisions for choosing representatives of the freemen, electing a governor and magistrates, limiting their terms of office, and ensuring equitable representation and taxation. The document is equally noteworthy because it was the first written constitution to create a government, not merely in America, but anywhere. With some additions and changes embodied in a royal charter granted in 1662, the Fundamental Orders remained the basis of Connecticut's government until 1818.

The Fundamental Orders of Connecticut

January 14, 1639

Forasmuch as it hath pleased the Almighty God by the wise disposition of His divine providence so to order and dispose of things that we the inhabitants and residents of Windsor, Hartford, and Wethersfield are now cohabiting and dwelling in and upon the river of Connecticut and the lands thereunto adjoining; and well knowing where a people are gathered together the word of

God requires that to maintain the peace and union of such a people there should be an orderly and decent government established according to God, to order and dispose of the affairs of the people at all seasons as occasion shall require; do therefore associate and conjoin ourselves to be as one public state or commonwealth; and do, for ourselves and our successors and such as shall be adjoined to us at any time hereafter, enter into combination and confederation together, to maintain and preserve the liberty and purity of the gospel of our Lord Jesus which we now profess, as also the discipline of the churches, which according to the truth of the said gospel is now practiced amongst us; as also in our civil affairs to be guided and governed according to such laws, rules, orders, and decrees as shall be made, ordered, and decreed, as followeth:

1. It is ordered that there shall be yearly two general assemblies or courts, the one the second Thursday in April, the other the second Thursday in September, following; the first shall be called the court of election, wherein shall be yearly chosen . . . . so many magistrates and other public officers as shall be found requisite: whereof one to be chosen governor for the year ensuing and until another be chosen, and no other magistrate to be chosen for more than one year; provided always there be six chosen beside the governor; which being chosen and sworn according to an oath recorded for that purpose shall have power to administer justice according to the laws here established, and for want thereof according to the rule of the word of God; which choice shall be made by all that are admitted freemen and have taken the oath of fidelity, and do cohabit within this jurisdiction (having been admitted inhabitants by the major part of the town wherein they live), or the major part of such as shall be then present. . . . .

4. It is ordered that no person be chosen governor above once in two years, and that the governor be always a member of some approved congregation, and formerly of the magistracy within this jurisdiction; and all the magistrates freemen of this commonwealth. . . . .

5. It is ordered that to the aforesaid court of election the several towns shall send their deputies; and when the elections are ended, they may proceed in any public service as at other courts. Also the other general court in September shall be for making of laws, and

any other public occasion which concerns the good of the commonwealth. . . . .

7. It is ordered that after there are warrants given out for any of the said general courts, the constable . . . . of each town shall forthwith give notice distinctly to the inhabitants of the same . . . . that at a place and time by him or them limited and set, they meet and assemble themselves together to elect and choose certain deputies to be at the general court then following to agitate the

affairs of the commonwealth; which said deputies shall be chosen by all that are admitted inhabitants in the several towns and have taken the oath of fidelity; provided that none be chosen a deputy for any general court which is not a freeman of this commonwealth. . . . .

8. It is ordered that Windsor, Hartford, and Wethersfield shall have power, each town, to send four of their freemen as deputies to every general court; and whatsoever other towns shall be hereafter added to this jurisdiction, they shall send so many deputies as the court shall judge meet, a reasonable proportion to the number of freemen that are in the said towns being to be attended therein; which deputies shall have the power of the whole town to give their votes and allowance to all such laws and orders as may be for the public good, and unto which the said towns are to be bound.

9. It is ordered that the deputies thus chosen shall have power and liberty to appoint a time and a place of meeting together before any general court to advise and consult of all such things as may

concern the good of the public, as also to examine their own elections. . . .

10. It is ordered that every general court . . . . shall consist of the governor, or some one chosen to moderate the court, and four other magistrates at least, with the major part of the deputies of the several towns legally chosen; and in case the freemen or major part of them, through neglect or refusal of the governor and major part of the magistrates, shall call a court, it shall consist of the major part of freemen that are present, or their deputies, with a moderator chosen by them: in which said general courts shall consist the supreme power of the commonwealth, and they only shall have power to make laws or repeal them, to grant levies, to admit of freemen, dispose of lands undisposed of to several towns or persons; and also shall have power to call either court or magistrate or any other person whatsoever into question for any misdemeanor; and may for just causes displace or deal otherwise according to the nature of the offense; and also may deal in any other matter that concerns the good of this commonwealth, except election of magistrates, which shall be done by the whole body of freemen.

In which court the governor or moderator shall have power to order the court to give liberty of speech and [to] silence unseasonable and disorderly speakings, to put all things to vote, and in case the vote be equal to have the casting voice. But none of these courts shall be adjourned or dissolved without the consent of the major part of the court.

11. It is ordered that when any general court upon the occasions of the commonwealth have agreed upon any sum or sums of money to be levied upon the several towns within this jurisdiction, that a committee be chosen to set out and appoint what shall be the proportion of every town to pay of the said levy, provided the committees be made up of an equal number out of each town.

ROGER WILLIAMS: LIBERTY IS NOT LICENSE

1655

Many a young Englishman must have envied Roger Williams. Born in London of prosperous parents, he had a "natural inclination to study," and at an early age attracted the attention of Sir Edward Coke, the great English jurist and political leader. Coke saw that the boy attended the Charterhouse School, and later, Cambridge, where he distinguished himself by winning one of the undergraduate honors. After graduating, Williams took holy orders and began a career as a priest of the Anglican Church. Intelligent, well-educated, handsome, charming to both men and women, he seemed to have an assured future.

But Roger Williams had an eager, questing mind which had already endowed him with a set of unpopular opinions. Convinced that there should be no connection between church and state, he became a Separatist and withdrew from the Established Church. In 1629, when he was twenty-six years of age, he received a pastoral call from New England. Late in the following year he turned his back on the land of his birth and took ship, with his wife, for Massachusetts.

Though welcomed as "a godly minister," Williams soon discovered that the Puritan system in Boston left no room for a nonconformist. He lived for a time at Plymouth and then at Salem where, in spite of the opposition of the authorities of the province, he was given charge of the church. By leading a movement for more democratic church government, he aroused the active enmity of the other ministers and the magistrates. In the fall of 1635 the General Court banished him from the colony.

In mid-winter Williams made his way to a settlement of friendly Indians at the head of Narragansett Bay. There, in the following spring, he founded the town of Providence. Other settlements—at

Portsmouth, Newport, and Warwick—marked the beginning of Rhode Island.

The Rhode Island towns, and Providence in particular, practiced the principles by which Williams guided his own life. These he proclaimed in one tract after another. The people, he held, were the ultimate source of political power, and could choose whatever form of government they wanted and limit its powers as they saw fit. Church and state should be completely independent, and every man had a right to believe and worship as his conscience dictated.

In holding to these beliefs, and founding a state upon them, Roger Williams was far ahead of his time. To his contemporaries the freedoms he expounded meant license to do as one chose, and there were settlers in the Rhode Island towns who acted upon this interpretation. One of these, in Providence, circulated a paper in which he contended that since all men were equal before Christ, it was contrary to the gospel to punish offenders against either individuals or the general welfare. To this argument Williams, then President of the Town of Providence, replied with a public letter that is a masterly exposition of the difference between liberty and license.

Letter to the Townsmen of Providence

January 1655

That ever I should speak or write a tittle that tends to such an infinite liberty of conscience is a mistake, and which I have ever disclaimed and abhorred. To prevent such mistakes, I shall at present only propose this case:

There goes many a ship to sea, with many hundred souls in one ship, whose weal and woe is common, and is a true picture of a commonwealth, or a human combination or society. It hath fallen out sometimes that both papists and protestants, Jews and Turks, may be embarked in one ship; upon which supposal I affirm, that all the liberty of conscience, that I ever pleaded for, turns upon these two hinges–that none of the papists, protestants, Jews, or Turks be forced to come to the ship's prayers or worship, nor compelled from their own particular prayers or worship, if they practice any. I further add, that I never denied, that notwithstanding this liberty, the commander of this ship ought to command the ship's course, yea, and also command that justice, peace, and sobriety be kept and practiced, both among the seamen and all the passengers.

If any of the seamen refuse to perform their services, or passengers to pay their freight; if any refuse to help, in person or purse, toward the common charges or defense; if any refuse to obey the common laws and orders of the ship, concerning their common peace or preservation; if any shall mutiny and rise up against their commanders and officers; if any should preach or write that there ought to be no commanders or officers, because all are equal in Christ, therefore no masters nor officers, no laws nor orders, nor corrections nor punishments–I say, I never denied, but in such cases, whatever is pretended, the commander or commanders may judge, resist, compel, and punish such transgressors, according to their deserts and merits.

This if seriously and honestly minded, may, if it so please the Father of lights, let in some light to such as willingly shut not their eyes.

I remain studious of your common peace and liberty.

Roger Williams

WILLIAM PENN GRANTS A FREEMAN'S GOVERNMENT

1675

If William Penn had been a docile young man, the growth of democratic government in America might have been less rapid than it was. Early in his life the son of Admiral Sir William Penn showed strong religious leanings. Those leanings, moreover, took the direction of Puritanism. As a student at Oxford, young Penn became such an outspoken nonconformist that his college expelled him. The Admiral, chagrined, prescribed a continental tour in the hope that the young man would become more worldly. For a time the prescription appeared to work; but after a few months the son enrolled at the Huguenot Academy at Saumur in western France. There, in two years, he found strong support for the unorthodox convictions he already held.

Called home by his father, Penn served briefly with the fleet, and again savored the pleasures of worldliness at the court of the Lord Lieutenant of Ireland. But not for long. A Quaker preacher stirred anew latent religious longings. Day by day Penn attended the meetings of the Friends, and as a result, soon found himself in prison. Upon his release and return to England he became an avowed Quaker. No one would have charged a man of his ample girth and beaming good nature with zealotry, yet he was not content with a passive role. With tongue and pen he preached the doctrines of peace and political liberty, suffered imprisonment for his temerity, and labored for the cause of the Friends in Holland and Germany.

Penn became interested in America almost by accident. In 1664 the Duke of York, later to be James II, had conveyed what is now New Jersey to two of his friends, Lord Berkeley and Sir George Carteret. Nine years later Berkeley sold his part of the grant, the western half, to two Quakers. As the arbiter of a dispute between the two Friends, and then as the trustee for the creditors of one of them, Penn took an active interest in the colonization of the province. Having a shipload of colonists about to depart from England, he prepared, on behalf of the proprietors, a charter of liberties and privileges, called the Concessions and Agreements of West Jersey. Into it went the convictions of a mature liberal—he was now thirty-two years of age—whose beliefs had stood the test of persecution.

Years later, in Pennsylvania, which he received by royal grant in 1681, William Penn would elaborate the principles of religious toleration, equality before the law, and government by the consent of the governed in a series of Frames of Government and in the final (1701) Charter of Privileges, under which the colony lived until 1776. The Concessions and Agreements of West Jersey, however, antedated all the Pennsylvania charters. A long document, it deals in considerable part with the division and apportionment of the land and with the organic framework of government. We give here only those provisions that led C. M. Andrews, an authority on colonial government, to characterize it as "the broadest, sanest, and most equitable charter draughted for any body of colonists up to this time."

The Concessions and Agreements of West Jersey

March 3, 1676

We do consent and agree, as the best present expedition, that such persons as shall be from time to time deputed, nominated, and appointed commissioners by the present proprietors or the major part of them, by writing, under their hands and seals, shall be commissioners for the time being and have power to order and manage the estate and affairs of the said Province of West New Jersey, according to these our concessions hereafter following; and to depute others in their place and authority in case of death or removal;

and to continue until some other persons be deputed, nominated, and appointed by the same proprietors, or the major part of them, to succeed them in that office and service. . . .

CHAPTER XI

They [the commissioners] are not to impose or suffer to be imposed any tax, custom, or subsidy, tollage, assessment, or any other duty whatsoever, upon any color or pretense, how specious soever, upon the said province and inhabitants thereof, without their own consent first had, or other than what shall be imposed by the authority and consent of the General Assembly, and that only in manner and for the good ends and uses as aforesaid. . . .

CHAPTER XIII

That the common law or fundamental rights and privileges of West New Jersey are individually agreed upon by the proprietors and freeholders thereof to be the foundation of the government, which is not to be altered by the legislative authority or free assembly hereafter mentioned and constituted; but that the said legislative authority is constituted according to these fundamentals, to make such laws as agree with and maintain the said fundamentals, and to make no laws that in the least contradict, differ, or vary from the said fundamentals, under what pretense or allegation soever. . . .

CHAPTER XVI

That no men, nor number of men upon earth, hath power or authority to rule over men's consciences in religious matters; therefore it is consented, agreed, and ordained that no person or persons whatsoever within the said province, at any time or times hereafter, shall be any ways upon any pretense whatsoever called in question, or in the least punished or hurt, either in person, estate, or privilege, for the sake of his opinion, judgment, faith or worship toward God in matters of religion. But that all and every such person, and persons, may from time to time, and at all times, freely and fully have and enjoy his and their judgments and the exercise of their consciences in matters of religious worship throughout all the said province.

CHAPTER XVII

That no proprietor, freeholder, or inhabitant of the said Province of West New Jersey shall be deprived or condemned of life, limb, liberty, estate, property, or any ways hurt in his or their privileges, freedoms, or franchises, upon any account whatsoever, without a due trial and judgment passed by twelve good and lawful men of his neighborhood first had; and that in all causes to be tried, and in all trials, the person or persons arraigned may except against [object to] any of the said neighborhood without any reason rendered (not exceeding thirty-five), and in case of any valid reason alleged, against every person nominated for that service. . . .

CHAPTER XXII

That the trials of all causes, civil and criminal, shall be heard and decided by the verdict or judgment of twelve honest men of the neighborhood, only to be summoned and presented by the sheriff of that division, or propriety, where the fact or trespass is committed; and that no person or persons shall be compelled to fee any attorney or counselor to plead his cause, but that all persons have free liberty to plead his own cause, if he please; and that no person nor persons imprisoned upon any account whatsoever within this province shall be obliged to pay any fees to the officer or officers of the said prison, either when committed or discharged.

CHAPTER XXIII

That in all public courts of justice for trials of causes, civil or criminal, any person or persons, inhabitants of the said province, may freely come into and attend the said courts, and hear and be present at all or any such trials as shall be there had or passed, that justice may not be done in a corner nor in any covert manner; being intended and resolved, by the help of the Lord, and by these our concessions and fundamentals, that all and every person and persons inhabiting the said province shall, as far as in us lies, be free from oppression and slavery. . . .

CHAPTER XXV

It is concluded and agreed that if any of the Indian natives within the said province shall or may do any wrong or injury to any of the proprietors, freeholders, or inhabitants, in person, estate, or otherways however, upon notice thereof, or complaint made to the commissioners, or any two of them, they [the commissioners] are to give notice to the sachem, or other chief person or persons, that hath authority over the said Indian native or natives, that justice may be done and satisfaction made to the person or persons offended, according to law and equity, and the nature and quality of the offense and injury done or committed.

And also in case any of the proprietors, freeholders, or inhabitants shall any wise wrong or injure any of the Indian natives there, in person, estate, or otherwise, the commissioners are to take care upon complaint to them made, or any one of them, either by the Indian natives [or others], that justice be done to the Indian natives and plenary satisfaction made them according to the nature and quality of the offense and injury.

And that in all trials wherein any of the said Indian natives are concerned, the trial to be by six of the neighborhood and six of the said Indian natives, to be indifferently and impartially chosen by order of the commissioners, and that the commissioners use their endeavor to persuade the natives to the like way of trial; when any of the natives do any ways wrong or injure the said proprietors, freeholders, or inhabitants, that they [the commissioners] choose six of the natives and six of the freeholders or inhabitants to judge of the wrong and injury done, and to proportion satisfaction accordingly.

CHAPTER XXVI

It is agreed when any land is to be taken up for settlement of towns or otherways, before it be surveyed, the commissioners or the major part of them are to appoint some persons to go to the chief of the natives concerned in that land, so intended to be taken up, to acquaint the natives of their intention and to give the natives what present they shall agree upon for their good will or consent, and take a grant of the same in writing under their hands and seals, or some other public way used in those parts of the world; which grant is to be registered in the public register, allowing also the natives (if they please) a copy thereof; and that no person or persons take up any land but by order from the commissioners for the time being. . . . .

CHAPTER XXXII

That so soon as divisions or tribes, or other such like distinctions are made, that then the inhabitants, freeholders, and proprietors, resident upon the said province, or several and respective tribes, or divisions or distinctions aforesaid, do yearly and every year meet on the first day of October, or the eighth month, and choose one proprietor or freeholder for each respective propriety in the said province (the said province being to be divided into one hundred proprieties) to be deputies, trustees, or representatives for the benefit, service, and behoof of the people of the said province; which body of deputies, trustees, or representatives, consisting of one hundred persons, chosen as aforesaid, shall be the General, Free, and Supreme Assembly of the said province for the year ensuing and no longer. And in case any member of the said assembly during the said year shall decease or otherwise be rendered incapable of that service, that then the inhabitants of the said propriety shall elect a new member to serve in his room for the remainder of the said year.

CHAPTER XXXIII

That no person or persons who shall give, bestow, or promise directly or indirectly to the said parties electing any meat, drink, money, or money's worth, for procurement of their choice and consent, shall be capable of being elected a member of the said assembly. And if any person or persons shall be at any time corruptly elected, and sufficient proof thereof made to the said free assembly, such person or persons so electing or elected shall be reckoned incapable to choose or sit in the said assembly, or execute any other public office of trust within the said province, for the space of seven years thence next ensuing. And also that all such elections as aforesaid be not determined by the common and confused way of cries and voices, but by putting balls into balloting boxes, to be provided for that purpose, for the prevention of all partiality, and whereby every man may freely choose according to his own judgment and honest intention. . . .

CHAPTER XXXVI

That in every General Free Assembly, every respective member hath liberty of speech; that no man be interrupted when speaking;

that all questions be stated with deliberation and liberty for amendments; that it be put by the chairman, by them to be chosen, and determined by plurality of votes. Also that every member has power of entering his protest and reasons of protestations. And that if any member of such assembly shall require to have the persons' names registered, according to their yeas and noes, that it be accordingly done; and that after debates are past, and the question agreed upon, the doors of the house be set open, and the people have liberty to come in to hear and be witnesses of the votes and the inclinations of the persons voting. . . .

CHAPTER XXXVIII

That it shall be lawful for any person or persons during the session of any General Free Assembly in that province to address, remonstrate, or declare any suffering, danger, or grievance, or to propose, tender, or request any privilege, profit, or advantage to the said province, they not exceeding the number of one hundred persons.

CHAPTER XXXIX

To enact and make all such laws, acts, and constitutions as shall be necessary for the well government of the said province (and them to repeal), provided that the same be, as near as may be conveniently agreeable, to the primitive, ancient, and fundamental laws of the nation of England. Provided also, that they be not against any of these our concessions and fundamentals before or hereafter mentioned. . . .

In testimony and witness of our consent to and affirmation of these present laws, concessions, and agreements, we the proprietors, freeholders, and inhabitants of the said Province of West New Jersey, whose names are underwritten, have to the same voluntarily and freely set our hands, dated this third day of the month commonly called March, in the year of our Lord one thousand six hundred and seventy-six.

[One hundred and fifty-one names follow.]

PETER ZENGER FIGHTS FOR FREEDOM OF THE PRESS

1735

Appointed Governor of the Royal Province of New York in the summer of 1732, William Cosby lost no time in making himself unpopular. A man of limited intelligence, imperfect education, and no prudence whatever, he had more than his share of greed, pomposity, and bad temper. By a grasping effort to deprive his predecessor of his share of the rewards of the office, Cosby won the contempt of a large proportion of the inhabitants. Contempt changed to bitter antagonism when the Governor refused to grant lands to settlers unless he received a share himself, oppressed the Quakers, and arbitrarily dismissed the Chief Justice of the Supreme Court. Within a few months Cosby's only supporters were the provincial officers and a number of other favored colonists who profited by his patronage.

Yet the popular party—a large majority of New York's ten thousand inhabitants—had no way of expressing their discontent. The proprietor of the only newspaper—the *New York Weekly Gazette*—was also the public printer, and would admit no criticism of the Governor to his columns. The leaders of the opposition decided to establish a paper of their own. For a dozen years John Peter Zenger had been scraping a lean living from a small print shop; now he was induced to establish the *New York Weekly Journal.* Zenger,

born in the Palatinate, was not too sure of English grammar and spelling, but his supporters supplied him with articles holding Cosby and the court party up to ridicule. New Yorkers read the *Journal,* sometimes in such numbers that extra editions had to be run off.

The Governor writhed. Twice he persuaded the Chief Justice to ask grand juries to indict Zenger for libel, but they refused. As a last resort the Governor's Council issued a warrant for Zenger's arrest—an act of doubtful legality—on the ground that he had published "seditious libels" which tended to raise "factions and tumults" among the people and to inflame their minds "with contempt of His Majesty's government." Failing to raise the excessive bail set by the court, Zenger remained in jail. While he was there, the Attorney General charged him by information (a method of instituting a criminal proceeding without an indictment) with having printed articles that were "false, scandalous, malicious, and seditious."

Zenger's attorneys, two prominent members of the popular party, began their defense by challenging the legality of the commissions of the two judges who composed the court. The judges retaliated by disbarring the attorneys, thus preventing them from representing Zenger at the trial. Having no confidence in the young lawyer whom the court had appointed to defend their client, Zenger's original lawyers quietly appealed to Andrew Hamilton of Philadelphia, reputed to be the ablest advocate in the colonies, to take the case. Hamilton accepted.

The judges, clad in black robes and heavy wigs, took their seats on the morning of August 4, 1735. The little courtroom was crowded to the limit, for the people of the province saw this case as the last stand against an arbitrary and oppressive administration. When Hamilton appeared, the members of the court party lost some of their aplomb. Although racked by gout and no longer young, his fine mind was vigorous as ever and his powers of persuasion known and feared.

As soon as the jury was chosen, the Attorney General opened the case by reading the information. Hamilton readily admitted that what Zenger had printed was libelous if false, but contended that the prosecution had to prove it to be false. The Attorney General, on the other hand, took the position that truth was no defense. Any statements, he asserted, that were "scandalous, seditious," and of a tendency "to disquiet the minds of the people" were libelous, even though true. Truth, in fact, made a libel the more malicious. This was the accepted law of England at the time, and the Chief Justice indicated plainly that he inclined to the prosecution's view of the case.

Hamilton's only hope was to convince the jury that this interpretation led inevitably to tyranny. His argument was lengthy, but the selection given below contains its essence.

The jury deliberated for only a few minutes before it brought in a verdict of not guilty. "Upon which," Zenger himself wrote, "there were three huzzas in the hall." The next day he was discharged.

On the night of the trial the popular party toasted Hamilton at the Black Horse Tavern. When he left for Philadelphia the following morning, ships lying in the harbor honored him with salutes.

A month later the Common Council voted him the freedom of the city, symbolized by a seal encased in a gold box purchased by public subscription.

After more than two centuries the freedom of the press has not been established beyond attack and dispute, but the gouty lawyer of Philadelphia still holds the honor of the first great victory over repression.

Andrew Hamilton's Argument

August 4, 1735

I beg leave to insist that the right of complaining or remonstrating is natural; and the restraint upon this natural right is the law only, and that those restraints can only extend to what is false; for as it is truth alone which can excuse or justify any man for complaining of a bad administration, I as frankly agree that nothing ought to excuse a man who raises a false charge or accusation, even against a private person, and that no manner of allowance ought to be made to him who does so against a public magistrate.

Truth ought to govern the whole affair of libels, and yet the party accused runs risk enough even then; for if he fails of proving every tittle of what he has wrote, and to the satisfaction of the court and jury too, he may find to his cost that when the prosecution is set on foot by men in power, it seldom wants friends to favor it. And from thence (it is said) has arisen the great diversity of opinions among judges about what words were or were not scandalous or libelous. I believe it will be granted that there is not greater uncertainty in any part of the law than about words of scandal; it would be misspending of the court's time to mention the cases, they may be said to be numberless; and therefore the uttermost care ought to be taken in following precedents. . . .

If . . . . there is so great an uncertainty among judges (learned and great men) in matters of this kind; if power has had so great an influence on judges, how cautious ought we to be in determining by their judgments, especially in the plantations, and in the case of libels? There is heresy in law, as well as in religion, and both have changed very much; and we well know that it is not two centuries ago that a man would have been burnt as an heretic for owning such opinions in matters of religion as are publicly wrote and printed at this day. They were fallible men, it seems, and we take the liberty not only to differ from them in religious opinion, but to condemn them and their opinions too; and I must presume that, in taking these freedoms in thinking and speaking about matters of faith and religion, we are in the right: for, though it is said there are very great liberties of this kind taken in New York, yet I have heard of no information preferred by Mr. Attorney for any offenses of this sort. From which I think it is pretty clear, that in New York a man may make very free with his God, but he must take special care what he says of his Governor.

It is agreed upon by all men that this is a reign of liberty, and while men keep within the bounds of truth, I hope they may with safety both speak and write their sentiments of the conduct of men in power—I mean of that part of their conduct only which affects the liberty or property of the people under their administration; were this to be denied, then the next step may make them slaves. For what notions can be entertained of slavery beyond that of suffering the greatest injuries and oppressions without the liberty of complaining; or if they do, to be destroyed, body and estate, for so doing?

It is said and insisted upon by Mr. Attorney that government is a sacred thing; that it is to be supported and reverenced; it is government that protects our persons and estates; that prevents treasons, murders, robberies, riots, and all the train of evils that overturns kingdoms and states and ruins particular persons; and if those in the administration, especially the supreme magistrate, must have all their conduct censured by private men, government cannot subsist. This is called a licentiousness not to be tolerated. It is said that it brings the rulers of the people into contempt, and their authority not to be regarded, and so in the end the laws cannot be put in execution. These I say, and such as these, are the general topics insisted upon by men in power, and their advocates.

But I wish it might be considered at the same time how often it has happened that the abuse of power has been the primary cause of these evils, and that it was the injustice and oppression of these great men, which has commonly brought them into contempt with the people. The craft and art of such men is great, and who, that

is the least acquainted with history or law, can be ignorant of the specious pretenses which have often been made use of by men in power to introduce arbitrary rule and destroy the liberties of a free people. . . .

The danger is great, in proportion to the mischief that may happen, through our too great credulity. A proper confidence in a court is commendable; but as the verdict (whatever it is) will be yours, you ought to refer no part of your duty to the discretion of other persons. If you should be of opinion that there is no falsehood in Mr. Zenger's papers, you will, nay (pardon me for the expression) you ought to say so; because you don't know whether others (I mean the court) may be of that opinion. It is your right to do so, and there is much depending upon your resolution, as well as upon your integrity.

The loss of liberty to a generous mind is worse than death; and yet we know there have been those in all ages, who for the sake of preferment, or some imaginary honor, have freely lent a helping hand to oppress, nay to destroy, their country.

This brings to my mind that saying of the immortal Brutus, when he looked upon the creatures of Caesar, who were very great men, but by no means good men. "You Romans," said Brutus, "if yet I may call you so, consider what you are doing; remember that you are assisting Caesar to forge those very chains which one day he will make yourselves wear." This is what every man (that values freedom) ought to consider: he should act by judgment and not by affection or self-interest; for, where those prevail, no ties of either country or kindred are regarded, as upon the other hand, the man who loves his country prefers its liberty to all other considerations, well knowing that without liberty, life is a misery. . . . .

Power may justly be compared to a great river: while kept within its due bounds, [it] is both beautiful and useful; but when it overflows its banks, it is then too impetuous to be stemmed—it bears down all before it and brings destruction and desolation wherever it comes. If then this is the nature of power, let us at least do our duty, and like wise men (who value freedom) use our utmost care to support liberty, the only bulwark against lawless power, which in all ages has sacrificed to its wild lust and boundless ambition the blood of the best men that ever lived.

I hope to be pardoned, Sir, for my zeal upon this occasion; it is an old and wise caution that when our neighbor's house is on fire, we ought to take care of our own. For though, blessed be God, I live in a government where liberty is well understood and freely enjoyed, yet experience has shown us all (I'm sure it has to me) that a bad precedent in one government is soon set up for an authority in another; and therefore I cannot but think it mine, and every honest man's duty, that (while we pay all due obedience to men in authority) we ought at the same time to be upon our guard against power wherever we apprehend that it may affect ourselves or our fellow-subjects.

I am truly very unequal to such an undertaking on many accounts. And you see I labor under the weight of many years, and am borne down with great infirmities of body; yet old and weak as I am, I should think it my duty, if required, to go to the utmost part of the land where my service could be of any use in assisting to quench the flame of prosecutions upon informations, set on foot by the government, to deprive a people of the right of remonstrating (and complaining too) of the arbitrary attempts of men in power. Men who injure and oppress the people under their administration provoke them to cry out and complain; and then make that very complaint the foundation for new oppressions and prosecutions. I wish I could say there were no instances of this kind.

But to conclude: The question before the court and you, gentlemen of the jury, is not of small nor private concern, it is not the cause of a poor printer, nor of New York alone, which you are now trying. No! It may in its consequence affect every freeman that lives under a British government on the main of America. It is the best cause. It is the cause of liberty; and I make no doubt but your upright conduct, this day, will not only entitle you to the love and esteem of your fellow-citizens, but every man who prefers freedom to a life of slavery will bless and honor you as men who have baffled the attempt of tyranny; and by an impartial and uncorrupt verdict, have laid a noble foundation for securing to ourselves, our posterity, and our neighbors, that to which nature and the laws of our country have given us a right—the liberty, both of exposing and opposing arbitrary power (in these parts of the world, at least), by speaking and writing truth.

JAMES OTIS DENOUNCES TYRANNY

1761

Great Britain was at war. Since 1754, in various coalitions, she had been grappling with France on the continent of North America, in Europe, in India, and on the seas. Victory seemed to be in sight, but two years would pass, after 1761, before a formal treaty would bring peace. In the meantime she needed money, huge sums of money, to maintain her own forces and to subsidize her allies. No source of revenue could be neglected.

On the statute books stood a series of Trade and Navigation Acts passed for the purpose of regulating the commerce of the Empire. Some of these imposed customs duties on the American colonists. For many years the Americans had ignored or evaded the duties which they found burdensome, but now, on the order of none other than the great Pitt, all were to be collected.

Heretofore customs officials who tried to break up smuggling found themselves helpless. Few colonists would furnish the evidence on which search warrants could be based, and without the right to search for and seize smuggled goods, the crown officers could not prosecute. The officials, consequently, resorted to "writs of assistance," which gave them the right to board any ship or enter any warehouse at their pleasure, even though no one had complained, under oath, that the ships or warehouses harbored smuggled commodities.

The writs, however, were valid only during the lifetime of the king in whose reign they were issued, and six months thereafter. George II died in October, 1760. New writs must be obtained if the customs officers were to collect the duties.

Nowhere in the colonies was the opposition to the hated search warrants more bitter than in Massachusetts. Now, with a new king on the throne, the opportunity for resistance had come. When the deputy collector at Salem applied for new writs, the merchants of the colony retained Oxenbridge Thacher, an able and respected lawyer, and James Otis, a brilliant but erratic younger member of the bar, to resist the application.

The hearing took place in February, 1761, in the council chamber of the Town House at Boston. Young John Adams, present as a spectator, sketched a memorable picture of the scene. Around a great fire sat the five judges of the court, all in robes of scarlet broadcloth, each wearing the huge wig that was his badge of office. Members of the bar of Boston, and of nearby towns, also wearing gowns and wigs, occupied a long table before the judges. Full-length portraits of Charles II and James II, painted in gleaming colors and superbly framed in gold, gave an added touch of dignity to a setting already impressive.

The attorney for the crown took the floor and argued with learning and ingenuity for the issuance of the writs. Thacher, cool, deft, persuasive, spoke in opposition. Then came Otis, thirty-six years of age, his amiable features concealing the pride and energy and impatience that made him, in the words of Adams, "a flame of fire." The cold print of his speech, amplified many years later from notes taken at the time, can convey only a faint idea of his impetuous eloquence.

"Every man of a crowded audience," John Adams wrote, "appeared to me to go away, as I did, ready to take arms against writs of assistance. Then and there was the first scene of the first act of opposition to the arbitrary claims of Great Britain. Then and there the child Independence was born."

Speech against Writs of Assistance

February 1761

May it please your Honors:

I was desired by one of the court to look into the books and consider the question now before them concerning writs of assistance. I have accordingly considered it, and now appear, not only in obedience to your order, but likewise in behalf of the inhabitants of this town, who have presented another petition, and out of regard to the liberties of the subject. And I take this opportunity to declare that, whether under a fee or not (for in such a case as this I despise a fee), I will to my dying day oppose, with all the powers and faculties God has given me, all such instruments of slavery on the one hand, and villainy on the other, as this writ of assistance is.

It appears to me the worst instrument of arbitrary power, the most destructive of English liberty and the fundamental principles of law, that ever was found in an English lawbook. I must, therefore, beg your Honors' patience and attention to the whole range of an argument, that may perhaps appear uncommon in many things, as well as to points of learning that are more remote and unusual; that the whole tendency of my design may the more easily be perceived, the conclusions better discerned, and the force of them be better felt.

I shall not think much of my pains in this cause, as I engaged in it from principle. I was solicited to argue this cause as advocate general; and because I would not, I have been charged with desertion from my office. To this charge I can give a very sufficient answer. I renounced that office, and I argue this cause, from the same principle; and I argue it with the greater pleasure, as it is in favor of British liberty, at a time when we hear the greatest monarch upon earth declaring from his throne that he glories in the name of Briton, and that the privileges of his people are dearer to him than the most valuable prerogatives of his crown; and as it is in opposition to a kind of power, the exercise of which, in former periods of English history, cost one King of England his head, and another his throne.

I have taken more pains in this cause than I ever will take again, although my engaging in this and another popular cause has raised much resentment. But I think I can sincerely declare that I cheerfully submit myself to every odious name for conscience' sake; and from my soul I despise all those whose guilt, malice, or folly has made them my foes.

Let the consequences be what they will, I am determined to

proceed. The only principles of public conduct, that are worthy of a gentleman, or a man, are to sacrifice estate, ease, health, and applause, and even life, to the sacred calls of his country. These manly sentiments, in private life, make the good citizen; in public life, the patriot and the hero. I do not say, that when brought to the test,

I shall be invincible. I pray God I may never be brought to the melancholy trial; but if ever I should, it will be then known how far I can reduce to practice principles which I know to be founded in truth. In the meantime I will proceed to the subject of this writ.

In the first place, may it please your Honors, I will admit that writs of one kind may be legal; that is, special writs, directed to special officers, and to search certain houses, etc., specially set forth in the writ, may be granted by the Court of Exchequer at home, upon oath made before the Lord Treasurer by the person who asks it, that he suspects such goods to be concealed in those very places he desires to search. The act of 14 Charles II, which Mr. Gridley mentions, proves this. And in this light the writ appears like a warrant from a justice of the peace to search for stolen goods.

Your Honors will find in the old books concerning the office of a justice of the peace, precedents of general warrants to search suspected houses. But in more modern books you will find only special warrants to search such and such houses specially named, in which the complainant has before sworn that he suspects his goods are concealed; and you will find it adjudged that special warrants only are legal.

In the same manner I rely on it [affirm it], that the writ prayed for in this petition, being general, is illegal. It is a power that places the liberty of every man in the hands of every petty officer. I say I admit that special writs of assistance, to search special places, may be granted to certain persons on oath; but I deny that the writ now prayed for can be granted, for I beg leave to make some observations on the writ itself before I proceed to other acts of Parliament.

In the first place, the writ is universal, being directed "to all and singular justices, sheriffs, constables, and all other officers and subjects"; so, that, in short, it is directed to every subject in the King's dominions. Every one with this writ may be a tyrant; if this commission be legal, a tyrant in a legal manner also may control, imprison, or murder any one within the realm. In the next place, it is perpetual; there is no return. A man is accountable to no person for his doings. Every man may reign secure in his petty tyranny, and spread terror and desolation around him. In the third place, a person with this writ, in the daytime, may enter all houses, shops, etc., at will, and command all to assist him. Fourthly, by this writ not only deputies, etc., but even their menial servants, are allowed to lord it over us.

Now one of the most essential branches of English liberty is the freedom of one's house. A man's house is his castle; and whilst he is quiet, he is as well guarded as a prince in his castle. This writ, if it should be declared legal, would totally annihilate this privilege. Customhouse officers may enter our houses, when they please; we are commanded to permit their entry. Their menial servants may enter, may break locks, bars, and everything in their way; and whether they break through malice or revenge, no man, no court, can inquire. Bare suspicion without oath is sufficient.

This wanton exercise of this power is not a chimerical suggestion of a heated brain. I will mention some facts. Mr. Pew had one of these writs, and when Mr. Ware succeeded him, he endorsed this writ over to Mr. Ware; so that these writs are negotiable from one officer to another; and so your Honors have no opportunity of judging the persons to whom this vast power is delegated. Another instance is this: Mr. Justice Walley had called this same Mr. Ware before him, by a constable, to answer for a breach of Sabbath-day acts, or that of profane swearing. As soon as he had finished, Mr. Ware asked him if he had done. He replied, yes. Well then, said Mr. Ware, I will show you a little of my power. I command you to permit me to search your house for uncustomed goods. And went on to search his house from the garret to the cellar; and then served the constable in the same manner.

But to show another absurdity in this writ: if it should be established, I insist upon it, every person by the 14 Charles II has this power as well as customhouse officers. The words are, "It shall be lawful for any person or persons authorized," etc. What a scene does this open! Every man, prompted by revenge, ill humor, or wantonness to inspect the inside of his neighbor's house, may get a writ of assistance. Others will ask it from self-defense; one arbitrary exertion will provoke another, until society be involved in tumult and in blood.

Again, these writs are not returned. Writs in their nature are temporary things. When the purposes for which they are issued are answered, they exist no more; but these live forever; no one can be called to account. Thus reason and the constitution are both against this writ. Let us see what authority there is for it. Not more than one instance can be found of it in all our lawbooks; and that was in the zenith of arbitrary power, namely, in the reign of Charles II, when star-chamber powers were pushed to extremity by some ignorant clerk of the exchequer. But had this writ been in any book whatever, it would have been illegal. All precedents are under the control of the principles of law. Lord Talbot says it is better to observe these than any precedents, though in the House of Lords, the last resort of the subject. No acts of Parliament can establish such a writ; though it should be made in the very words of the petition, it would be void. An act against the constitution is void.

But these prove no more than what I before observed, that special writs may be granted *on oath and probable suspicion.* The acts of

7 & 8 William III, that the officers of the plantations shall have the same powers, etc., is confined to this sense; that an officer should show probable ground; should take his oath of it; should do this before a magistrate; and that such magistrate, if he think proper, should issue a special warrant to a constable to search the places. That of 6 Anne can prove no more.

THE COLONIES RESIST A HATED TAX

1765

For England, the Seven Years' War ended in glorious victory. France, a threat to the English colonies in North America for more than a century, ceded all of Canada and her possessions east of the Mississippi to her rival. Spain took Louisiana, and at the same time surrendered the Floridas to the British. At one stroke the tight little island doubled the extent of her North American empire.

But the outcome of the war was not the unmixed blessing that it at first seemed. If Britain's empire had doubled, so had her debt, and her yearly cost of government had tripled. The ministers in London considered it only fair that the colonists, now safe from the menace of France, should bear their share of the increase. The Americans, on the other hand, felt that they were already overburdened with taxation. They resented the effort of the mother country to draw increased revenue from them, and when that effort took the form of the Stamp Act, resentment boiled over. This measure, which placed a tax on legal documents of all kinds, and newspapers, pamphlets, even playing cards, was not only a nuisance; it was a tax levied on the people without their consent. And that was something no self-respecting Englishman, at home or in the colonies, intended to tolerate.

George III signed the Stamp Act in March, 1765. Even before the ship bearing the news reached the colonies, an angry determination to resist the act had spread from South Carolina to New England. Virginia, spurred by the eloquence of Patrick Henry, passed resolutions denouncing the stamp duties in ringing terms. Massachusetts followed the lead of the Old Dominion, and went further by proposing that a congress, consisting of delegates from all the colonies, meet in New York to protest this invasion of the rights of true Englishmen.

The delegates gathered in early October. Among them were men of local fame whose reputations were already spreading to distant colonies—from South Carolina, Christopher Gadsden, hot-tempered and impetuous; John Rutledge, eloquent and able; Thomas Lynch, plain, unpretentious, but shrewd and sensible; from New York, Robert R. Livingston, whose levelheadedness matched his amiability; from Delaware, Caesar Rodney, tall, thin as a broomstick, but full of spirit, wit, and humor; from Pennsylvania, John Dickinson, outspoken in opposition to British oppression, but equally opposed to violent resistance; and from Massachusetts, James Otis, grown even more fiery in his defiance of the mother country than he had been four years earlier, when he had thrilled the opponents of writs of assistance by his eloquence.

When all were present, twenty-eight delegates represented nine colonies. At the City Hall, they met in an atmosphere charged with tension. Only a few days earlier a British officer, busying himself with strengthening the King's fortifications, had boasted: "I will cram the stamps down their throats with the end of my sword. If they attempt to rise, I will drive them all out of the town for a pack of rascals." The temper of the New Yorkers, on the other hand, was expressed by the motto of a newspaper published shortly before the delegates met: "Join or die."

After deliberating for two weeks, the congress adopted resolutions defining the rights of the colonies and expressing their grievances. The British ministry, impressed by the extent and gravity of the opposition, made no serious attempt to enforce the Stamp Act, and soon repealed it.

Resolutions of the Stamp Act Congress

October 19, 1765

The members of this congress, sincerely devoted with the warmest sentiments of affection and duty to His Majesty's person and government, inviolably attached to the present happy establishment of the Protestant succession, and with minds deeply impressed by a sense of the present and impending misfortunes of the British colonies on this continent, having considered as maturely as time would permit, the circumstances of the said colonies, esteem it our

indispensable duty to make the following declarations of our humble opinion respecting the most essential rights and liberties of the colonists, and of the grievances under which they labor, by reason of several late acts of Parliament.

I. That His Majesty's subjects in these colonies owe the same allegiance to the Crown of Great Britain that is owing from his subjects born within the realm, and all due subordination to that august body, the Parliament of Great Britain.

II. That His Majesty's liege subjects in these colonies are entitled to all the inherent rights and privileges of his natural-born subjects within the kingdom of Great Britain.

III. That it is inseparably essential to the freedom of a people, and the undoubted rights of Englishmen, that no taxes should be imposed on them but with their own consent, given personally or by their representatives.

IV. That the people of these colonies are not, and from their local circumstances cannot be, represented in the House of Commons in Great Britain.

V. That the only representatives of the people of these colonies are persons chosen therein by themselves; and that no taxes ever have been or can be, constitutionally imposed on them, but by their respective legislatures.

VI. That all supplies to the Crown, being free gifts of the people, it is unreasonable and inconsistent with the principles and spirit of the British constitution for the people of Great Britain to grant to His Majesty the property of the colonists.

VII. That trial by jury is the inherent and invaluable right of every British subject in these colonies.

VIII. That the late act of Parliament, entitled *An Act for granting and applying certain stamp duties, and other duties, in the British colonies and plantations in America, etc.*, by imposing taxes on the inhabitants of these colonies; and the said act, and several other acts, by extending the jurisdiction of the courts of admiralty beyond its ancient limits, have a manifest tendency to subvert the rights and liberties of the colonists.

IX. That the duties imposed by several late acts of Parliament, from the peculiar circumstances of these colonies, will be extremely burthensome and grievous; and from the scarcity of specie, the payment of them absolutely impracticable.

X. That as the profits of the trade of these colonies ultimately center in Great Britain, to pay for the manufactures which they are obliged to take from thence, they eventually contribute very largely to all supplies granted there to the Crown.

XI. That the restrictions imposed by several late acts of Parliament on the trade of these colonies will render them unable to purchase the manufactures of Great Britain.

XII. That the increase, prosperity, and happiness of these colonies depend on the full and free enjoyment of their rights and liberties, and an intercourse with Great Britain mutually affectionate and advantageous.

XIII. That it is the right of the British subjects in these colonies to petition the King or either house of Parliament.

Lastly, that it is the indispensable duty of these colonies to the best of sovereigns, to the mother country, and to themselves, to endeavor by a loyal and dutiful address to His Majesty, and humble application to both houses of Parliament, to procure the repeal of the act for granting and applying certain stamp duties, of all clauses of any other acts of Parliament whereby the jurisdiction of the admiralty is extended as aforesaid, and of the other late acts for the restriction of the American commerce.

THE UNITED COLONISTS ASSERT THEIR RIGHTS

1774

In mid-December, 1773, three ships carrying tea owned by the British East India Company lay in Boston Harbor. For days their masters had hoped to discharge the cargoes, but had not dared to make the attempt. In 1770, the British Government had repealed all duties on goods imported by the colonists except the tax on tea, and had then given the East India Company a monopoly on that commodity. Now the company proposed to sell the tea, used by almost everyone, through it own agents, and thus stop the smuggling at which the colonial merchants were adept. If the scheme succeeded, the right of Parliament to tax the colonies would be established.

On the night of December 16, Governor Hutchinson announced that if the tea were not landed the next day, with the duty paid, the customs officers would sell it at auction. Within minutes a band of men disguised as Mohawk Indians boarded the ships, broke open the hatches, and threw the chests of tea over the sides. John Adams spoke for a cheering crowd on the wharf when he wrote: "Many persons wish that as many dead carcasses were floating in the harbor as there are chests of tea."

As soon as word of the "tea party" reached London, the ministry took severe measures. Laws were passed closing the port of Boston, increasing the powers of the royal officers in the province, and providing that certain offenders be taken to England for trial. Up and down the seaboard the colonies rallied to the support of Massachusetts, for what had happened to her could happen to any of them. Out of protest meetings held in state houses, courthouses, and stores at country crossroads came a demand for a congress to meet at Philadelphia in the fall of the year, there "to consult upon the present unhappy State of the Colonies."

Delegates began to arrive at the Quaker city as summer changed to early fall. John Adams' account of one of his first days in Philadelphia revealed the temper of the gathering. In the morning he went with several other members of the congress to the store of William Barrell, where they drank punch and ate smoked sprats; in the afternoon he dined with other delegates; that evening, in a larger group at Mr. Mifflin's, he partook of an "elegant supper" and "drank sentiments till eleven o'clock." The "sentiments" reflected the prevailing point of view:

"May the collision of British flint and American steel produce that spark of liberty which shall illumine the latest posterity. . . .

"Wisdom to Britain, and firmness to the colonies; may Britain be wise, and America free. . . .

"Union of Britain and the colonies on a constitutional foundation."

On September 5, 1774, fifty-five delegates representing all the colonies except Georgia opened the First Continental Congress in Carpenters' Hall. Many were men of mark, and some would be far better known as the years passed. The Virginian, Peyton Randolph, was chosen as presiding officer; his delegation included Colonel George Washington, whom Silas Deane of Connecticut described as "hard" of countenance, "yet with a very young look, and an easy, soldier-like air and gesture"; Edmund Pendleton, "a lawyer of eminence, of easy and cheerful countenance, polite in address, and elegant if not eloquent in style and elocution." What Pendleton lacked in oratorical fervor was offset by Patrick Henry, whom Deane called "the completest speaker" he had ever heard. And as an orator, Richard Henry Lee was said to be Henry's equal.

Other delegates took shape in John Adams' diary–Thomas Johnson of Maryland, a man with "a clear and cool head, an extensive knowledge of trade as well as law"; Joseph Galloway, also of Maryland, and James Duane of New York, conservatives both, "sensible and learned, but cold speakers"; John Rutledge of South Carolina, a member of the Stamp Act Congress, accompanied by his brother Edward, "young"–he was twenty-four–"zealous," and "a little unsteady and unjudicious."

Among the New England members two stood out–John Adams himself, grave of mien, imposing in appearance, yet capable of hot anger when aroused; and his distant relative Samuel Adams who, as one of the delegates wrote, ate little, drank little, slept little, thought much, and devoted himself tirelessly to his one object–independence from Britain.

"The Congress," John Adams reflected, "is such an assembly as never before came together, on a sudden, in any part of the world. Here are fortunes, abilities, learning, eloquence, acuteness equal to any I ever met with in my life. Here is a diversity of religions, educations, manners, interests, such as it would seem almost impossible to unite in one plan of conduct." Yet, in little more than a month, they did unite, adopting, on October 14, 1774, a calm and moderate declaration and series of resolutions which Parliament and the British ministry would have been wise to heed.

Even more important than the declaration and resolutions was the Continental Association, by which the delegates agreed that their constituents would import no more British goods, deny themselves all luxuries, and encourage their own manufactures until the mother country should redress their grievances. In this way they forged into a national weapon coercive measures that had so far been only local and unorganized, and took a long step on the road to independence.

Declarations and Resolves of the First Continental Congress

October 14, 1774

Whereas, Since the close of the last war, the British Parliament, claiming a power of right to bind the people of America by statute in all cases whatsoever, hath in some acts expressly imposed taxes on them, and in others, under various pretenses, but in fact for the purpose of raising a revenue, hath imposed rates and duties payable in these colonies, established a board of commissioners with unconstitutional powers, and extended the jurisdiction of courts of admiralty not only for collecting the said duties, but for the trial of causes merely arising within the body of a county.

And whereas, In consequence of other statutes, judges who before held only estates at will in their offices have been made dependent on the Crown alone for their salaries; and standing armies kept in times of peace. And it has lately been resolved in Parliament that by force of a statute made in the thirty-fifth year of the reign of King Henry the Eighth, colonists may be transported to England and tried there upon accusations for treasons and misprisions, or concealments of treasons committed in the colonies; and by a late statute, such trials have been directed in cases therein mentioned.

And whereas, In the last session of Parliament, three statutes were made . . . . [the Boston Port Act, the Massachusetts Government Act, the Administration of Justice Act], and another statute was then made [the Quebec Act]. . . . All which statutes are impolitic, unjust, and cruel, as well as unconstitutional, and most dangerous and destructive of American rights.

And whereas, Assemblies have been frequently dissolved, contrary to the rights of the people, when they attempted to deliberate on grievances; and their dutiful, humble, loyal, and reasonable petitions to the Crown for redress have been repeatedly treated with contempt by His Majesty's ministers of state:

The good people of the several colonies of New Hampshire, Massachusetts Bay, Rhode Island and Providence Plantations, Connecticut, New York, New Jersey, Pennsylvania, Newcastle, Kent and Sussex on Delaware, Maryland, Virginia, North Carolina, and South Carolina, justly alarmed at these arbitrary proceedings of Parliament and administration, have severally elected, constituted, and appointed deputies to meet and sit in general congress, in the city of Philadelphia, in order to obtain such establishment as that their religion, laws, and liberties may not be subverted:

Whereupon the deputies so appointed being now assembled, in a full and free representation of these colonies, taking into their most serious consideration the best means of attaining the ends aforesaid, do in the first place, as Englishmen their ancestors in like cases have usually done, for asserting and vindicating their rights and liberties, declare,

That the inhabitants of the English colonies in North America, by the immutable laws of nature, the principles of the English constitution, and the several charters or compacts, have the following rights:

Resolved, ...

1. That they are entitled to life, liberty, and property, and they have never ceded to any sovereign power whatever a right to dispose of either without their consent.

2. That our ancestors, who first settled these colonies, were, at the time of their emigration from the mother country, entitled to all the rights, liberties, and immunities of free and natural-born subjects within the realm of England.

3. That by such emigration they by no means forfeited, surrendered, or lost any of those rights, but that they were, and their descendants now are, entitled to the exercise and enjoyment of all such of them as their local and other circumstances enable them to exercise and enjoy.

4. That the foundation of English liberty, and of all free government, is a right in the people to participate in their legislative council: and as the English colonists are not represented, and from their local and other circumstances, cannot properly be represented in the British Parliament, they are entitled to a free and exclusive power of legislation in their several provincial legislatures, where their right of representation can alone be preserved, in all cases of taxation and internal polity, subject only to the negative of their sovereign, in such manner as has been heretofore used and ac-

customed. But, from the necessity of the case, and a regard to the mutual interest of both countries, we cheerfully consent to the operation of such acts of the British Parliament as are bona fide restrained to the regulation of our external commerce, for the purpose of securing the commercial advantages of the whole empire to the mother country, and the commercial benefits of its respective members, excluding every idea of taxation, internal or external, for raising a revenue on the subjects in America without their consent.

5. That the respective colonies are entitled to the common law of England, and more especially to the great and inestimable privilege of being tried by their peers of the vicinage, according to the course of that law.

6. That they are entitled to the benefit of such of the English statutes as existed at the time of their colonization; and which they have, by experience, respectively found to be applicable to their several local and other circumstances.

7. That these, His Majesty's colonies, are likewise entitled to all the immunities and privileges granted and confirmed to them by royal charters, or secured by their several codes of provincial laws.

8. That they have a right peaceably to assemble, consider of their grievances, and petition the King; and that all prosecutions, prohibitory proclamations, and commitments for the same, are illegal.

9. That the keeping a standing army in these colonies, in times of peace, without the consent of the legislature of that colony in which such army is kept, is against law.

10. It is indispensably necessary to good government, and rendered essential by the English constitution, that the constituent branches of the legislature be independent of each other; that, therefore, the exercise of legislative power in several colonies, by a council appointed during pleasure, by the Crown, is unconstitutional, dangerous, and destructive to the freedom of American legislation.

All and each of which the aforesaid deputies, in behalf of themselves, and their constituents, do claim, demand, and insist on, as their indubitable rights and liberties; which cannot be legally taken from them, altered or abridged by any power whatever, without their own consent, by their representatives in their several provincial legislatures.

In the course of our inquiry, we find many infringements and violations of the foregoing rights, which, from an ardent desire that harmony and mutual intercourse of affection and interest may be restored, we pass over for the present, and proceed to state such acts and measures as have been adopted since the last war, which demonstrate a system formed to enslave America.

Resolved, That the following acts of Parliament are infringements and violations of the rights of the colonists; and that the repeal of them is essentially necessary, in order to restore harmony between Great Britain and the American colonies, viz.:

The several Acts of 4 Geo. III, ch. 15 & ch. 34; 5 Geo. III, ch. 25; 6 Geo. III, ch. 52; 7 Geo. III, ch. 41 & 46; 8 Geo. III, ch. 22; which impose duties for the purpose of raising a revenue in America, extend the powers of the admiralty courts beyond their ancient limits, deprive the American subject of trial by jury, authorize the judges' certificate to indemnify the prosecutor from damages that he might otherwise be liable to, requiring oppressive security from a claimant of ships and goods seized before he shall be allowed to defend his property; and are subversive of American rights.

Also the 12 Geo. III, ch. 24, entitled "An act for the better securing His Majesty's dockyards, magazines, ships, ammunition, and stores," which declares a new offense in America, and deprives the American subject of a constitutional trial by a jury of the vicinage, by authorizing the trial of any person charged with the committing any offense described in the said act, out of the realm, to be indicted and tried for the same in any shire or county within the realm.

Also the three acts passed in the last session of Parliament, for stopping the port and blocking up the harbor of Boston, for altering the charter and government of the Massachusetts Bay, and that which is entitled "An Act for the better administration of Justice," etc.

Also the act passed the same session for establishing the Roman Catholic religion in the province of Quebec, abolishing the equitable system of English laws, and erecting a tyranny there, to the great danger, from so great a dissimilarity of religion, law, and government, of the neighboring British colonies, by the assistance of whose blood and treasure the said country was conquered from France.

Also the act passed the same session for the better providing suitable quarters for officers and soldiers in His Majesty's service in North America.

Also, that the keeping a standing army in several of these colonies, in time of peace, without the consent of the legislature of that colony in which the army is kept, is against law.

To these grievous acts and measures Americans cannot submit; but in hopes that their fellow-subjects in Great Britain will, on a revision of them restore us to that state in which both countries found happiness and prosperity, we have for the present only resolved to pursue the following peaceable measures: (1) To enter into a nonimportation, nonconsumption, and nonexportation agreement or association. (2) To prepare an address to the people of Great Britain, and a memorial to the inhabitants of British America, and (3) To prepare a loyal address to His Majesty, agreeable to resolutions already entered into.

FREE AND INDEPENDENT STATES

1776

When the delegates to the First Continental Congress left for their homes at the end of October, 1774, they agreed to meet again on May 10, 1775, if the colonies and Great Britain were still at odds. The winter passed with little friction, but in the spring the smoldering fire of revolt broke into flame. In mid-April the British military governor of Massachusetts heard that the colonists had collected a supply of muskets and gunpowder at Concord. On the evening of the eighteenth he ordered a detachment of regulars to march out from Boston and seize the supplies. And that was the night when Paul Revere, anxiously watching the belfry of the Old North Church, saw a single light—"One if by land, and two if by sea"—and leaped on his horse to warn the countryside that the British were marching.

A hurry of hoofs in a village street,
A shape in the moonlight, a bulk in the dark,
And beneath, from the pebbles, in passing, a spark
Struck out by a steed flying fearless and fleet:
That was all! And yet, through the gloom and the light,
The fate of a nation was riding that night. . . .

The next day, at Lexington and Concord, men and boys who had considered themselves loyal Englishmen died for what they believed to be their rights—and exacted a toll from His Majesty's redcoats far heavier than they themselves paid.

So the members of the Continental Congress met again—at Philadelphia, as they had planned, and on the tenth of May, 1775. Many had served in the first Congress, but there were new faces, too—John Hancock, the wealthiest merchant in Massachusetts, who would preside in place of Peyton Randolph, soon to die; Thomas Jefferson, only thirty-two, but already marked as a man of learning and literary skill; and above all the venerable and respected Doctor Franklin, finally convinced that the last hope of peaceful settlement had vanished. In the ears of the delegates rang the words of Patrick Henry, uttered when the news of Lexington reached Virginia:

"Gentlemen may cry 'peace, peace' but there is no peace. The war is actually begun! The next gale that sweeps from the north will bring to our ears the clash of resounding arms! Our brethren are already in the field! Why stand we here idle?"

And as they pondered this stirring challenge, the delegates could see, in their minds, Ethan Allen and his Green Mountain Boys crashing through the defenses of Fort Ticonderoga and accepting the surrender of that outpost in the name of the Congress of which they were members. A few weeks later George Washington rode off from Philadelphia to take command of the Continental Army that had besieged the British in Boston. It was ominous that he should be met on the way by couriers with news of Bunker Hill —a defeat which American heroism, and the heavy losses inflicted on the finest troops of Europe, made almost as sweet as victory.

The members of the Second Continental Congress met, in the main, as loyal Englishmen. But when King George, in the late summer of 1775, issued a proclamation calling the colonists rebels and warning all persons not to give them aid and comfort, public opinion began to change. On January 1, 1776, Washington, who had declared six months earlier that he would make every effort to restore peace and harmony with the mother country, raised the Con-

tinental flag in front of his headquarters at Cambridge; and a few weeks later he openly advocated independence. At the same time Thomas Paine's pamphlet, *Common Sense*, swept through edition after edition and converted thousands to the necessity of separation.

By May, 1776, a majority of the delegates to the Congress had come to favor independence. All that was needed was an impulse, and that was provided when a convention sitting in Virginia instructed her delegates to move a resolution declaring the colonies to be free and independent states. On June 7, Richard Henry Lee, chairman of the Virginia delegation to the Congress, made the motion. John Adams, in one of the proudest moments of his life, offered a quick second. Debate began, but three days later the question was postponed until July 1.

At the same time a committee consisting of Jefferson, Adams, Franklin, Roger Sherman, and Robert R. Livingston was appointed to draft a "declaration" in support of the resolution. Jefferson, steeped in the writings of John Locke, the English philosopher and political theorist, set himself to the task, working in the second-floor bedroom and parlor which he had rented for the duration of the Congress. After incorporating several suggestions offered by Adams and Franklin, he had the declaration in what he hoped would be its final form by the end of June.

On July 1, when the great debate was to take place, Congress listened first to the reading of a gloomy report from General Washington on the state of the Continental Army. Next came a more cheerful communication reporting that the Maryland convention had voted unanimously for independence. After that had been heard, Congress resolved itself into a committee of the whole to consider the resolution that Richard Henry Lee had offered three weeks earlier. For a few minutes silence prevailed, for no one could escape the feeling that one of the most momentous decisions in the history of the world would soon be made. John Dickinson broke the spell by taking the floor to summarize, deferentially but with all the eloquence at his command, the arguments against independence. John Adams replied in a ringing speech, and the session ended.

The next day, July 2, Congress passed the Lee Resolution: "These United Colonies are, and of right ought to be, free and independent States." Then the declaration was taken up, argued over, and amended while Jefferson squirmed with the pain that all authors experience when outsiders tamper with their brain-children. By the late afternoon of July 4, the delegates were satisfied, and the Unanimous Declaration of the Thirteen United States of America, known to us as the Declaration of Independence, was adopted to justify to a curious and skeptical world the founding of a new nation.

Contrary to widespread belief, no one signed the Declaration on July 4. Two weeks passed before the Congress ordered it to be engrossed, and it was not until August 2 that the delegates who were present on that day signed their names. Others added their signatures from time to time for the next several months.

The Declaration, however, was published and circulated immediately after July 4. Throughout the colonies—now to be called states—it was received with acclamation. As militia officers read it to their companies, as heads of councils or assemblies proclaimed it to eager crowds, drums rattled, fifes shrilled, bells rang, and cannon boomed—always thirteen times—while rowdy patriots tore down tavern signs like the "Lion and Crown," burned King George in effigy, and drank endless toasts in celebration. The years of hardship, bloodshed, and dissension were yet to come.

The Declaration of Independence

July 4, 1776

When in the course of human events, it becomes necessary for one people to dissolve the political bands which have connected them with another, and to assume among the powers of the earth the separate and equal station to which the laws of nature and of nature's God entitle them, a decent respect to the opinions of mankind requires that they should declare the causes which impel them to the separation.

We hold these truths to be self-evident: that all men are created equal, that they are endowed by their Creator with certain unalienable rights, that among these are life, liberty, and the pursuit of happiness. That to secure these rights, governments are instituted among men, deriving their just powers from the consent of the governed; that whenever any form of government becomes destructive of these ends, it is the right of the people to alter or to abolish it, and to institute new government, laying its foundation on such principles and organizing its powers in such form, as to them shall seem most likely to effect their safety and happiness.

Prudence, indeed, will dictate that governments long established should not be changed for light and transient causes; and accordingly all experience hath shown, that mankind are more disposed to suffer, while evils are sufferable, than to right themselves by abolishing the forms to which they are accustomed. But when a long train of abuses and usurpations, pursuing invariably the same object, evinces a design to reduce them under absolute despotism, it is their right, it is their duty, to throw off such government, and to provide new guards for their future security. Such has been the patient sufferance of these colonies; and such is now the necessity which constrains them to alter their former systems of government.

The history of the present King of Great Britain is a history of repeated injuries and usurpations, all having in direct object the establishment of an absolute tyranny over these states. To prove this, let facts be submitted to a candid world.

He has refused his assent to laws, the most wholesome and necessary for the public good.

He has forbidden his governors to pass laws of immediate and pressing importance, unless suspended in their operation till his assent should be obtained; and when so suspended, he has utterly neglected to attend to them.

He has refused to pass other laws for the accommodation of large districts of people, unless those people would relinquish the right of representation in the legislature, a right inestimable to them and formidable to tyrants only.

He has called together legislative bodies at places unusual, uncomfortable, and distant from the depository of their public records, for the sole purpose of fatiguing them into compliance with his measures.

He has dissolved representative houses repeatedly for opposing with manly firmness his invasions on the rights of the people.

He has refused for a long time, after such dissolutions, to cause others to be elected; whereby the legislative powers, incapable of annihilation, have returned to the people at large for their exercise; the state remaining in the meantime exposed to all the dangers of invasion from without, and convulsions within.

He has endeavored to prevent the population of these states; for that purpose obstructing the laws for naturalization of foreigners; refusing to pass others to encourage their migration hither, and raising the conditions of new appropriations of lands.

He has obstructed the administration of justice, by refusing his assent to laws for establishing judiciary powers.

He has made judges dependent on his will alone, for the tenure of their offices, and the amount and payment of their salaries.

He has erected a multitude of new offices, and sent hither swarms of officers to harass our people and eat out their substance.

He has kept among us, in times of peace, standing armies without the consent of our legislature.

He has affected to render the military independent of and superior to the civil power.

He has combined with others to subject us to a jurisdiction foreign to our constitution, and unacknowledged by our laws; giving his assent to their acts of pretended legislation:

For quartering large bodies of armed troops among us;

For protecting them, by a mock trial, from punishment for any murders which they should commit on the inhabitants of these states;

For cutting off our trade with all parts of the world;

For imposing taxes on us without our consent;

For depriving us, in many cases, of the benefits of trial by jury;

For transporting us beyond seas to be tried for pretended offenses;

For abolishing the free system of English laws in a neighboring province, establishing therein an arbitrary government, and enlarging its boundaries so as to render it at once an example and fit instrument for introducing the same absolute rule into these colonies;

For taking away our charters, abolishing our most valuable laws, and altering fundamentally the forms of our governments;

For suspending our own legislatures, and declaring themselves invested with power to legislate for us in all cases whatsoever.

He has abdicated government here by declaring us out of his protection and waging war against us.

He has plundered our seas, ravaged our coasts, burnt our towns, and destroyed the lives of our people.

He is at this time transporting large armies of foreign mercenaries to complete the works of death, desolation, and tyranny, already begun with circumstances of cruelty and perfidy scarcely paralleled in the most barbarous ages, and totally unworthy the head of a civilized nation.

He has constrained our fellow-citizens taken captive on the high seas to bear arms against their country, to become the executioners of their friends and brethren, or to fall themselves by their hands.

He has excited domestic insurrections amongst us, and has endeavored to bring on the inhabitants of our frontiers, the merciless Indian savages, whose known rule of warfare is an undistinguished destruction of all ages, sexes, and conditions.

In every stage of these oppressions we have petitioned for redress in the most humble terms; our repeated petitions have been answered only by repeated injury. A prince, whose character is thus marked by every act which may define a tyrant, is unfit to be the ruler of a free people.

Nor have we been wanting in attention to our British brethren. We have warned them from time to time of attempts by their legislature to extend an unwarrantable jurisdiction over us. We have reminded them of the circumstances of our emigration and settlement here. We have appealed to their native justice and magnanimity, and we have conjured them by the ties of our common kindred to disavow these usurpations, which would inevitably interrupt our connections and correspondence. They too have been deaf to the voice of justice and of consanguinity. We must, therefore, acquiesce in the necessity which denounces our separation, and hold them, as we hold the rest of mankind, enemies in war, in peace, friends.

We, therefore, the representatives of the United States of America, in general congress assembled, appealing to the Supreme Judge of the world for the rectitude of our intentions, do, in the name and by authority of the good people of these colonies, solemnly publish and declare, that these united colonies are, and of right ought to be, free and independent states; that they are absolved from all allegiance to the British Crown, and that all political connection between them and the state of Great Britain is, and ought to be, totally dissolved; and that as free and independent states they have full power to levy war, conclude peace, contract alliances, establish commerce, and to do all other acts and things which independent states may of right do. And for the support of this declaration, with a firm reliance on the protection of Divine Providence, we mutually pledge to each other our lives, our fortunes, and our sacred honor.

John Hancock

New Hampshire
Josiah Bartlett
Wm. Whipple
Matthew Thornton

Massachusetts Bay
Saml. Adams
John Adams
Robt. Treat Paine
Elbridge Gerry

Rhode Island
Step. Hopkins
William Ellery

Connecticut
Roger Sherman
Sam'el. Huntington
Wm. Williams
Oliver Wolcott

New York
Wm. Floyd
Phil. Livingston
Frans. Lewis
Lewis Morris

Georgia
Button Gwinnett
Lyman Hall
Geo. Walton

Maryland
Samuel Chase
Wm. Paca
Thos. Stone
Charles Carroll of Carrollton

Virginia
George Wythe
Richard Henry Lee
Th. Jefferson
Benja. Harrison
Thos. Nelson, Jr.
Francis Lightfoot Lee
Carter Braxton

North Carolina
Wm. Hooper
Joseph Hewes
John Penn

Pennsylvania

ROBT. MORRIS
BENJAMIN RUSH
BENJA. FRANKLIN
JOHN MORTON
GEO. CLYMER
JAS. SMITH
GEO. TAYLOR
JAMES WILSON
GEO. ROSS

Delaware

CAESAR RODNEY
GEO. READ
THO. M'KEAN

South Carolina

EDWARD RUTLEDGE
THOS. HEYWARD, JUNR.
THOMAS LYNCH, JUNR.
ARTHUR MIDDLETON

New Jersey

RICHD. STOCKTON
JNO. WITHERSPOON
FRAS. HOPKINSON
JOHN HART
ABRA. CLARK

THE STATES ADOPT THEIR FIRST CONSTITUTION

1781

When Richard Henry Lee, on the seventh of June, 1776, introduced his momentous resolution that the colonies declare themselves to be free and independent states, he also moved that "a plan of confederation" be prepared. Wise men among the delegates to the Congress—indeed, wise men in all the colonies—knew that if independence were to become a reality, some form of union must be adopted. Yet many difficulties stood in the way.

For long years the colonists had thought of themselves as Virginians or New Yorkers or Rhode Islanders, and no small degree of ignorance, provincialism, and jealousy colored their attitudes toward each other. A young Jerseyman, visiting Virginia in 1773, could pass the harsh judgment that in that province the possession of large estates "blows up the owners to an imagination . . . . that they are exalted as much above other Men in worth & precedency, as . . . . in their property." In the same year a visitor from Massachusetts could comment, in his private journal, on the addiction of the South Carolinians to "cards, dice, the bottle and horses"; on the "odious character" of the middle class; on the widespread desecration of the Sabbath; and on the baneful effect of slavery on the manners and conduct of the people generally.

A dozen years earlier Lewis Morris of New York had provided in his will that his son Gouverneur should not be educated in Connecticut "lest he should imbibe in his youth that lowe craft and cunning so incident to the People of that Colony." "Low cunning" was the term that Edward Rutledge applied to New England leaders in the summer of 1776 when the colonies were on the verge of declaring their independence. A few weeks later George Washington felt the necessity of issuing a general order denouncing the "jealousies &c." that had arisen among the troops from different provinces and admonishing all men in the service to sink "distinctions of Nations, Countries, and Provinces" in the name American.

Prejudices were strengthened by honest differences regarding the form a union should take. Many members of the Continental Congress, still smarting from Britain's attempts at dictation and not forgetting the efforts of royal governors to seize power at the expense of colonial legislatures, insisted upon the complete independence of the states. Others placed their faith in a central government with power enough to suppress uprisings, settle disputes between the states, regulate commerce, and control the western lands that invited the new nation to expansion.

On July 12, 1776, eight days after the adoption of the Declaration of Independence, a committee charged with formulating the plan of union made its report. A few days later Congress began to debate the subject, but one event after another distracted the attention of the delegates. Washington, hard pressed, yielded New York to the British in the early fall, but a few months later, on Christmas night, he crossed the Delaware and inflicted a stinging defeat on the Hessians at Trenton. The next year "Gentleman Johnny" Burgoyne came down from Canada, terrified the New Yorkers, but ended by surrendering his army to Gates at Saratoga. Always, between battles, problems of recruiting, supply, and finance demanded attention.

As a result, it was not until November 15, 1777–seventeen

months after the submission of the first draft—that Congress approved the Articles of Confederation. And that was only the first step. Every one of the thirteen states would have to ratify the new plan of government before it could go into effect. The congressional letter of transmittal approached the apologetic:

"Hardly is it to be expected," the delegates confessed, "that any plan . . . . should exactly correspond with the maxims and political views of every particular State. . . . . This is proposed as the best which could be adapted to the circumstances of all; and as that alone which affords any tolerable prospect of a general ratification." Yet, imperfect as this form of government might be, circumstances demanded its adoption. "It will confound our foreign enemies," Congress predicted, "defeat the flagitious practices of the disaffected, strengthen and confirm our friends, support our public credit, restore the value of our money, enable us to maintain our fleets and armies, and add weight and respect to our councils at home, and to our treaties abroad. In short, this salutary measure can no longer be deferred."

By the end of July, 1778, ten states had responded to this appeal. But New Jersey, Delaware, and Maryland held off. Small, with definite boundaries, they feared that in the new union they would be overshadowed by the larger states, whose original charters gave them claims to vast expanses of unsettled land to the west. New Jersey gave up its scruples in November, 1778; Delaware yielded hers six months later; but Maryland held out until March, 1781. Thus, after nearly five years of debate, indecision, and controversy, the Articles of Confederation became the framework of union, and the first of the two constitutions of the United States.

In the light of history, one is inclined to magnify the defects of the Articles of Confederation. They provided for no independent executive, no national system of courts and judges. Each state retained its full sovereignty, and in Congress, where it possessed one vote, equaled any other in power. In order to pass important legislation, nine states had to agree, and the Articles could be amended only by a unanimous vote. Congress had the right to make war or peace, borrow money, and administer a postal service, but it could raise an army or navy only by requesting the states to fill the quotas it set. It had no means of enforcing its requests, and no power to levy taxes on the people or to regulate interstate commerce.

Yet the Articles served a purpose. The mere fact that they could be adopted in the face of provincial jealousies proved that the concept of a nation was gaining ground. In a few years, moreover, they would demonstrate that pure democracy needed to be qualified to fit hard reality.

The Articles of Confederation

March 1, 1781

To all to whom these presents shall come, we the undersigned delegates of the states affixed to our names send greeting. WHEREAS the delegates of the United States of America in Congress assembled did on the fifteenth day of November in the year of our Lord one thousand seven hundred and seventy-seven, and in the second year of the independence of America, agree to certain articles of confederation and perpetual union between the states of New Hampshire, Massachusetts Bay, Rhode Island and Providence Plantations, Connecticut, New York, New Jersey, Pennsylvania, Delaware, Maryland, Virginia, North Carolina, South Carolina, and Georgia in the words following, viz.,

"Articles of Confederation and perpetual union between the states of New Hampshire, Massachusetts Bay, Rhode Island and Providence Plantations, Connecticut, New York, New Jersey, Pennsylvania, Delaware, Maryland, Virginia, North Carolina, South Carolina, and Georgia."

ARTICLE I. The style of this confederacy shall be "The United States of America."

THE SOVEREIGNTY OF THE STATES

ARTICLE II. Each state retains its sovereignty, freedom, and independence, and every power, jurisdiction, and right, which is not by this confederation expressly delegated to the United States, in Congress assembled.

ARTICLE III. The said states hereby severally enter into a firm league of friendship with each other for their common defense, the security of their liberties, and their mutual and general welfare, binding themselves to assist each other against all force offered to, or attacks made upon them, or any of them, on account of religion, sovereignty, trade, or any other pretense whatever.

NATIONAL CITIZENSHIP

ARTICLE IV. The better to secure and perpetuate mutual friendship and intercourse among the people of the different states in this union, the free inhabitants of each of these states—paupers, vagabonds, and fugitives from justice excepted—shall be entitled to all privileges and immunities of free citizens in the several states; and the people of each state shall have free ingress and regress to and from any other state, and shall enjoy therein all the privileges of trade and commerce, subject to the same duties, impositions, and restrictions as the inhabitants thereof respectively, provided that such restrictions shall not extend so far as to prevent the removal of property imported into any state, to any other state of which the owner is an inhabitant; provided also that no imposition, duties, or restriction shall be laid by any state on the property of the United States, or either of them.

If any person guilty of, or charged with treason, felony, or other high misdemeanor in any state shall flee from justice, and be found in any of the United States, he shall upon demand of the governor or executive power of the state from which he fled be delivered up and removed to the state having jurisdiction of his offense.

Full faith and credit shall be given in each of these states to the records, acts, and judicial proceedings of the courts and magistrates of every other state.

THE CONGRESS

ARTICLE V. For the more convenient management of the general interests of the United States, delegates shall be annually appointed in such manner as the legislature of each state shall direct, to meet in Congress on the first Monday in November, in every year, with a power reserved to each state to recall its delegates, or any of them, at any time within the year, and to send others in their stead for the remainder of the year.

No state shall be represented in Congress by less than two, nor by more than seven members; and no person shall be capable of being a delegate for more than three years in any term of six years; nor shall any person, being a delegate, be capable of holding any office under the United States for which he, or another for his benefit, receives any salary, fees, or emolument of any kind.

Each state shall maintain its own delegates in a meeting of the states, and while they act as members of the committee of the states.

In determining questions in the United States in Congress assembled, each state shall have one vote.

Freedom of speech and debate in Congress shall not be impeached or questioned in any court, or place out of Congress, and the members of Congress shall be protected in their persons from arrests and imprisonments during the time of their going to and from, and attendance on Congress, except for treason, felony, or breach of the peace.

LIMITATIONS ON THE POWERS OF THE STATES

ARTICLE VI. No state without the consent of the United States in Congress assembled shall send any embassy to, or receive any embassy from, or enter into any conference, agreement, or alliance or treaty with any king, prince, or state; nor shall any person holding any office of profit or trust under the United States, or any of them, accept of any present, emolument, office, or title of any kind whatever from any king, prince, or foreign state; nor shall the United States in Congress assembled, or any of them, grant any title of nobility.

No two or more states shall enter into any treaty, confederation, or alliance whatever between them without the consent of the United Sates in Congress assembled, specifying accurately the purposes for which the same is to be entered into, and how long it shall continue.

No state shall lay any imposts or duties which may interfere with any stipulations in treaties entered into by the United States in Congress assembled, with any king, prince, or state, in pursuance of any treaties already proposed by Congress to the courts of France and Spain.

No vessels of war shall be kept up in time of peace by any state, except such number only as shall be deemed necessary by the United States in Congress assembled, for the defense of such state, or its trade; nor shall any body of forces be kept up by any state in time of peace, except such number only as in the judgment of the United States, in Congress assembled, shall be deemed requisite to garrison the forts necessary for the defense of such state; but every state shall always keep up a well-regulated and disciplined militia, sufficiently armed and accoutered, and shall provide and constantly have ready for use, in public stores, a due number of field pieces and tents, and a proper quantity of arms, ammunition, and camp equipage.

No state shall engage in any war without the consent of the United States in Congress assembled, unless such state be actually invaded by enemies, or shall have received certain advice of a resolution being formed by some nation of Indians to invade such state, and the danger is so imminent as not to admit of a delay till the United States in Congress assembled can be consulted: nor shall any state grant commissions to any ships or vessels of war, nor letters of marque or reprisal, except it be after a declaration of war by the United States in Congress assembled, and then only against the kingdom or state and the subjects thereof, against which war has been so declared, and under such regulations as shall be established by the United States in Congress assembled, unless such state be infested by pirates, in which case vessels of war may be fitted out for that occasion and kept so long as the danger shall continue, or until the United States in Congress assembled shall determine otherwise.

Article VII. When land forces are raised by any state for the common defense, all officers of or under the rank of colonel shall be appointed by the legislature of each state respectively by whom such forces shall be raised, or in such manner as such state shall direct, and all vacancies shall be filled up by the state which first made the appointment.

RAISING A REVENUE

Article VIII. All charges of war, and all other expenses that shall be incurred for the common defense or general welfare, and allowed by the United States in Congress assembled, shall be defrayed out of a common treasury, which shall be supplied by the several states in proportion to the value of all land within each state, granted to or surveyed for any person, as such land and the buildings and improvements thereon shall be estimated according to such mode as the United States in Congress assembled shall from time to time direct and appoint. The taxes for paying that proportion shall be laid and levied by the authority and direction of the legislatures of the several states within the time agreed upon by the United States in Congress assembled.

FOREIGN AFFAIRS

ARTICLE IX. The United States in Congress assembled shall have the sole and exclusive right and power of determining on peace and war, except in the cases mentioned in the sixth article—of sending and receiving ambassadors—[of] entering into treaties and alliances, provided that no treaty of commerce shall be made whereby the legislative power of the respective states shall be restrained from imposing such imposts and duties on foreigners, as their own people are subjected to, or from prohibiting the exportation or importation of any species of goods or commodities whatsoever—of establishing rules for deciding in all cases, what captures on land or water shall be legal, and in what manner prizes taken by land or naval forces in the service of the United States shall be divided or appropriated—of granting letters of marque and reprisal in times of peace—[of] appointing courts for the trial of piracies and felonies committed on the high seas and establishing courts for receiving and determining finally appeals in all cases of captures, provided that no member of Congress shall be appointed a judge of any of the said courts.

DISPUTES BETWEEN STATES

The United States in Congress assembled shall also be the last resort on appeal in all disputes and differences now subsisting or that hereafter may arise between two or more states concerning boundary, jurisdiction, or any other cause whatever; which authority shall always be exercised in the manner following:

Whenever the legislative or executive authority or lawful agent of any state in controversy with another shall present a petition to Congress, stating the matter in question and praying for a hearing, notice thereof shall be given by order of Congress to the legislative or executive authority of the other state in controversy, and a day assigned for the appearance of the parties by their lawful agents, who shall then be directed to appoint by joint consent, commissioners or judges to constitute a court for hearing and determining the matter in question: but if they cannot agree, Congress shall name three persons out of each of the United States, and from the list of such persons each party shall alternately strike out one, the petitioners beginning, until the number shall be reduced to thirteen; and from that number not less than seven nor more than nine names, as Congress shall direct, shall in the presence of Congress be drawn out by lot, and the persons whose names shall be so drawn, or any five of them, shall be commissioners or judges to hear and finally determine the controversy; so always as a major part of the judges who shall hear the cause shall agree in the determination: and if either party shall neglect to attend at the day appointed, without showing reasons, which Congress shall judge sufficient, or being present shall refuse to strike, the Congress shall proceed to nominate three persons out of each state, and the secretary of Congress shall strike in behalf of such party absent or refusing; and the judgment and sentence of the court to be appointed, in the manner before prescribed, shall be final and conclusive; and if any one of the parties shall refuse to submit to the authority of such court, or to appear to defend their claim or cause, the court shall nevertheless proceed to pronounce sentence, or judgment, which shall in like manner be final and decisive, the judgment or sentence and other proceedings being in either case transmitted to Congress and lodged among the acts of Congress for the security of the parties concerned: provided that every commissioner, before he sits in judgment, shall take an oath to be administered by one of the judges of the supreme or superior court of the state where the cause shall be tried, "well and truly to hear and determine the matter in question, according to the best of his judgment, without favor, affection, or hope of reward": provided also that no state shall be deprived of territory for the benefit of the United States.

All controversies concerning the private right of soil claimed under different grants of two or more states, whose jurisdiction as they may respect such lands, and the states which passed such grants are adjusted, the said grants or either of them being at the same time claimed to have originated antecedent to such settlement of jurisdiction, shall on the petition of either party to the Congress of the United States, be finally determined as near as may be in the same manner as is before prescribed for deciding disputes respecting territorial jurisdiction between different states.

POWERS OF THE CONGRESS

The United States in Congress assembled shall also have the sole and exclusive right and power of regulating the alloy and value of coin struck by their own authority, or by that of the respective states—fixing the standard of weights and measures throughout the United States—regulating the trade and managing all affairs with the Indians, not members of any of the states, provided that the legislative right of any state within its own limits be not infringed or violated—establishing and regulating post offices from one state to another throughout all the United States, and exacting such postage on the papers passing through the same as may be requisite to defray the expenses of the said office—appointing all officers of the land forces in the service of the United States, excepting regimental officers—appointing all the officers of the naval forces, and commissioning all officers whatever in the service of the United States—making rules for the government and regulation of the said land and naval forces, and directing their operations.

The United States in Congress assembled shall have authority to appoint a committee to sit in the recess of Congress, to be denominated a "Committee of the States," and to consist of one delegate from each state; and to appoint such other committees and civil officers as may be necessary for managing the general affairs of the United States under their direction—to appoint one of their number to preside, provided that no person be allowed to serve in the office of president more than one year in any term of three years; to ascertain the necessary sums of money to be raised for the service of the United States, and to appropriate and apply the same for defraying the public expenses—to borrow money or emit bills on the credit of the United States, transmitting every half-year to the respective states an account of the sums of money so borrowed or emitted—to build and equip a navy—to agree upon the number of land forces, and to make requisitions from each state for its quota in proportion to the number of white inhabitants in each state; which requisition shall be binding, and thereupon the legislature of each state shall appoint the regimental officers, raise the men, and clothe, arm, and equip them in a soldier-like manner at the expense of the United States, and the officers and men so clothed, armed, and equipped shall march to the place appointed, and within the time agreed on by the United States in Congress assembled: but if the United States in Congress assembled shall, on consideration of circumstances, judge proper that any state should not raise men, or should raise a smaller number of men than the quota thereof, and that any other state should raise a greater number of men than the quota thereof, such extra number shall be raised, officered, clothed, armed, and equipped in the same manner as the quota of such state unless the legislature of such state shall judge that such extra number cannot be safely spared out of the same, in which case they shall raise, officer, clothe, arm, and equip as many of such extra number as they judge can be safely spared. And the officers and men so clothed, armed, and equipped shall march to the place appointed, and within the time agreed on by the United States in Congress assembled.

The United States in Congress assembled shall never engage in a war, nor grant letters of marque and reprisal in time of peace, nor enter into any treaties or alliances, nor coin money, nor regulate the value thereof, nor ascertain the sums and expenses necessary for the defense and welfare of the United States, or any of them, nor emit bills, nor borrow money on the credit of the United States, nor appropriate money, nor agree upon the number of vessels of war to be built or purchased, nor the number of land or sea forces to be raised, nor appoint a commander-in-chief of the army or navy, unless nine states assent to the same: nor shall a question on any other point, except for adjourning from day to day, be determined unless by the votes of a majority of the United States in Congress assembled.

The Congress of the United States shall have power to adjourn to any time within the year, and to any place within the United States, so that no period of adjournment be for a longer duration than the space of six months, and shall publish the journal of their proceedings monthly, except such parts thereof relating to treaties, alliances, or military operations, as in their judgment require secrecy; and the yeas and nays of the delegates of each state on any question shall be entered on the journal when it is desired by any delegate; and the delegates of a state, or any of them, at his or their request shall be furnished with a transcript of the said journal, except such parts as are above excepted, to lay before the legislatures of the several states.

THE EXECUTIVE POWER

Article X. The committee of the states, or any nine of them, shall be authorized to execute, in the recess of Congress, such of the powers of Congress as the United States in Congress assembled, by the consent of nine states, shall from time to time think expedient to vest them with; provided that no power be delegated to the said committee for the exercise of which, by the Articles of Confederation, the voice of nine states in the Congress of the United States assembled is requisite.

CANADA

Article XI. Canada acceding to this confederation, and joining in the measures of the United States, shall be admitted into, and entitled to all the advantages of this union: but no other colony shall be admitted into the same unless such admission be agreed to by nine states.

THE NATIONAL DEBT

Article XII. All bills of credit emitted, monies borrowed, and debts contracted by, or under the authority of Congress, before the assembling of the United States, in pursuance of the present confederation, shall be deemed and considered as a charge against the United States, for payment and satisfaction whereof the said United States and the public faith are hereby solemnly pledged.

A PERPETUAL UNION

Article XIII. Every state shall abide by the determinations of the United States in Congress assembled on all questions which, by this confederation, are submitted to them. And the articles of this confederation shall be inviolably observed by every state, and the union shall be perpetual; nor shall any alteration at any time hereafter be made in any of them, unless such alteration be agreed to in a Congress of the United States, and be afterward confirmed by the legislatures of every state.

And Whereas, It hath pleased the Great Governor of the World to incline the hearts of the legislatures we respectively represent in Congress to approve of, and to authorize us to ratify, the said Articles of Confederation and perpetual union: Know Ye, That we the undersigned delegates, by virtue of the power and authority to us given for that purpose, do by these presents, in the name and in behalf of our respective constituents, fully and entirely ratify and confirm each and every of the said Articles of Confederation and perpetual union, and all and singular the matters and things therein contained: and we do further solemnly plight and engage the faith of our respective constituents, that they shall abide by the determinations of the United States in Congress assembled, on all questions which, by the said confederation, are submitted to them. And that the articles thereof shall be inviolably observed by the states we respectively represent, and that the union shall be perpetual. In witness whereof we have hereunto set our hands in Congress.

Done at Philadelphia in the State of Pennsylvania the ninth day of July in the year of our Lord one thousand seven hundred and seventy-eight, and in the third year of the independence of America.

JOSIAH BARTLETT JOHN WENTWORTH JUN[R] *August 8, 1778*	On the part and behalf of the State of New Hampshire
JOHN HANCOCK SAMUEL ADAMS ELBRIDGE GERRY FRANCIS DANA JAMES LOVELL SAMUEL HOLTEN	On the part and behalf of the State of Massachusetts Bay
WILLIAM ELLERY HENRY MARCHANT JOHN COLLINS	On the part and behalf of the State of Rhode Island and Providence Plantations
ROGER SHERMAN SAMUEL HUNTINGTON OLIVER WOLCOTT TITUS HOSMER ANDREW ADAMS	On the part and behalf of the State of Connecticut

Ja[s] Duane Fra[s] Lewis W[m] Duer Gouv. Morris	On the part and behalf of the State of New York
Jno. Witherspoon Nath[l] Scudder	On the part and in behalf of the State of New Jersey. *Nov. 26, 1778*
Rob[t] Morris Daniel Roberdeau Jon[a] Bayard Smith William Clingan Joseph Reed *July 22, 1778*	On the part and behalf of the State of Pennsylvania
Tho. M:Kean *Feb. 12, 1779* John Dickinson *May 5, 1779* Nicholas Van Dyke	On the part and behalf of the State of Delaware
John Hanson *March 1, 1781* Daniel Carroll d[o]	On the part and behalf of the State of Maryland
Richard Henry Lee John Banister Thomas Adams Jn[o] Harvie Francis Lightfoot Lee	On the part and behalf of the State of Virginia
John Penn *July 21, 1778* Corn[s] Harnett Jn[o] Williams	On the part and behalf of the State of North Carolina

HENRY LAURENS WILLIAM HENRY DRAYTON JNO MATHEWS RICHD HUTSON THOS HEYWARD JUNR	On the part and behalf of the State of South Carolina
JNO WALTON *July 24, 1778* EDWD TELFAIR EDWD LANGWORTHY	On the part and behalf of the State of Georgia

VIRGINIA ESTABLISHES RELIGIOUS FREEDOM

1786

In September, 1776, Thomas Jefferson withdrew from the Continental Congress, partly to be closer to his ailing wife, and partly to have a share, as a member of the Virginia House of Delegates, in reforming the government of his state.

Virginia needed change. Here an entrenched aristocracy stubbornly resisted the demands of the majority for the abolition of privilege and an equal share in government. The ruling class derived its power from wealth, and its wealth stemmed from the ownership of huge estates. The laws of entail and primogeniture, which assured that estates would descend intact to the oldest son, kept unassailable the dominance of a few families.

Sharing the privileges of the aristocracy were the clergy of the Church of England. Enjoying the sole right to hold religious services, supporting its clergy by taxation, and conducting its affairs through self-perpetuating vestries, the Church relished its position and resisted change as fervently as the great landowners.

Jefferson made his way to the dusty little capital of Williamsburg with high hopes of liberalizing this antiquated social structure. Thirty-three years of age, tall, angular, sandy-haired, he had the frame of the Scotch-Irish from whom he descended, the mind of a sophisticated son of the French enlightenment, and the zeal of the reformer who had not yet sensed to the full the perversity, stupidity, and selfishness of humanity. He would abolish entail and primogeniture, disestablish the Church of England, and provide for complete freedom of religious worship; institute a system of free schools so that the sharers of the new democracy would enjoy at least the fundamentals of education, abolish the slave trade, and frame a new code of laws that would be suited to the needs of a progressive, republican state.

In the main he succeeded, but that is another story. Here we are concerned only with his battle for religious freedom. None knew better than he how bitterly he would be opposed—by the clergy, who had no desire to see their easy livings disturbed; by the propertied class, who much preferred to have the churches supported by a tax on all the people rather than by contributions which would come from their own pockets; by the vestrymen, who coveted the influence their positions gave them; by zealous members of the Church itself, who could conceive of no other road to salvation than their own; by blind conservatives, who resisted change simply because it was change. Support, on the other hand, could be expected from the Presbyterians of the Piedmont region; from the growing numbers of Methodists and Baptists, who could worship in their own ways only at the risk of jail sentences; and from a few free spirits like himself.

Four days after the Virginia Assembly convened, Jefferson was appointed to the Committee on Religion. Petitions showered in from the frontier counties, demanding the separation of church and state; the Church struck back with counter-memorials. Although a majority of the committee were supporters of the Establishment, Jefferson attracted strong allies in George Mason, the liberal planter to whom freedom admitted of no qualifications, and James Madison, a frail young man of twenty-six already distinguished by erudition and philosophical attitude.

Leading the opposition were Edmund Pendleton, conservative to his fingertips, suave, respected, and a master-strategist in parliamentary maneuver; and Robert Carter Nicholas, devout member of the Established Church and deeply devoted to its interests.

The fight for disestablishment took place in stages. By a resolution here, a law there, Jefferson and his associates whittled at the power of the Church, but always the defenders of the Establishment managed to preserve something of its privileged position. Not until the summer of 1779 did the reformers feel confident enough to attempt a definitive test. By this time Jefferson occupied the Governor's Palace. From there he sent down the ordinance for religious freedom, which Madison attempted to push through the Assembly. The result was a storm of opposition so noisy and violent that Madison made no serious effort to secure passage.

Jefferson served two years as Governor, retired to Monticello, became a delegate in the Congress under the Articles of Confederation, and in 1784 went to France to represent his country as a special envoy, and later, as minister. By this time, in his own state, public opinion had taken the turn he had foreseen ten years earlier. The disfranchised had gained strength and the supporters of special privilege knew themselves to be vanquished. Once again Madison took up the bill for religious freedom, and on January 16, 1786, it became the law of the state.

After Jefferson's death his own sketch of a monument, with the draft of an epitaph, was found among his papers. The man who had occupied the Presidency and a host of other positions only less important, who had attained distinction in more fields than any other American of his time, wanted to be remembered for only three achievements. One of these was the authorship of the Virginia Statute for Religious Freedom.

The Virginia Statute for Religious Freedom

January 16, 1786

An Act for establishing Religious Freedom. I. *Whereas* Almighty God hath created the mind free; that all attempts to influence it by temporal punishments or burthens, or by civil incapacitations, tend only to beget habits of hypocrisy and meanness, and are a departure from the plan of the Holy Author of our religion, who being Lord both of body and mind, yet chose not to propagate it by coercions on either, as was in his Almighty Power to do; that the impious presumption of legislators and rulers, civil as well as ecclesiastical, who being themselves but fallible and uninspired men, have assumed dominion over the faith of others, setting up their own opinions and modes of thinking as the only true and infallible, and as such endeavoring to impose them on the others, hath established and maintained false religions over the greatest part of the world, and through all time; that to compel a man to furnish contributions of money for the propagation of opinions which he disbelieves is sinful and tyrannical; that even the forcing him to support this or that teacher of his own religious persuasion, is depriving him of the comfortable liberty of giving his contributions to the particular pastor, whose morals he would make his pattern, and whose powers he feels most persuasive to righteousness, and is withdrawing from the ministry those temporary rewards, which proceeding from an approbation of their personal conduct, are an additional incitement to earnest and unremitting labors for the instruction of mankind; that our civil rights have no dependence on our religious opinions, any more than our opinions in physics or geometry; that therefore the proscribing any citizen as unworthy the public confidence, by laying upon him an incapacity of being called to offices of trust and emolument unless he profess or renounce this or that religious opinion, is depriving him injuriously of those privileges and advantages to which in common with his fellow-citizens he has a natural right; that it tends only to corrupt the principles of that religion it is meant to encourage, by bribing with a monopoly of worldly honors and emoluments those who will externally profess and conform to it; that though indeed these are criminal who do not withstand such temptation, yet neither are those innocent who lay the bait in their way; that to suffer the civil magistrate to intrude his powers into the field of opinion, and to restrain the profession or propagation of principles on supposition of their ill tendency, is a dangerous fallacy which at once destroys all religious liberty, because he [the civil magistrate] being of course judge of that tendency will make his opinions the rule of judgment, and approve or condemn the sentiments of others only as they shall square with or differ from his own; that it is time enough, for the rightful purposes of civil government, for its officers to interfere when principles break out into overt acts against peace and good order; and finally, that truth is great and will prevail if left to herself, that she is the proper and sufficient antagonist to error, and has nothing to fear from the conflict unless by human interposition disarmed of her natural weapons—free argument and debate, errors ceasing to be dangerous when it is permitted freely to contradict them:

II. *Be it enacted by the General Assembly*, That no man shall be compelled to frequent or support any religious worship, place, or ministry whatsoever, nor shall be enforced, restrained, molested, or burthened in his body or goods, nor shall otherwise suffer on account of his religious opinions or belief; but that all men shall be free to profess, and by argument to maintain, their opinion in matters of religion; and that the same shall in no wise diminish, enlarge, or affect their civil capacities.

III. And though we well know that this assembly, elected by the people for the ordinary purposes of legislation only, have no power to restrain the acts of succeeding assemblies, constituted with powers equal to our own, and that therefore to declare this act to be irrevocable would be of no effect in law; yet we are free to declare, and do declare, that the rights hereby asserted are of the natural rights of mankind, and that if any act shall be hereafter passed to repeal the present, or to narrow its operation, such act will be an infringement of natural right.

WESTWARD THE COURSE OF DEMOCRATIC GOVERNMENT

1787

By the Treaty of Paris, which brought the War for Independence to an end, the United States came into undisputed possession of the territory extending from the original states to the Mississippi. Here was an empire of incredible diversity and fabulous wealth. Steep hills bordering on the upper Ohio shaded into gentle swells that held promise of fertile farms once the covering of oak, hickory, maple, walnut, and other hardwoods should be felled. The rolling land turned into sealike prairies, matted with tangled grasses higher than a horse's head. West of Lake Erie, and east and west of Lake Michigan, where sunny openings shone at frequent intervals in the oaken groves, the wooded country shaded into forests so thick with pines that the sun's rays rarely reached the ground. Rivers great and small —the Ohio, Muskingum, Miami, Wabash, Kankakee, Fox, Wisconsin, Illinois—gave access to the interior and promised to float the produce of future farms to markets not yet in existence. None could guess, even, at the wealth in coal and iron and other minerals that lay beneath the surface of prairie and forest.

A handful of villages—Detroit, Michilimackinac, Green Bay, Peoria, Kaskaskia, Vincennes—stood as remnants of the colonial empire that France had relinquished twenty years earlier. But for the most part Indian tribes roamed the region as they had for cen-

turies, living on the game and fish that abounded, and trading pelts for such of the white man's goods as they had come to depend on. Yet it was plain that their day would soon end. Explorers and soldiers had already spread the fame of the "west" among the land-hungry settlers of the eastern states, and a rush of emigrants awaited only the organization of the new territory.

To this task the Congress set itself as early as 1784. In that year it adopted an ordinance drafted by Thomas Jefferson, delegate from Virginia, which provided for temporary governments to be followed by new states. The ordinance, superseded before it went into effect, is remembered now principally for the classical names with which Jefferson bedecked the ten states for which it provided—Cheronesus, Polypotamia, Pelisipia, and others equally fanciful. The following year Congress took a second step by adopting, in the Ordinance of 1785, a scientific system of surveying and describing land which, because it provided for unmistakable designations, turned out to be one of government's greatest contributions to a people.

Recognizing that Jefferson's Ordinance of 1784 was impractical in many respects, Congress took up again the problem of forming a government for the new territory. The pressure for action mounted steadily. American settlers had already moved into southern Illinois, others had made clearings in the river valleys of eastern and southern Ohio, and thousands of Revolutionary veterans held bounty land warrants that they wanted to exchange for farms. Yet the delegates dawdled month after month with reports and resolutions.

Had it not been for a determined group of New Englanders, the Congress under the Articles of Confederation might have gone out of existence without adopting what has long been recognized as its greatest claim to fame—the Ordinance of 1787. The story begins, properly, in June, 1783, when 288 officers in Washington's army petitioned Congress to provide bounty lands in the Ohio country. As usual, that body procrastinated. These petitioners, however, were determined men. They kept the subject alive, and eventually formed the Ohio Company of Associates to achieve their purpose. The essence of their plan was the purchase of a large tract of land with the continental certificates—worthless in ordinary use—which they had received for their military services. And they intended to see to it that the Continental Congress acted.

As a first move, they submitted a memorial explaining their organization and its purpose. Nothing happened, so they sent a representative, Samuel Parsons, to try personal persuasion. The delegates were so indifferent, however, that not even a quorum could be brought together. But early in July, 1787, when the Reverend Manasseh Cutler of Ipswich, Massachusetts, took Parsons' place, the situation changed. This robust Congregational clergyman, who had served as a Revolutionary chaplain, had practiced medicine, and had won a wide reputation as a scientist, now demonstrated that he possessed no small talent as a lobbyist. Armed with many letters of introduction, he quickly ingratiated himself with delegates and officers of the government. By a combination of arguments, threats, pressures, and trades he induced Congress to do in three weeks what it had failed to do on its own initiative in three years—that is, to devise an acceptable frame of government for the new territory, and sell land located there on terms that would attract sturdy and industrious settlers. And all this the good clergyman had accomplished, as he wrote when he reluctantly started home, "in a constant round of pleasure."

The Ordinance of 1787 contained many notable features—guarantees of freedom of worship, of the benefits of the writ of habeas corpus, of trial by jury, of the sanctity of contracts; and it struck a new note in prohibiting slavery by national action. But its true greatness derives from the article which deals with the creation of new states. Here, for the first time in modern history, a nation provided that newly acquired territory, when properly settled and organized, would become an integral part of the parent country rather than a subordinate colony.

The Ohio Company moved quickly to take advantage of the land purchase that Cutler had engineered. On April 7, 1788, forty-eight men, led by General Rufus Putnam, arrived at the junction of the Muskingum and Ohio rivers. There they proceeded to found the town of Marietta. They were the vanguard of the thousands who would settle Ohio and bring that state—the first to be created out of the Northwest Territory—into the Union in 1803.

By that time the process of making new states was under way in other parts of the country. Vermont had been admitted to the Union in 1791, Kentucky in 1792, Tennessee in 1796. None of these commonwealths was directly affected by the Ordinance of 1787, but its great principle of expansion—that new states should be full participating members of the Union—was followed as each won admission. Thus the Ordinance insured the expansion of democratic government, and established the rule which the nation followed in its march across the continent.

The Ordinance of July 13, 1787

An Ordinance for the Government of the Territory of the United States Northwest of the River Ohio

Be it ordained by the United States in Congress assembled, That the said territory, for the purposes of temporary government, be one district, subject, however, to be divided into two districts as future circumstances may, in the opinion of Congress, make it expedient.

DESCENT AND CONVEYANCE OF PROPERTY

Be it ordained by the authority aforesaid, That the estates, both of resident and nonresident proprietors in the said territory, dying intestate, shall descend to, and be distributed among, their children and the descendants of a deceased child in equal parts; the descendants of a deceased child or grandchild to take the share of their deceased parent in equal parts among them; and where there shall be no children or descendants, then in equal parts to the next of kin in equal degree; and among collaterals, the children of a deceased brother or sister of the intestate shall have, in equal parts among them, their deceased parents' share; and there shall in no case be a distinction between kindred of the whole and half-blood; saving, in all cases, to the widow of the intestate her third part of the real estate for life, and one-third part of the personal estate; and this law relative to descents and dower shall remain in full force until altered by the legislature of the district.

And until the governor and judges shall adopt laws as hereinafter mentioned, estates in the said territory may be devised or bequeathed by wills in writing, signed and sealed by him or her in whom the estate may be (being of full age) and attested by three witnesses;

and real estates may be conveyed by lease and release, or bargain and sale, signed, sealed, and delivered by the person, being of full age, in whom the estate may be, and attested by two witnesses, provided such wills be duly proved and such conveyances be acknowledged, or the execution thereof duly proved, and be recorded within one year after proper magistrates, courts and registers shall be appointed for that purpose; and personal property may be transferred by delivery, saving, however, to the French and Canadian inhabitants, and other settlers of the Kaskaskies, St. Vincents, and the neighboring villages who have heretofore professed themselves citizens of Virginia, their laws and customs now in force among them, relative to the descent and conveyance of property.

THE FRAMEWORK AND POWERS OF GOVERNMENT

Be it ordained by the authority aforesaid, That there shall be appointed, from time to time, by Congress, a governor, whose commission shall continue in force for the term of three years, unless sooner revoked by Congress; he shall reside in the district, and have a freehold estate therein, in one thousand acres of land while in the exercise of his office.

There shall be appointed from time to time, by Congress, a secretary, whose commission shall continue in force for four years unless sooner revoked; he shall reside in the district, and have a freehold estate therein, in five hundred acres of land while in the exercise of his office. It shall be his duty to keep and preserve the acts and laws passed by the legislature, and the public records of the district, and the proceedings of the governor in his executive department, and transmit authentic copies of such acts and proceedings every six months to the Secretary of Congress. There shall also be appointed a court, to consist of three judges, any two of whom to form a court, who shall have a common law jurisdiction, and reside in the district, and have each therein a freehold estate in five hundred acres of land while in the exercise of their offices; and their commissions shall continue in force during good behavior.

The governor and judges, or a majority of them, shall adopt and publish in the district such laws of the original states, criminal and civil, as may be necessary and best suited to the circumstances of the district, and report them to Congress from time to time; which laws shall be in force in the district until the organization of the general assembly therein, unless disapproved of by Congress; but afterward the legislature shall have authority to alter them as they shall think fit.

The governor, for the time being, shall be commander-in-chief of the militia, appoint and commission all officers in the same below the rank of general officers; all general officers shall be appointed and commissioned by Congress.

Previous to the organization of the general assembly, the governor shall appoint such magistrates and other civil officers in each county or township as he shall find necessary for the preservation of the peace and good order in the same. After the general assembly shall be organized, the powers and duties of the magistrates and other civil officers shall be regulated and defined by the said assembly; but all magistrates and other civil officers not herein otherwise directed shall, during the continuance of this temporary government, be appointed by the governor.

For the prevention of crimes and injuries, the laws to be adopted or made shall have force in all parts of the district, and for the execution of process, criminal and civil, the governor shall make proper divisions thereof; and he shall proceed from time to time, as circumstances may require, to lay out the parts of the district in which the Indian titles shall have been extinguished, into counties and townships, subject, however, to such alterations as may thereafter be made by the legislature.

So soon as there shall be five thousand free male inhabitants of full age in the district, upon giving proof thereof to the governor, they shall receive authority, with time and place, to elect representatives from their counties or townships to represent them in the general assembly:

Provided, That, for every five hundred free male inhabitants, there shall be one representative, and so on, progressively, with the number of free male inhabitants, shall the right of representation increase, until the number of representatives shall amount to twenty-five; after which, the number and proportion of representatives shall be regulated by the legislature:

Provided, That no person be eligible or qualified to act as a representative unless he shall have been a citizen of one of the

United States three years, and be a resident in the district, or unless he shall have resided in the district three years; and, in either case, shall likewise hold in his own right, in fee simple, two hundred acres of land within the same:

Provided, also, That a freehold in fifty acres of land in the district, having been a citizen of one of the states, and being resident in the district, or the like freehold and two years' residence in the district, shall be necessary to qualify a man as an elector of a representative.

The representatives thus elected shall serve for the term of two years; and in case of the death of a representative, or removal from office, the governor shall issue a writ to the county or township, for which he was a member, to elect another in his stead to serve for the residue of the term.

The general assembly or legislature shall consist of the governor, legislative council, and a house of representatives. The legislative council shall consist of five members, to continue in office five years unless sooner removed by Congress; any three of whom to be a quorum: and the members of the council shall be nominated and appointed in the following manner, to wit:

As soon as representatives shall be elected, the governor shall appoint a time and place for them to meet together; and, when met, they shall nominate ten persons, residents in the district and each possessed of a freehold in five hundred acres of land, and return their names to Congress; five of whom Congress shall appoint and commission to serve as aforesaid; and, whenever a vacancy shall happen in the council, by death or removal from office, the house of representatives shall nominate two persons, qualified as aforesaid, for each vacancy, and return their names to Congress; one of whom Congress shall appoint and commission for the residue of the term; and every five years, four months at least before the expiration of the time of service of the members of the council, the said house shall nominate ten persons, qualified as aforesaid, and return their names to Congress; five of whom Congress shall appoint and commission to serve as members of the council five years, unless sooner removed.

And the governor, legislative council, and house of representatives shall have authority to make laws, in all cases, for the good government of the district, not repugnant to the principles and articles in this ordinance established and declared. And all bills, having passed by a majority in the house, and by a majority in the council, shall be referred to the governor for his assent; but no bill, or legislative act whatever, shall be of any force without his assent. The governor shall have power to convene, prorogue, and dissolve the general assembly when, in his opinion, it shall be expedient.

The governor, judges, legislative council, secretary, and such other officers as Congress shall appoint in the district, shall take an oath or affirmation of fidelity and of office; the governor before the president of Congress, and all other officers before the governor. As soon as a legislature shall be formed in the district, the council and house assembled in one room, shall have authority, by joint ballot, to elect a delegate to Congress, who shall have a seat in Congress, with a right of debating, but not of voting, during this temporary government.

THE RIGHTS AND DUTIES OF FREEMEN

And, for extending the fundamental principles of civil and religious liberty, which form the basis whereon these republics, their laws and constitutions are erected; to fix and establish those principles as the basis of all laws, constitutions, and governments, which forever hereafter shall be formed in the said territory; to provide also for the establishment of states, and permanent government therein, and for their admission to a share in the federal councils on an equal footing with the original states, at as early periods as may be consistent with the general interest:

It is hereby ordained and declared by the authority aforesaid, That the following articles shall be considered as articles of compact, between the original states and the people and states in the said territory, and forever remain unalterable, unless by common consent, to wit:

ARTICLE 1. No person, demeaning himself in a peaceable and orderly manner, shall ever be molested on account of his mode of worship or religious sentiments in the said territory.

ARTICLE 2. The inhabitants of the said territory shall always be entitled to the benefits of the writ of habeas corpus and of the trial by jury; of a proportionate representation of the people in the legislature; and of judicial proceedings according to the course of the common law. All persons shall be bailable, unless for capital offenses, where the proof shall be evident, or the presumption great. All fines shall be moderate; and no cruel or unusual punishments shall be inflicted. No man shall be deprived of his liberty or property, but by the judgment of his peers or the law of the land; and should the public exigencies make it necessary, for the common preservation, to take any person's property, or to demand his particular services, full compensation shall be made for the same. And, in the just preservation of rights and property, it is understood and declared, that no law ought ever to be made or have force in the said territory, that shall, in any manner whatever, interfere with or affect private contracts or engagements, bona fide, and without fraud previously formed.

ARTICLE 3. Religion, morality, and knowledge being necessary to good government and the happiness of mankind, schools and the means of education shall forever be encouraged. The utmost good faith shall always be observed toward the Indians; their lands and property shall never be taken from them without their consent; and in their property, rights, and liberty they shall never be invaded or disturbed unless in just and lawful wars authorized by Congress; but laws founded in justice and humanity shall from time to time be made for preventing wrongs being done to them, and for preserving peace and friendship with them.

Article 4. The said territory, and the states which may be formed therein, shall forever remain a part of this confederacy of the United States of America, subject to the Articles of Confederation, and to such alterations therein as shall be constitutionally made; and to all the acts and ordinances of the United States in Congress assembled, conformable thereto.

The inhabitants and settlers in the said territory shall be subject to pay a part of the federal debts contracted, or to be contracted, and a proportional part of the expenses of government to be apportioned on them by Congress, according to the same common rule and measure by which apportionments thereof shall be made on other states; and the taxes for paying their proportion shall be laid and levied by the authority and direction of the legislatures of the district or districts, or new states, as in the original states, within the time agreed upon by the United States in Congress assembled.

The legislatures of those districts, or new states, shall never interfere with the primary disposal of the soil by the United States in Congress assembled, nor with any regulations Congress may find necessary for securing the title in such soil to the bona fide purchasers. No tax shall be imposed on land the property of the United States; and, in no case shall nonresident proprietors be taxed higher than residents.

The navigable waters leading into the Mississippi and St. Lawrence, and the carrying places between the same, shall be common highways and forever free, as well to the inhabitants of the said territory as to the citizens of the United States, and those of any other states that may be admitted into the confederacy, without any tax, impost, or duty therefor.

THE FORMING OF NEW STATES

Article 5. There shall be formed in the said territory not less than three nor more than five states; and the boundaries of the states, as soon as Virginia shall alter her act of cession and consent to the same, shall become fixed and established as follows, to wit: The western state, in the said territory, shall be bounded by the Mississippi, the Ohio, and Wabash rivers; a direct line drawn from the Wabash and Post Vincents due north to the territorial line between the United States and Canada; and, by the said territorial line, to the Lake of the Woods and [the] Mississippi. The middle state shall be bounded by the said direct line, the Wabash from Post Vincents to the Ohio, by the Ohio, by a direct line drawn due north from the mouth of the Great Miami to the said territorial line, and by the said territorial line. The eastern state shall be bounded by the last mentioned direct line, the Ohio, Pennsylvania, and the said territorial line:

Provided, however, And it is further understood and declared that the boundaries of these three states shall be subject so far to be altered, that, if Congress shall hereafter find it expedient, they shall have authority to form one or two states in that part of the said territory which lies north of an east-and-west line drawn through the southerly bend or extreme of Lake Michigan. And whenever any of the said states shall have sixty thousand free inhabitants therein, such state shall be admitted, by its delegates, into the Congress of the United States on an equal footing with the original states, in all respects whatever; and shall be at liberty to form a permanent constitution and state government:

Provided, The constitution and government so to be formed shall be republican, and in conformity to the principles contained in these articles; and, so far as it can be consistent with the general interest of the confederacy, such admission shall be allowed at an earlier period, and when there may be a less number of free inhabitants in the state than sixty thousand.

PROHIBITION OF SLAVERY

Article 6. There shall be neither slavery nor involuntary servitude in the said territory, otherwise than in punishment of crimes whereof the party shall have been duly convicted: *Provided, always,* That any person escaping into the same, from whom labor or service is lawfully claimed in any one of the original states, such fugitive may be lawfully reclaimed, and conveyed to the person claiming his or her labor or services as aforesaid.

Be it ordained by the authority aforesaid, That the resolutions of the 23rd of April 1784, relative to the subject of this ordinance, be, and the same are hereby repealed and declared null and void.

TO FORM A MORE PERFECT UNION

1788

Troubles plagued the new nation. Under the Articles of Confederation the federal government could only call upon the states for the funds it needed for its own operations, and the states could not, or would not, meet more than a fraction of the demands. Everyone, it seemed, was in debt—farmers to merchants, merchants to bankers, taxpayers to the states, the states to the central government. Currency of uncertain value made trade difficult, while the states threw up additional barriers by imposing tariffs favoring their own citizens. Farm products went begging, trade stagnated. Spain threatened to close the Mississippi to the produce of the frontier, and the Barbary pirates took heavy toll of American ships whose masters ventured into the Mediterranean. The government, unable to induce the states to act in unison, could not protect its people, and the foreign offices of European nations confidently expected the new country to fall apart.

In Massachusetts, where conditions were more unsettled than

elsewhere, discontent flared into rebellion. In the fall of 1786 mobs of farmers, determined that there should be no judgments for debts, began to prevent the courts from meeting. Outlawed, they banded together under the leadership of a former army captain, Daniel Shays, and attempted to seize the federal arsenal at Springfield. Militiamen put down the revolt and dispersed the rebels, but the incident led sober citizens to believe that the country wavered on the brink of civil war, and that the underlying cause of very real grievances—a weak central government—had better be remedied.

While Shays's Rebellion was at its height, delegates from five states were meeting at Annapolis, Maryland. Attempting to settle vexatious problems of commercial relations, they soon concluded that the problem was too far-reaching to be dealt with by a minority of the states, and decided to recommend that a general convention be called "to take into consideration the situation of the United States," and to adopt such action as should be necessary "to render the constitution of the federal government adequate to the exigencies of the Union."

This recommendation sprang from the ingenious brain and determined will of a man who was to leave a deep mark on the history of his country. Alexander Hamilton had been born on the island of Nevis in the British West Indies. As a youth he had come to New York to study at King's College (now Columbia) and had quickly thrown himself into the Revolutionary cause. He soon discarded pamphlets for guns, attracted Washington's attention by his skillful conduct during the early stages of the war, and became the Commander-in-Chief's private secretary and aide-de-camp. With victory assured, Hamilton left the army [illegible]ve a year in Congress and then established a lucrative law [illegible]ice in New York.

Hamilton believed that the United States could not survive as a nation unless it had a central government strong enough to suppress such disorders as Shays's Rebellion, establish public credit and a sound currency, regulate trade between the states, maintain an army and navy, and conduct foreign affairs with authority. The Articles of Confederation, he well knew, conferred no such powers, but he hoped that a convention, if one were called as a result of the action of the Annapolis meeting, would see the need as he saw it, and act accordingly.

The Congress of the Confederation fell in line by inviting all the states to send delegates to Philadelphia on May 14, 1787, though the purpose of the gathering was explicitly limited to the revising of the Articles of Confederation. Eleven states responded promptly, New Hampshire came in later, and Rhode Island held aloof.

In talent and prestige the assembly was the most notable ever held in the country, and probably none since has equaled it. George Washington, honored above all men for his successful prosecution of the War for Independence, agreed to serve as a delegate from Virginia, and was unanimously chosen as the presiding officer. James Madison, though only thirty-six, could be counted on for a ripe knowledge of all the forms of government with which men had experimented in historic times. Hamilton appeared, endowed with such set purpose, acute mind, extraordinary power of debate, and personal charm that even his enemies resisted with difficulty. Gouverneur Morris, highly intelligent, urbane, sophisticated, and Robert Morris, the financier of the Revolution, were members of the Pennsylvania delegation. No one brought more distinction, however, than Benjamin Franklin, eighty-one years old but still blessed with liveliness, full mentality, and the abundance of common sense that had characterized him for more than half a century of public life.

Almost at the outset the delegates decided to disregard their instructions and devise an entirely new form of government. Virginia, through Edmund Randolph, proposed a plan that provided for a legislature of two houses in which each state would be represented in accordance with its wealth and population. The legislature would have the power to tax individuals directly instead of making levies on the states. There would also be a national executive and a federal judicial system. New Jersey, on behalf of the small states, countered with a plan that merely strengthened the Articles of Confederation without going to the root of the national necessity.

The two plans led to prolonged, and at times excited, debate. A series of compromises resulted. The delegates decided upon a legislature of two houses—to be called the Congress—in one of which the states would be represented according to population, while in the other their representation would be equal. Representation by population raised the question of the slaves: Should they be counted, or not, in the apportionment? The solution: a compromise by which three-fifths of the slaves were to be counted. The controversy over this point brought up the related issue of the slave trade. The northern states opposed it; the southern states wanted it retained. In the end, it was agreed that the trade should not be abolished for twenty years.

With great reluctance, because they distrusted power in the hands of one man, the delegates settled upon an elected chief executive, or President, and a federal judiciary to be appointed for life. At the same time they devised a system of checks and balances so that no branch of government could increase its authority at the expense of the other branches.

On September 15, 1787, all the states, through their delegates, approved the Constitution and ordered it to be engrossed. Two days later a clerk read the engrossed copy. When he had finished, the venerable Franklin took the floor and asked his colleague from Pennsylvania, James Wilson, to read a few remarks that he had reduced to writing. The Constitution, Franklin admitted, was far from perfect, but on the whole it was the best frame of government that could be devised under the circumstances. "I cannot help expressing a wish," he concluded, "that every member of the Convention, who may still have objections to it, would with me, on this occasion, doubt a little of his own infallibility, and, to make manifest our unanimity, put his name to this instrument."

There was argument over the form in which the members should subscribe their names, and in the end only thirty-nine of the fifty-five delegates who had attended the convention signed. Of the other sixteen, some were absent, and several ranged themselves in opposition.

James Madison drew a little pen picture of one of the most momentous events in American history. "Whilst the last members were signing," he wrote in a note that did not come to light until long afterward, "Dr. Franklin, looking towards the president's chair, at the back of which a rising sun happened to be painted, observed to a few members near him, that painters had found it difficult to distinguish, in their art, a rising from a setting sun. 'I have,' said he, 'often and often, in the course of the session, and the vicissitudes of my hopes and fears as to its issue, looked at that behind the president, without being able to tell whether it was rising or setting; but now, at length, I have the happiness to know that it is a rising, and not a setting sun.' "

The Constitution would go into effect, so Article VII read, when it should be ratified by nine of the thirteen states. A spirited campaign began immediately. Strong opposition developed. Many resented the undoubted fact that the delegates had exceeded their authority; others believed that the new government went too far in the direction of centralized power. Nevertheless, the dangers confronting the country were real and pressing, and there might not be time for perfecting an ideal system. Reasoning thus, the state conventions began to pass ordinances of ratification—Delaware, the first, on December 7, 1787, Pennsylvania five days later, New Jersey on December 18. New Hampshire, the ninth state to ratify, acted on June 21, 1788.

Technically, the Constitution would now go into effect, yet everyone knew that without New York and Virginia the new government would fail. In the Old Dominion, James Madison pleaded for ratification, George Washington came to his support, and the convention voted favorably on June 25, 1788. In New York, Alexander Hamilton, through his contributions to the series of newspaper articles that we know as *The Federalist*, and by the force of his arguments in the state convention, produced the margin of victory, and the state fell in line with Virginia. A few weeks later the old Congress chose New York City as the seat of the new government, fixed dates for the appointment of presidential electors, and specified that the first Congress to be elected under the Constitution would convene on March 4, 1789.

Much of the criticism of the Constitution stemmed from the fact that it did not contain guarantees of individual rights. The ratifications of several states were accompanied by recommendations that a bill of rights be added, and it was soon evident that public opinion favored this course. At the urging of Madison, the House of Representatives recommended, on September 9, 1789, twelve amendments that embodied the specific guarantees proposed by the conventions that had ratified the Constitution. In substance the amendments comprised the historic rights of Englishmen, reaffirmed by the Americans in such documents as the Declarations and Resolves of the Continental Congress and the Declaration of Independence. Of the twelve, ten were ratified and went into effect on December 15, 1791.

The Bill of Rights is the American citizen's sturdiest protection against tyranny, whether it be the tyranny of government or the tyranny of the popular majority. In times of stress some of the guarantees of freedom have been called into question, but in well over a century and a half they have suffered no serious impairment.

The Constitution of the United States

June 21, 1788

We the people of the United States, in order to form a more perfect union, establish justice, insure domestic tranquillity, provide for the common defense, promote the general welfare, and secure the blessings of liberty to ourselves and our posterity, do ordain and establish this Constitution for the United States of America.

THE LEGISLATIVE DEPARTMENT

ARTICLE I

SECTION 1. All legislative powers herein granted shall be vested in a Congress of the United States, which shall consist of a Senate and House of Representatives.

SECTION 2. The House of Representatives shall be composed of members chosen every second year by the people of the several states, and the electors in each state shall have the qualifications requisite for electors of the most numerous branch of the state legislature.

No person shall be a Representative who shall not have attained to the age of twenty-five years, and been seven years a citizen of the United States, and who shall not, when elected, be an inhabitant of that state in which he shall be chosen.

Representatives and direct taxes shall be apportioned among the several states which may be included within this Union, according to their respective numbers, which shall be determined by adding to the whole number of free persons, including those bound to service for a term of years, and excluding Indians not taxed, three-fifths of all other persons. The actual enumeration shall be made within three years after the first meeting of the Congress of the United States, and within every subsequent term of ten years, in such manner as they shall by law direct. The number of Representatives shall not exceed one for every thirty thousand, but each state shall have at least one Representative; and until such enumeration shall be made, the State of New Hampshire shall be entitled to choose three, Massachusetts eight, Rhode Island and Providence Plantations one, Connecticut five, New York six, New Jersey four, Pennsylvania eight, Delaware one, Maryland six, Virginia ten, North Carolina five, South Carolina five, and Georgia three.

When vacancies happen in the representation from any state, the executive authority thereof shall issue writs of election to fill such vacancies.

The House of Representatives shall choose their speaker and other officers; and shall have the sole power of impeachment.

SECTION 3. The Senate of the United States shall be composed of two Senators from each state, chosen by the legislature thereof, for six years; and each Senator shall have one vote.

Immediately after they shall be assembled in consequence of the first election, they shall be divided as equally as may be into three

classes. The seats of the Senators of the first class shall be vacated at the expiration of the second year, of the second class at the expiration of the fourth year, and of the third class at the expiration of the sixth year, so that one third may be chosen every second year; and if vacancies happen by resignation, or otherwise, during the recess of the legislature of any state, the executive thereof may make temporary appointments until the next meeting of the legislature, which shall then fill such vacancies.

No person shall be a Senator who shall not have attained to the age of thirty years, and been nine years a citizen of the United States, and who shall not, when elected, be an inhabitant of that state for which he shall be chosen.

The Vice-President of the United States shall be President of the Senate, but shall have no vote, unless they be equally divided.

The Senate shall choose their other officers, and also a president pro tempore, in the absence of the Vice-President, or when he shall exercise the office of President of the United States.

The Senate shall have the sole power to try all impeachments. When sitting for that purpose, they shall be on oath or affirmation. When the President of the United States is tried, the Chief Justice shall preside: And no person shall be convicted without the concurrence of two-thirds of the members present.

Judgment in cases of impeachment shall not extend further than to removal from office, and disqualification to hold and enjoy any office of honor, trust or profit under the United States: but the party convicted shall nevertheless be liable and subject to indictment, trial, judgment and punishment, according to law.

SECTION 4. The times, places and manner of holding elections for Senators and Representatives, shall be prescribed in each state by the legislature thereof; but the Congress may at any time by law make or alter such regulations, except as to the places of choosing Senators.

The Congress shall assemble at least once in every year, and such meeting shall be on the first Monday in December, unless they shall by law appoint a different day.

SECTION 5. Each House shall be the judge of the elections, returns and qualifications of its own members, and a majority of each shall constitute a quorum to do business; but a smaller number may adjourn from day to day, and may be authorized to compel the attendance of absent members, in such manner, and under such penalties as each House may provide.

Each House may determine the rules of its proceedings, punish its members for disorderly behavior, and, with the concurrence of two-thirds, expel a member.

Each House shall keep a journal of its proceedings, and from time to time publish the same, excepting such parts as may in their judgment require secrecy; and the yeas and nays of the members of either House on any question shall, at the desire of one-fifth of those present, be entered on the journal.

Neither House, during the session of Congress, shall, without the consent of the other, adjourn for more than three days, nor to any other place than that in which the two Houses shall be sitting.

SECTION 6. The Senators and Representatives shall receive a compensation for their services, to be ascertained by law, and paid out of the Treasury of the United States. They shall in all cases, except treason, felony and breach of the peace, be privileged from arrest during their attendance at the session of their respective Houses, and in going to and returning from the same; and for any speech or debate in either House, they shall not be questioned in any other place.

No Senator or Representative shall, during the time for which he was elected, be appointed to any civil office under the authority of the United States, which shall have been created, or the emoluments whereof shall have been increased during such time; and no person holding any office under the United States, shall be a member of either House during his continuance in office.

SECTION 7. All bills for raising revenue shall originate in the House of Representatives; but the Senate may propose or concur with amendments as on other bills.

Every bill which shall have passed the House of Representatives and the Senate, shall, before it become a law, be presented to the President of the United States; if he approve he shall sign it, but if not he shall return it, with his objections to that House in which it shall have originated, who shall enter the objections at large on their journal, and proceed to reconsider it. If after such reconsideration two-thirds of that House shall agree to pass the bill, it shall be sent, together with the objections, to the other House, by which it shall likewise be reconsidered, and if approved by two-thirds of that House, it shall become a law. But in all such cases the votes of both Houses shall be determined by yeas and nays, and the names of the persons voting for and against the bill shall be entered on the journal of each House respectively. If any bill shall not be returned by the President within ten days (Sundays excepted) after it shall have been presented to him, the same shall be a law, in like manner as if he had signed it, unless the Congress by their adjournment prevent its return, in which case it shall not be a law.

Every order, resolution, or vote to which the concurrence of the Senate and House of Representatives may be necessary (except on a question of adjournment) shall be presented to the President of the United States; and before the same shall take effect, shall be approved by him, or being disapproved by him, shall be repassed by two-thirds of the Senate and House of Representatives, according to the rules and limitations prescribed in the case of a bill.

SECTION 8. The Congress shall have power to lay and collect taxes, duties, imposts and excises, to pay the debts and provide for the common defense and general welfare of the United States; but all duties, imposts and excises shall be uniform throughout the United States;

To borrow money on the credit of the United States;

To regulate commerce with foreign nations, and among the several states, and with the Indian tribes;

To establish an uniform rule of naturalization, and uniform laws on the subject of bankruptcies throughout the United States;

To coin money, regulate the value thereof, and of foreign coin, and fix the standard of weights and measures;

To provide for the punishment of counterfeiting the securities and current coin of the United States;

To establish post offices and post roads;

To promote the progress of science and useful arts, by securing for limited times to authors and inventors the exclusive right to their respective writings and discoveries;

To constitute tribunals inferior to the Supreme Court;

To define and punish piracies and felonies committed on the high seas, and offenses against the law of nations;

To declare war, grant letters of marque and reprisal, and make rules concerning captures on land and water;

To raise and support armies, but no appropriation of money to that use shall be for a longer term than two years;

To provide and maintain a navy;

To make rules for the government and regulation of the land and naval forces;

To provide for calling forth the militia to execute the laws of the Union, suppress insurrections and repel invasions;

To provide for organizing, arming, and disciplining, the militia, and for governing such part of them as may be employed in the service of the United States, reserving to the states respectively, the appointment of the officers, and the authority of training the militia according to the discipline prescribed by Congress;

To exercise exclusive legislation in all cases whatsoever, over such district (not exceeding ten miles square) as may, by cession of particular states, and the acceptance of Congress, become the seat of the government of the United States, and to exercise like authority over all places purchased by the consent of the legislature of the state in which the same shall be, for the erection of forts, magazines, arsenals, dockyards, and other needful buildings; and—

To make all laws which shall be necessary and proper for carrying into execution the foregoing powers, and all other powers vested by this Constitution in the government of the United States, or in any department or officer thereof.

SECTION 9. The migration or importation of such persons as any of the states now existing shall think proper to admit, shall not be prohibited by the Congress prior to the year one thousand eight hundred and eight, but a tax or duty may be imposed on such importation, not exceeding ten dollars for each person.

The privilege of the writ of habeas corpus shall not be suspended, unless when in cases of rebellion or invasion the public safety may require it.

No bill of attainder or ex post facto law shall be passed.

No capitation, or other direct, tax shall be laid, unless in proportion to the census or enumeration herein before directed to be taken.

No tax or duty shall be laid on articles exported from any state.

No preference shall be given by any regulation of commerce or revenue to the ports of one state over those of another; nor shall vessels bound to, or from, one state, be obliged to enter, clear or pay duties in another.

No money shall be drawn from the treasury, but in consequence of appropriations made by law; and a regular statement and account of the receipts and expenditures of all public money shall be published from time to time.

No title of nobility shall be granted by the United States: and no person holding any office of profit or trust under them, shall, without the consent of the Congress, accept of any present, emolument, office, or title, of any kind whatever, from any king, prince, or foreign state.

SECTION 10. No state shall enter into any treaty, alliance, or confederation; grant letters of marque and reprisal; coin money; emit bills of credit; make anything but gold and silver coin a tender in payment of debts; pass any bill of attainder, ex post facto law, or law impairing the obligation of contracts, or grant any title of nobility.

No state shall, without the consent of the Congress, lay any imposts or duties on imports or exports, except what may be absolutely necessary for executing its inspection laws: and the net produce of all duties and imposts, laid by any state on imports or exports, shall be for the use of the Treasury of the United States; and all such laws shall be subject to the revision and control of the Congress.

No state shall, without the consent of Congress, lay any duty of tonnage, keep troops, or ships of war in time of peace, enter into any agreement or compact with another state, or with a foreign power, or engage in war, unless actually invaded, or in such imminent danger as will not admit of delay.

THE EXECUTIVE DEPARTMENT

ARTICLE II

SECTION 1. The executive power shall be vested in a President of the United States of America. He shall hold his office during the

term of four years, and, together with the Vice-President, chosen for the same term, be elected, as follows.

Each state shall appoint, in such manner as the legislature thereof may direct, a number of electors, equal to the whole number of

Senators and Representatives to which the state may be entitled in the Congress: but no Senator or Representative, or person holding an office of trust or profit under the United States, shall be appointed an elector.

The electors shall meet in their respective states, and vote by ballot for two persons, of whom one at least shall not be an inhabitant of the same state with themselves. And they shall make a list of all the persons voted for, and of the number of votes for each; which list they shall sign and certify, and transmit sealed to the seat of the government of the United States, directed to the President of the Senate. The President of the Senate shall, in the presence of the Senate and House of Representatives, open all the certificates, and the votes shall then be counted. The person having the greatest number of votes shall be the President, if such number be a majority of the whole number of electors appointed; and if there be more than one who have such majority, and have an equal number of votes, then the House of Representatives shall immediately choose by ballot one of them for President; and if no person have a majority, then from the five highest on the list the said House shall in like manner choose the President. But in choosing the President, the votes shall be taken by states, the representation from each state having one vote; a quorum for this purpose shall consist of a member or members from two-thirds of the states, and a majority of all the states shall be necessary to a choice. In every case, after the choice of the President, the person having the greatest number of votes of the electors shall be the Vice-President. But if there should remain two or more who have equal votes, the Senate shall choose from them by ballot the Vice-President.

The Congress may determine the time of choosing the electors, and the day on which they shall give their votes; which day shall be the same throughout the United States.

No person except a natural-born citizen, or a citizen of the United States, at the time of the adoption of this Constitution, shall be eligible to the office of President; neither shall any person be eligible to that office who shall not have attained to the age of thirty-five years, and been fourteen years a resident within the United States.

In case of the removal of the President from office, or of his death, resignation, or inability to discharge the powers and duties of the said office, the same shall devolve on the Vice-President, and the Congress may by law provide for the case of removal, death, resignation or inability, both of the President and Vice-President, declaring what officer shall then act as President, and such officer shall act accordingly, until the disability be removed, or a President shall be elected.

The President shall, at stated times, receive for his services, a compensation, which shall neither be increased nor diminished during the period for which he shall have been elected, and he shall not receive within that period any other emolument from the United States, or any of them.

Before he enter on the execution of his office, he shall take the following oath or affirmation: "I do solemnly swear (or affirm) that I will faithfully execute the office of President of the United States, and will to the best of my ability, preserve, protect and defend the Constitution of the United States."

SECTION 2. The President shall be commander-in-chief of the army and navy of the United States, and of the militia of the several states, when called into the actual service of the United States; he may require the opinion, in writing, of the principal officer in each of the executive departments, upon any subject relating to the duties of their respective offices, and he shall have power to grant reprieves and pardons for offenses against the United States, except in cases of impeachment.

He shall have power, by and with the advice and consent of the Senate, to make treaties, provided two-thirds of the Senators present concur; and he shall nominate, and by and with the advice and consent of the Senate, shall appoint ambassadors, other public ministers and consuls, judges of the Supreme Court, and all other officers of the United States, whose appointments are not herein otherwise provided for, and which shall be established by law: but the Congress may by law vest the appointment of such inferior officers, as they think proper, in the President alone, in the courts of law, or in the heads of departments.

The President shall have power to fill up all vacancies that may happen during the recess of the Senate, by granting commissions which shall expire at the end of their next session.

SECTION 3. He shall from time to time give to the Congress information of the state of the Union, and recommend to their consideration such measures as he shall judge necessary and expedient; he may, on extraordinary occasions, convene both Houses, or either of them, and in case of disagreement between them, with respect to the time of adjournment, he may adjourn them to such time as he shall think proper; he shall receive ambassadors and other public ministers; he shall take care that the laws be faithfully executed, and shall commission all the officers of the United States.

SECTION 4. The President, Vice-President and all civil officers of the United States, shall be removed from office on impeachment for, and conviction of, treason, bribery, or other high crimes and misdemeanors.

THE JUDICIAL DEPARTMENT

ARTICLE III

SECTION 1. The judicial power of the United States, shall be vested in one Supreme Court, and in such inferior courts as the Congress may from time to time ordain and establish. The judges, both of the supreme and inferior courts, shall hold their offices during good behavior, and shall, at stated times, receive for their services, a compensation, which shall not be diminished during their continuance in office.

SECTION 2. The judicial power shall extend to all cases, in law and equity, arising under this Constitution, the laws of the United States, and treaties made, or which shall be made, under their authority; to all cases affecting ambassadors, other public ministers and consuls; to all cases of admiralty and maritime jurisdiction; to controversies to which the United States shall be a party; to controversies between two or more states—between a state and citizens of another state—between citizens of different states—between citizens of the same state claiming lands under grants of different states, and between a state, or the citizens thereof, and foreign states, citizens or subjects.

In all cases affecting ambassadors, other public ministers and consuls, and those in which a state shall be party, the Supreme Court shall have original jurisdiction. In all the other cases before mentioned, the Supreme Court shall have appellate jurisdiction, both as to law and fact, with such exceptions, and under such regulations as the Congress shall make.

The trial of all crimes, except in cases of impeachment, shall be by jury; and such trial shall be held in the state where the said crimes shall have been committed; but when not committed within any state, the trial shall be at such place or places as the Congress may by law have directed.

SECTION 3. Treason against the United States, shall consist only in levying war against them, or in adhering to their enemies, giving them aid and comfort. No person shall be convicted of treason unless on the testimony of two witnesses to the same overt act, or on confession in open court.

The Congress shall have power to declare the punishment of treason, but no attainder of treason shall work corruption of blood, or forfeiture except during the life of the person attainted.

FEDERAL AND STATE GOVERNMENTS

ARTICLE IV

SECTION 1. Full faith and credit shall be given in each state to the public acts, records, and judicial proceedings of every other state. And the Congress may by general laws prescribe the manner in which such acts, records and proceedings shall be proved, and the effect thereof.

SECTION 2. The citizens of each state shall be entitled to all privileges and immunities of citizens in the several states.

A person charged in any state with treason, felony, or other crime, who shall flee from justice, and be found in another state, shall on demand of the executive authority of the state from which he fled, be delivered up, to be removed to the state having jurisdiction of the crime.

No person held to service or labor in one state, under the laws thereof, escaping into another, shall, in consequence of any law or regulation therein, be discharged from such service or labor, but shall be delivered up on claim of the party to whom such service or labor may be due.

SECTION 3. New states may be admitted by the Congress into this Union; but no new state shall be formed or erected within the jurisdiction of any other state; nor any state be formed by the junction of two or more states, or parts of states, without the consent of the legislatures of the states concerned as well as of the Congress.

The Congress shall have power to dispose of and make all needful rules and regulations respecting the territory or other property belonging to the United States; and nothing in this Constitution shall be so construed as to prejudice any claims of the United States, or of any particular state.

SECTION 4. The United States shall guarantee to every state in this Union a republican form of government, and shall protect each of them against invasion; and on application of the legislature, or of the executive (when the legislature cannot be convened) against domestic violence.

PROVISION FOR AMENDMENTS

ARTICLE V

The Congress, whenever two-thirds of both Houses shall deem it necessary, shall propose amendments to this Constitution, or, on the application of the legislatures of two-thirds of the several states, shall call a convention for proposing amendments, which, in either case, shall be valid to all intents and purposes, as part of this Constitution, when ratified by the legislatures of three-fourths of the several states, or by conventions in three-fourths thereof, as the one or the other mode of ratification may be proposed by the Congress; provided that no amendment which may be made prior to the year one thousand eight hundred and eight shall in any manner affect the first and fourth clauses in the ninth section of the first article; and that no state, without its consent, shall be deprived of its equal suffrage in the Senate.

THE SUPREME LAW OF THE LAND

ARTICLE VI

All debts contracted and engagements entered into, before the adoption of this Constitution, shall be as valid against the United States under this Constitution, as under the Confederation.

This Constitution, and the laws of the United States which shall be made in pursuance thereof; and all treaties made, or which shall be made, under the authority of the United States, shall be the supreme law of the land; and the judges in every state shall be bound thereby, anything in the constitution or laws of any state to the contrary notwithstanding.

The Senators and Representatives before mentioned, and the members of the several state legislatures, and all executive and judicial officers, both of the United States and of the several states, shall be bound by oath or affirmation, to support this Constitution; but no religious test shall ever be required as a qualification to any office or public trust under the United States.

PROVISION FOR RATIFICATION

ARTICLE VII

The ratification of the conventions of nine states, shall be sufficient for the establishment of this Constitution between the states so ratifying the same.

Done in convention by the unanimous consent of the states present the seventeenth day of September in the year of our Lord one thousand seven hundred and eighty-seven and of the Independence of the United States of America the twelfth. In witness whereof we have hereunto subscribed our names.

Go Washington, *President and deputy from Virginia*

Attest: William Jackson, *Secretary*

Connecticut
Wm. Saml. Johnson
Roger Sherman

New York
Alexander Hamilton

New Jersey
Wil: Livingston
David Brearley
Wm. Paterson
Jona. Dayton

Pennsylvania
B. Franklin
Thomas Mifflin
Robt. Morris
Geo. Clymer
Thos FitzSimons
Jared Ingersoll
James Wilson
Gouv Morris

Delaware
Geo: Read
Gunning Bedford jun.
John Dickinson
Richard Bassett
Jaco: Broom

Maryland
James McHenry
Dan of St. Thos. Jenifer
Danl. Carroll

Virginia
John Blair
James Madison Jr.

North Carolina
Wm. Blount
Richd. Dobbs Spaight
Hu Williamson

New Hampshire
John Langdon
Nicholas Gilman

Massachusetts
Nathaniel Gorham
Rufus King

Georgia
William Few
Abr Baldwin

South Carolina
J. Rutledge
Charles Cotesworth Pinckney
Charles Pinckney
Pierce Butler

Articles in addition to, and amendment of the Constitution of the United States of America, proposed by Congress, and ratified by the legislatures of the several states, pursuant to the fifth article of the original Constitution.

THE BILL OF RIGHTS

Declared ratified December 15, 1791

ARTICLE I

Congress shall make no law respecting an establishment of religion, or prohibiting the free exercise thereof; or abridging the freedom of speech, or of the press; or the right of the people peaceably to assemble, and to petition the government for a redress of grievances.

ARTICLE II

A well-regulated militia, being necessary to the security of a free state, the right of the people to keep and bear arms, shall not be infringed.

ARTICLE III

No soldier shall, in time of peace be quartered in any house, without the consent of the owner, nor in time of war, but in a manner to be prescribed by law.

ARTICLE IV

The right of the people to be secure in their persons, houses, papers, and effects, against unreasonable searches and seizures, shall not be violated, and no warrants shall issue, but upon probable cause, supported by oath or affirmation, and particularly describing the place to be searched, and the persons or things to be seized.

ARTICLE V

No person shall be held to answer for a capital, or otherwise infamous crime, unless on a presentment or indictment of a grand jury, except in cases arising in the land or naval forces, or in the militia, when in actual service in time of war or public danger; nor shall any person be subject for the same offense to be twice put in jeopardy of life or limb; nor shall be compelled in any criminal case to be a witness against himself, nor be deprived of life, liberty, or property, without due process of law; nor shall private property be taken for public use, without just compensation.

ARTICLE VI

In all criminal prosecutions, the accused shall enjoy the right to a speedy and public trial, by an impartial jury of the state and district wherein the crime shall have been committed, which district shall have been previously ascertained by law, and to be informed of the nature and cause of the accusation; to be confronted with the witnesses against him; to have compulsory process for obtaining witnesses in his favor, and to have the assistance of counsel for his defense.

ARTICLE VII

In suits at common law, where the value in controversy shall exceed twenty dollars, the right of trial by jury shall be preserved, and no fact tried by a jury, shall be otherwise re-examined in any court of the United States, than according to the rules of the common law.

ARTICLE VIII

Excessive bail shall not be required, nor excessive fines imposed, nor cruel and unusual punishments inflicted.

ARTICLE IX

The enumeration in the Constitution, of certain rights, shall not be construed to deny or disparage others retained by the people.

ARTICLE X

The powers not delegated to the United States by the Constitution, nor prohibited by it to the states, are reserved to the states respectively, or to the people.

LATER AMENDMENTS

ARTICLE XI

Declared ratified January 8, 1798

The judicial power of the United States shall not be construed to extend to any suit in law or equity, commenced or prosecuted against one of the United States by citizens of another state, or by citizens or subjects of any foreign state.

ARTICLE XII

Declared ratified September 25, 1804

The electors shall meet in their respective states and vote by ballot for President and Vice-President, one of whom, at least, shall not be an inhabitant of the same state with themselves; they shall name in their ballots the person voted for as President, and in distinct ballots the person voted for as Vice-President, and they shall make distinct lists of all persons voted for as President, and of all persons voted for as Vice-President, and of the number of votes for each, which lists they shall sign and certify, and transmit sealed to the seat of the government of the United States, directed to the President of the Senate.

The President of the Senate shall, in the presence of the Senate and House of Representatives, open all the certificates and the votes shall then be counted; the person having the greatest number of votes for President, shall be the President, if such number be a majority of the whole number of electors appointed; and if no person have such majority, then from the persons having the highest numbers not exceeding three on the list of those voted for as President, the House of Representatives shall choose immediately, by ballot, the President. But in choosing the President, the votes shall be taken by states, the representation from each state having one vote; a quorum for this purpose shall consist of a member or members from two-thirds of the states, and a majority of all the states shall be necessary to a choice. And if the House of Representatives shall not choose a President whenever the right of choice shall devolve upon them, before the fourth day of March next following, then the Vice-President shall act as President, as in the case of the death or other constitutional disability of the President.

The person having the greatest number of votes as Vice-President, shall be the Vice-President, if such number be a majority of the whole number of electors appointed, and if no person have a majority, then from the two highest numbers on the list, the Senate shall choose the Vice-President; a quorum for the purpose shall consist of two-thirds of the whole number of Senators, and a majority of the whole number shall be necessary to a choice. But no person constitutionally ineligible to the office of President shall be eligible to that of Vice-President of the United States.

ARTICLE XIII

Declared ratified December 18, 1865

Section 1. Neither slavery nor involuntary servitude, except as a punishment for crime whereof the party shall have been duly convicted, shall exist within the United States, or any place subject to their jurisdiction.

Section 2. Congress shall have power to enforce this article by appropriate legislation.

ARTICLE XIV

Declared ratified July 28, 1868

SECTION 1. All persons born or naturalized in the United States, and subject to the jurisdiction thereof, are citizens of the United States and of the state wherein they reside. No state shall make or enforce any law which shall abridge the privileges or immunities of citizens of the United States; nor shall any state deprive any person of life, liberty, or property, without due process of law; nor deny to any person within its jurisdiction the equal protection of the laws.

SECTION 2. Representatives shall be apportioned among the several states according to their respective numbers, counting the whole number of persons in each state, excluding Indians not taxed. But when the right to vote at any election for the choice of electors for President and Vice-President of the United States, Representatives in Congress, the executive and judicial officers of a state, or the members of the legislature thereof, is denied to any of the male inhabitants of such state, being twenty-one years of age, and citizens of the United States, or in any way abridged, except for participation in rebellion, or other crime, the basis of representation therein shall be reduced in the proportion which the number of such male citizens shall bear to the whole number of male citizens twenty-one years of age in such state.

SECTION 3. No person shall be a Senator or Representative in Congress, or elector of President and Vice-President, or hold any office, civil or military, under the United States, or under any state, who, having previously taken an oath, as a member of Congress, or as an officer of the United States, or as a member of any state legislature, or as an executive or judicial officer of any state, to support the Constitution of the United States, shall have engaged in insurrection or rebellion against the same, or given aid and comfort to the enemies thereof. But Congress may by a vote of two-thirds of each House, remove such disability.

SECTION 4. The validity of the public debt of the United States, authorized by law, including debts incurred for payment of pensions and bounties for services in suppressing insurrection or rebellion, shall not be questioned. But neither the United States nor any state shall assume or pay any debt or obligation incurred in aid of insurrection or rebellion against the United States, or any claim for the loss or emancipation of any slave; but all such debts, obligations and claims shall be held illegal and void.

SECTION 5. The Congress shall have power to enforce, by appropriate legislation, the provisions of this article.

ARTICLE XV

Declared ratified March 30, 1870

SECTION 1. The right of citizens of the United States to vote shall not be denied or abridged by the United States or by any state on account of race, color, or previous condition of servitude.

SECTION 2. The Congress shall have power to enforce this article by appropriate legislation.

ARTICLE XVI

Declared ratified February 25, 1913

The Congress shall have power to lay and collect taxes on incomes, from whatever source derived, without apportionment among the several states, and without regard to any census or enumeration.

ARTICLE XVII

Declared ratified May 31, 1913

The Senate of the United States shall be composed of two Senators from each state, elected by the people thereof, for six years; and each Senator shall have one vote. The electors in each state shall have the qualifications requisite for electors of the most numerous branch of the state legislatures.

When vacancies happen in the representation of any state in the Senate, the executive authority of such state shall issue writs of election to fill such vacancies: *Provided*, That the legislature of any state may empower the executive thereof to make temporary appointments until the people fill the vacancies by election as the legislature may direct.

This amendment shall not be so construed as to affect the election or term of any Senator chosen before it becomes valid as part of the Constitution.

ARTICLE XVIII

Declared ratified January 29, 1919

Repealed by the Twenty-first Amendment

SECTION 1. After one year from the ratification of this article the manufacture, sale, or transportation of intoxicating liquors within, the importation thereof into, or the exportation thereof from the United States and all territory subject to the jurisdiction thereof for beverage purposes is hereby prohibited.

SECTION 2. The Congress and the several states shall have concurrent power to enforce this article by appropriate legislation.

SECTION 3. This article shall be inoperative unless it shall have been ratified as an amendment to the Constitution by the legislatures of the several states, as provided in the Constitution, within seven years from the date of the submission hereof to the states by the Congress.

ARTICLE XIX

Declared ratified August 26, 1920

The right of citizens of the United States to vote shall not be denied or abridged by the United States or by any state on account of sex.

Congress shall have power to enforce this article by appropriate legislation.

ARTICLE XX

Declared ratified February 6, 1933

SECTION 1. The terms of the President and Vice-President shall end at noon on the twentieth day of January, and the terms of Senators and Representatives at noon on the third day of January, of the years in which such terms would have ended if this article had not been ratified; and the terms of their successors shall then begin.

Section 2. The Congress shall assemble at least once in every year, and such meeting shall begin at noon on the third day of January, unless they shall by law appoint a different day.

Section 3. If, at the time fixed for the beginning of the term of the President, the President-elect shall have died, the Vice-President-elect shall become President. If a President shall not have been chosen before the time fixed for the beginning of his term, or if the President-elect shall have failed to qualify, then the Vice-President-elect shall act as President until a President shall have qualified; and the Congress may by law provide for the case wherein neither a President-elect nor a Vice-President-elect shall have qualified, declaring who shall then act as President, or the manner in which one who is to act shall be selected, and such person shall act accordingly until a President or Vice-President shall have qualified.

Section 4. The Congress may by law provide for the case of the death of any of the persons from whom the House of Representatives may choose a President whenever the right of choice shall have devolved upon them, and for the case of the death of any of the persons from whom the Senate may choose a Vice-President whenever the right of choice shall have devolved upon them.

Section 5. Sections 1 and 2 shall take effect on the fifteenth day of October following the ratification of this article.

Section 6. This article shall be inoperative unless it shall have been ratified as an amendment to the Constitution by the legislatures of three-fourths of the several states within seven years from the date of its submission.

ARTICLE XXI

Declared ratified December 5, 1933

Section 1. The eighteenth article of amendment to the Constitution of the United States is hereby repealed.

Section 2. The transportation or importation into any state, territory, or possession of the United States for delivery or use therein of intoxicating liquors, in violation of the laws thereof, is hereby prohibited.

Section 3. This article shall be inoperative unless it shall have been ratified as an amendment to the Constitution by conventions in the several states, as provided in the Constitution, within seven years from the date of the submission hereof to the states by the Congress.

ARTICLE XXII

Declared ratified February 26, 1951

SECTION 1. No person shall be elected to the office of the President more than twice, and no person who has held the office of President, or acted as President, for more than two years of a term to which some other person was elected President shall be elected to the office of the President more than once. But this article shall not apply to any person holding the office of President when this article was proposed by the Congress, and shall not prevent any person who may be holding the office of President, or acting as President, during the term within which this article becomes operative from holding the office of President or acting as President during the remainder of such term.

SECTION 2. This article shall be inoperative unless it shall have been ratified as an amendment to the Constitution by the legislatures of three-fourths of the several states within seven years from the date of its submission to the states by the Congress.

WASHINGTON ASSUMES THE PRESIDENCY

1789

By the fourth of March, 1789, the day appointed for the government under the new Constitution to begin operations, only a handful of members of the Congress had reached New York. Day after day those who were present anxiously awaited the arrival of their colleagues, but a month passed before a sufficient number of Senators were on hand to count the electoral votes. Washington was the first choice of every elector; John Adams, with the next largest number, won the Vice-Presidency. Messengers set out at once to notify the two men of their election.

Washington left Mount Vernon on April 16. In every village through which he passed the people dropped their work and turned out to honor the man to whom they owed their independence. Several cities detained him for formal ceremonies. As a result, seven days went by before he boarded the barge that was to take him from the Jersey shore to the tip of Manhattan Island. As thirteen "pilots" in white uniforms pulled on the oars, thousands of patriots cheered from the flag-decked craft that crowded the harbor. The Spanish warship *Galveston* saluted with thirteen guns, and the U.S.S. *North Carolina* replied.

An artillery company fired a third salute as Washington, dressed in a plain suit of blue and buff, mounted the crimson-carpeted steps of the wharf to be greeted by the Governor of New York and the members of the Senate and House of Representatives. Declining a carriage, he walked to the house that had been prepared for him. That night bonfires turned the sky red and revelers crowded the taverns and coffeehouses.

With Federal Hall, designed by the same L'Enfant who would plan the city of Washington, still unfinished, the inauguration ceremonies were postponed until April 30. On that morning thousands thronged the churches to pray for the success of the new government and the safety of the President. At noon, precisely, the presidential escort headed for Federal Hall. At the entrance the troops divided, and Washington passed through the stiff lines to the Senate Chamber where he was formally presented to the members of both houses. There John Adams, who had already been inaugurated, informed the President that the time for administering the oath of office had come. Washington rose, and walked to the balcony.

From Wall Street and Broad Street the crowds looked up to a man soberly dressed in dark brown, with white stockings and buckled shoes. Although he was nearing sixty, no stoop marred his tall and well-proportioned figure, and no one could fail to be impressed by the quiet dignity of his bearing. The Chancellor of New York administered the oath, turned toward the people, and called to the thousands below: "Long live George Washington, President of the United States!" The cry returned like rolling thunder.

With the cheers ringing in his ears, the President turned from the balcony to the Senate Chamber. There, in a voice so low as to be barely audible, and with some agitation and embarrassment, he read his inaugural address.

The address embodied no program, no ringing call to action. It did, however, breathe the spirit of public service, and summoned all men to sink selfishness and partisanship in a larger concern for the success of the experiment on which the nation was embarking.

Washington's First Inaugural Address

April 30, 1789

Fellow-citizens of the Senate and of the House of Representatives: Among the vicissitudes incident to life, no event could have filled me with greater anxieties than that of which the notification was transmitted by your order, and received on the fourteenth day of the present month.

On the one hand, I was summoned by my country, whose voice I can never hear but with veneration and love, from a retreat which I had chosen with the fondest predilection, and, in my flattering hopes, with an immutable decision, as the asylum of my declining years—a retreat which was rendered every day more necessary as well as more dear to me by the addition of habit to inclination, and of frequent interruptions in my health to the gradual waste committed on it by time.

On the other hand, the magnitude and difficulty of the trust to which the voice of my country called me, being sufficient to awaken in the wisest and most experienced of her citizens a distrustful scrutiny into his qualifications, could not but overwhelm with despondence one who (inheriting inferior endowments from nature and unpracticed in the duties of civil administration) ought to be peculiarly conscious of his own deficiencies.

In this conflict of emotions all I dare aver is, that it has been my faithful study to collect my duty from a just appreciation of every circumstance, by which it might be affected. All I dare hope is that if, in executing this task, I have been too much swayed by a grateful remembrance of former instances, or by an affectionate sensibility to this transcendent proof of the confidence of my fellow-citizens, and have thence too little consulted my incapacity as well as disinclination for the weighty and untried cares before me, my error will be palliated by the motives which misled me, and its consequences be judged by my country, with some share of the partiality in which they originated.

Such being the impressions under which I have, in obedience to the public summons, repaired to the present station, it would be peculiarly improper to omit in this first official act, my fervent supplications to that Almighty Being who rules over the universe, who presides in the councils of nations, and whose providential aids can supply every human defect, that His benediction may consecrate to the liberties and happiness of the people of the United States, a government instituted by themselves for these essential purposes, and may enable every instrument employed in its administration to execute with success the functions allotted to his charge.

In tendering this homage to the Great Author of every public and private good, I assure myself that it expresses your sentiments not less than my own, nor those of my fellow-citizens at large, less than either. No people can be bound to acknowledge and adore the Invisible Hand which conducts the affairs of men more than the people of the United States. Every step by which they have advanced to the character of an independent nation seems to have been distinguished by some token of providential agency. And in the important revolution just accomplished in the system of their united government, the tranquil deliberations and voluntary consent of so many distinct communities, from which the event has resulted, cannot be compared with the means by which most governments have been established, without some return of pious gratitude, along with an humble anticipation of the future blessings which the past seem to presage.

These reflections, arising out of the present crisis, have forced themselves too strongly on my mind to be suppressed. You will join with me, I trust, in thinking that there are none under the influence of which the proceedings of a new and free government can more auspiciously commence.

By the article establishing the executive department it is made the duty of the President "to recommend to your consideration such measures as he shall judge necessary and expedient." The circumstances under which I now meet you will acquit me from entering into that subject farther than to refer to the great constitutional charter under which you are assembled, and which, in defining your powers, designates the objects to which your attention is to be given.

It will be more consistent with those circumstances, and far more congenial with the feelings which actuate me, to substitute, in place of a recommendation of particular measures, the tribute that is due to the talents, the rectitude, and the patriotism which adorn the characters selected to devise and adopt them. In these honorable qualifications I behold the surest pledges that as on one side, no local prejudices or attachments, no separate views nor party animosities, will misdirect the comprehensive and equal eye which ought to watch over this great assemblage of communities and interests: so, on another, that the foundations of our national policy will be laid in the pure and immutable principles of private morality; and the pre-eminence of free government be exemplified by all the attributes which can win the affections of its citizens, and command the respect of the world.

I dwell on this prospect with every satisfaction which an ardent love for my country can inspire, since there is no truth more thoroughly established than that there exists in the economy and course of nature an indissoluble union between virtue and happiness—between duty and advantage—between the genuine maxims of an honest and magnanimous policy and the solid rewards of public prosperity and felicity; since we ought to be no less persuaded that the propitious smiles of Heaven can never be expected on a nation that disregards the external rules of order and right which Heaven itself has ordained; and since the preservation of the sacred fire of liberty and the destiny of the republican model of government are justly considered as deeply, perhaps as finally staked, on the experiment entrusted to the hands of the American people.

Besides the ordinary objects submitted to your care, it will remain with your judgment to decide how far an exercise of the occasional power delegated by the fifth article of the Constitution is rendered expedient, at the present juncture, by the nature of objections which have been urged against the system, or by the degree of inquietude which has given birth to them.

Instead of undertaking particular recommendations on this subject, in which I could be guided by no lights derived from official opportunities, I shall again give way to my entire confidence in your discernment and pursuit of the public good; for I assure myself that whilst you carefully avoid every alteration which might endanger the benefits of an united and effective government, or which ought to await the future lessons of experience, a reverence for the characteristic rights of freemen and a regard for the public harmony will sufficiently influence your deliberations on the question how far the former can be impregnably fortified, or the latter be safely and advantageously promoted.

To the foregoing observations I have one to add, which will be most properly addressed to the House of Representatives. It concerns myself, and will therefore be as brief as possible.

When I was first honored with a call into the service of my country, then on the eve of an arduous struggle for its liberties, the light in which I contemplated my duty required that I should renounce every pecuniary compensation. From this resolution I have in no instance departed. And being still under the impressions which produced it, I must decline as inapplicable to myself, any share in the personal emoluments which may be indispensably included in a permanent provision for the executive department, and must accordingly pray that the pecuniary estimates for the station in which I am placed may, during my continuance in it, be limited to such actual expenditures as the public good may be thought to require.

Having thus imparted to you my sentiments as they have been awakened by the occasion which brings us together, I shall take my present leave; but not without resorting once more to the benign Parent of the Human Race, in humble supplication that since He has been pleased to favor the American people with opportunities for deliberating in perfect tranquillity, and [with] dispositions for deciding with unparalleled unanimity on a form of government for the security of their union, and the advancement of their happiness, so His divine blessing may be equally conspicuous in the enlarged views, the temperate consultations, and the wise measures on which the success of this government must depend.

WASHINGTON COUNSELS HIS COUNTRYMEN

1796

Three years passed, and then four more. The man who had been the unanimous choice of the electors in 1789, and who had received all but three electoral votes in 1792, found himself reviled on every hand. Contrary to his fervent hope, parties had taken shape, and the Republicans—followers of Thomas Jefferson—had become outspoken in their opposition to a President who supported, in the main, the Federalist measures of Alexander Hamilton. Washington's refusal to allow the young nation to become involved in the wars of the French Revolution, with which many thousands sympathized, aroused bitter resentment. His suppression of the Whisky Rebellion made enemies.

But it was the Jay Treaty, by which, in 1794, the United States settled long-standing differences with Great Britain, that brought the full stream of abuse. By consenting to the treaty, Washington had violated the Constitution—so his detractors maintained—and heaped insults upon the people. He was an Anglomaniac, a monocrat, a tyrant who must now ride in a closed carriage drawn by more horses than were needed rather than make his way on foot or by horseback. The pettiest slight came on February 22, 1796, when the House of Representatives refused to congratulate the President, as it had done on each anniversary of his birth since he had held office.

Washington had consented to re-election with the utmost reluctance; now he made up his mind that he would not serve a third term under any circumstances. His reasons, he wrote to Hamilton, were various, but high among them was "a disinclination to be longer buffeted in the public prints by a set of infamous scribblers." He decided to announce his decision in a letter, or address, to his countrymen, and as early as May, 1796, he had enlisted Hamilton's help in its preparation. Letters that passed between the two men in the ensuing months show the great pains that Washington took with the document, and reveal his concern that it should reach a large and attentive audience. By mid-September he was satisfied with both form and content. After showing the address to his cabinet, he sent for David C. Claypoole, editor and proprietor of the Philadelphia *Daily American Advertiser*.

"I waited on him at the apointed time," Claypoole wrote, in describing the interview, "and found him sitting alone in the Drawing Room. He received me very kindly, and . . . . desired me to take a seat near him; then addressing himself to me, said, that he had for some time contemplated withdrawing from Public Life, and had at length concluded to do so at the end of the present term; that he had some Thoughts and Reflections on the occasion, which he deemed proper to communicate to the People of the United States, and which he wished to appear in the *Daily Advertiser*. . . ."

The two men agreed that the address should be published on September 19, and Washington promised that his secretary would deliver the copy the next day. Claypoole's account continues:

"After the Proof sheet had been carefully compared with the Copy and corrected by myself, I carried two different Revises [revised proofs] to be examined by the President, who made but few alterations from the Original, except in the punctuation, in which he was very minute. The publication of the address bearing the same date with the Paper, September 19th, 1796, being completed, I waited on the President with the Original, and in presenting it to him, expressed how much I should be gratified by being permitted to retain it; upon which in the most obliging manner, he handed it back to me, saying, that if I wished for it, I might keep it; —and I took my leave."

In the Farewell Address, Washington explained his reasons for retiring, justified certain measures of his administration, and propounded general principles that he hoped the nation would follow in the future. Few if any American pronouncements have had comparable influence on the course of history.

Washington's Farewell Address

September 19, 1796

Friends and Fellow-Citizens: The period for a new election of a citizen to administer the executive government of the United States being not far distant, and the time actually arrived when your thoughts must be employed in designating the person who is to be clothed with that important trust, it appears to me proper, especially as it may conduce to a more distinct expression of the public voice, that I should now apprise you of the resolution I have formed to decline being considered among the number of those out of whom a choice is to be made.

I beg you at the same time to do me the justice to be assured that this resolution has not been taken without a strict regard to all the considerations appertaining to the relation which binds a dutiful citizen to his country; and that in withdrawing the tender of service, which silence in my situation might imply, I am influenced by no diminution of zeal for your future interest, no deficiency of grateful respect for your past kindness, but am supported by a full conviction that the step is compatible with both.

The acceptance of and continuance hitherto in the office to which your suffrages have twice called me, have been a uniform sacrifice of inclination to the opinion of duty, and to a deference for what appeared to be your desire. I constantly hoped that it would have been much earlier in my power, consistently with motives which I was not at liberty to disregard, to return to that retirement from which I had been reluctantly drawn. The strength of my inclination to do this previous to the last election had even led to the preparation of an address to declare it to you; but mature reflection on the then perplexed and critical posture of our affairs with foreign nations, and the unanimous advice of persons entitled to my confidence, impelled me to abandon the idea.

I rejoice that the state of your concerns, external as well as internal, no longer renders the pursuit of inclination incompatible with the sentiment of duty or propriety, and am persuaded, whatever partiality may be retained for my services, that in the present circumstances of our country you will not disapprove my determination to retire.

The impressions with which I first undertook the arduous trust were explained on the proper occasion. In the discharge of this trust I will only say that I have, with good intentions, contributed toward the organization and administration of the government the best exertions of which a very fallible judgment was capable.

Not unconscious, in the outset, of the inferiority of my qualifications, experience in my own eyes, perhaps still more in the eyes of others, has strengthened the motives to diffidence of myself; and every day the increasing weight of years admonishes me more and more that the shade of retirement is as necessary to me as it will be welcome. Satisfied that if any circumstances have given peculiar value to my services, they were temporary, I have the consolation to believe that, while choice and prudence invite me to quit the political scene, patriotism does not forbid it.

In looking forward to the moment which is intended to terminate the career of my political life, my feelings do not permit me to suspend the deep acknowledgment of that debt of gratitude which I owe to my beloved country for the many honors it has conferred upon me; still more for the steadfast confidence with which it has supported me, and for the opportunities I have thence enjoyed of manifesting my inviolable attachment by services faithful and persevering, though in usefulness unequal to my zeal.

If benefits have resulted to our country from these services, let it always be remembered to your praise, and as an instructive example in our annals, that under circumstances in which the passions, agitated in every direction, were liable to mislead, amidst appearances sometimes dubious, vicissitudes of fortune often discouraging, in situations in which not unfrequently want of success has countenanced the spirit of criticism, the constancy of your support was the essential prop of the efforts, and a guarantee of the plans by which they were effected.

Profoundly penetrated with this idea, I shall carry it with me to my grave as a strong incitement to unceasing vows that Heaven may continue to you the choicest tokens of its beneficence; that your union and brotherly affection may be perpetual; that the free Constitution which is the work of your hands may be sacredly maintained; that its administration in every department may be stamped with wisdom and virtue; that, in fine, the happiness of the people of these states, under the auspices of liberty, may be made complete by so careful a preservation and so prudent a use of this blessing as will acquire to them the glory of recommending it to the applause, the affection, and adoption of every nation which is yet a stranger to it.

Here, perhaps, I ought to stop. But a solicitude for your welfare, which cannot end but with my life, and the apprehension of danger natural to that solicitude, urge me on an occasion like the present to offer to your solemn contemplation, and to recommend to your frequent review, some sentiments which are the result of much reflection, of no inconsiderable observation, and which appear to me all important to the permanency of your felicity as a people. These will be offered to you with the more freedom as you can only see in them the disinterested warnings of a parting friend, who can possibly have no personal motive to bias his counsel. Nor can I forget as an encouragement to it, your indulgent reception of my sentiments on a former and not dissimilar occasion.

Interwoven as is the love of liberty with every ligament of your hearts, no recommendation of mine is necessary to fortify or confirm the attachment.

The unity of government which constitutes you one people is also now dear to you. It is justly so, for it is a main pillar in the edifice of your real independence, the support of your tranquillity at home, your peace abroad, of your safety, of your prosperity, of that very liberty which you so highly prize.

But as it is easy to foresee that from different causes and from different quarters much pains will be taken, many artifices employed, to weaken in your minds the conviction of this truth, as this is the point in your political fortress against which the batteries of internal and external enemies will be most constantly and actively (though often covertly and insidiously) directed, it is of infinite moment that you should properly estimate the immense value of your national union to your collective and individual happiness; that you should cherish a cordial, habitual, and immovable attachment to it; accustoming yourselves to think and speak of it as of the palladium of your political safety and prosperity; watching for its preservation with jealous anxiety; discountenancing whatever may suggest even a suspicion that it can in any event be abandoned; and indignantly frowning upon the first dawning of every attempt to alienate any portion of our country from the rest, or to enfeeble the sacred ties which now link together the various parts.

For this you have every inducement of sympathy and interest. Citizens by birth or choice of a common country, that country has a right to concentrate your affections. The name of American, which belongs to you in your national capacity, must always exalt the just pride of patriotism more than any appellation derived from local discriminations. With slight shades of difference, you have the same religion, manners, habits, and political principles. You have in a common cause fought and triumphed together. The independence and liberty you possess are the work of joint councils and joint efforts, of common dangers, sufferings, and successes.

But these considerations, however powerfully they address themselves to your sensibility, are greatly outweighed by those which apply more immediately to your interest. Here every portion of our country finds the most commanding motives for carefully guarding and preserving the union of the whole.

The North, in an unrestrained intercourse with the South, protected by the equal laws of a common government, finds in the productions of the latter great additional resources of maritime and commercial enterprise and precious materials of manufacturing industry. The South, in the same intercourse, benefiting by the agency of the North, sees its agriculture grow and its commerce expand. Turning partly into its own channels the seamen of the North, it finds its particular navigation invigorated; and while it contributes in different ways to nourish and increase the general mass of the national navigation, it looks forward to the protection of a maritime strength to which itself is unequally adapted.

The East, in a like intercourse with the West, already finds, and in the progressive improvement of interior communications by land and water will more and more find, a valuable vent for the commodities which it brings from abroad or manufactures at home. The West derives from the East supplies requisite to its growth and comfort, and what is perhaps of still greater consequence, it must of necessity owe the secure enjoyment of indispensable outlets for its own productions to the weight, influence, and the future maritime strength of the Atlantic side of the Union, directed by an indissoluble community of interest as one nation. Any other tenure by which the West can hold this essential advantage, whether derived from its own separate strength or from an apostate and unnatural connection with any foreign power, must be intrinsically precarious.

While, then, every part of our country thus feels an immediate and particular interest in union, all the parts combined cannot fail to find in the united mass of means and efforts greater strength, greater resource, proportionably greater security from external danger, a less frequent interruption of their peace by foreign nations; and, what is of inestimable value, they must derive from union an exemption from those broils and wars between themselves, which so frequently afflict neighboring countries not tied together by the same government, which their own rivalships alone would be sufficient to produce, but which opposite foreign alliances, attachments, and intrigues would stimulate and embitter.

Hence, likewise, they will avoid the necessity of those overgrown military establishments which, under any form of government, are inauspicious to liberty, and which are to be regarded as particularly hostile to republican liberty. In this sense it is that your union ought to be considered as a main prop of your liberty, and that the love of the one ought to endear to you the preservation of the other.

These considerations speak a persuasive language to every reflecting and virtuous mind, and exhibit the continuance of the Union as a primary object of patriotic desire. Is there a doubt whether a common government can embrace so large a sphere? Let experience solve it. To listen to mere speculation in such a case were criminal. We are authorized to hope that a proper organization of the whole, with the auxiliary agency of governments for the respective subdivisions, will afford a happy issue to the experiment. 'Tis well worth a fair and full experiment. With such powerful and obvious motives to union affecting all parts of our country, while experience shall not have demonstrated its impracticability, there will always be reason to distrust the patriotism of those who in any quarter may endeavor to weaken its bands.

In contemplating the causes which may disturb our Union, it occurs as matter of serious concern that any ground should have been furnished for characterizing parties by geographical discriminations—Northern and Southern, Atlantic and Western—whence designing men may endeavor to excite a belief that there is a real difference of local interests and views. One of the expedients of party to acquire influence within particular districts is to misrepresent the opinions and aims of other districts. You cannot shield yourselves too much against the jealousies and heartburnings which spring from these misrepresentations. They tend to render alien to each other those who ought to be bound together by fraternal affection.

The inhabitants of our western country have lately had a useful lesson on this head. They have seen, in the negotiation by the Executive, and in the unanimous ratification by the Senate of the treaty with Spain, and in the universal satisfaction at that event throughout the United States, a decisive proof how unfounded were the suspicions propagated among them of a policy in the general government and in the Atlantic states unfriendly to their interests in regard to the Mississippi. They have been witnesses to the formation of two treaties—that with Great Britain and that with Spain—which secure to them everything they could desire in respect to our foreign relations, toward confirming their prosperity. Will it not be their wisdom to rely for the preservation of these advantages on the Union by which they were procured? Will they not henceforth be deaf to those advisers, if such there are, who would sever them from their brethren and connect them with aliens?

To the efficacy and permanency of your Union a government for the whole is indispensable. No alliances, however strict, between the parts can be an adequate substitute. They must inevitably experience the infractions and interruptions which all alliances in all times have experienced. Sensible of this momentous truth, you have improved upon your first essay by the adoption of a constitution of government better calculated than your former for an intimate union, and for the efficacious management of your common concerns.

This government, the offspring of our own choice, uninfluenced and unawed, adopted upon full investigation and mature deliberation, completely free in its principles, in the distribution of its powers, uniting security with energy, and containing within itself a provision for its own amendment, has a just claim to your confidence and your support. Respect for its authority, compliance with its laws, acquiescence in its measures, are duties enjoined by the fundamental maxims of true liberty. The basis of our political systems is the right of the people to make and to alter their constitutions of government. But the constitution which at any time exists, till changed by an explicit and authentic act of the whole people, is sacredly obligatory upon all. The very idea of the power and the right of the people to establish government presupposes the duty of every individual to obey the established government.

All obstructions to the execution of the laws, all combinations and associations, under whatever plausible character, with the real design to direct, control, counteract, or awe the regular deliberation and action of the constituted authorities are destructive of this fundamental principle and of fatal tendency. They serve to organize faction; to give it an artificial and extraordinary force; to put in the place of the delegated will of the nation the will of a party, often a small but artful and enterprising minority of the community; and, according to the alternate triumphs of different parties, to make the public administration the mirror of the ill-concerted and incongruous projects of faction, rather than the organ of consistent and wholesome plans, digested by common counsels and modified by mutual interests.

However combinations or associations of the above description may now and then answer popular ends, they are likely, in the course of time and things, to become potent engines by which cunning, ambitious, and unprincipled men will be enabled to subvert the power of the people, and to usurp for themselves the reins of government, destroying afterward the very engines which have lifted them to unjust dominion.

Toward the preservation of your government and the permanency of your present happy state, it is requisite not only that you steadily discountenance irregular oppositions to its acknowledged authority, but also that you resist with care the spirit of innovation upon its principles, however specious the pretexts. One method of assault may be to effect in the forms of the Constitution alterations which will impair the energy of the system, and thus to undermine what cannot be directly overthrown.

In all the changes to which you may be invited, remember that time and habit are at least as necessary to fix the true character of governments as of other human institutions; that experience is the surest standard by which to test the real tendency of the existing constitution of a country; that facility in changes upon the credit of mere hypotheses and opinion exposes to perpetual change, from the endless variety of hypotheses and opinion; and remember, especially, that for the efficient management of your common interests in a country so extensive as ours, a government of as much vigor as is consistent with the perfect security of liberty is indispensable. Liberty itself will find in such a government, with powers properly distributed and adjusted, its surest guardian. It is, indeed, little else than a name where the government is too feeble to withstand the enterprises of faction, to confine each member of the society within the limits prescribed by the laws, and to maintain all in the secure and tranquil enjoyment of the rights of person and property.

I have already intimated to you the danger of parties in the state, with particular reference to the founding of them on geographical discriminations. Let me now take a more comprehensive view, and warn you in the most solemn manner against the baneful effects of the spirit of party generally.

This spirit, unfortunately, is inseparable from our nature, having its root in the strongest passions of the human mind. It exists under different shapes in all governments, more or less stifled, controlled, or repressed; but in those of the popular form it is seen in its greatest rankness and is truly their worst enemy.

The alternate domination of one faction over another, sharpened by the spirit of revenge natural to party dissension, which in different ages and countries has perpetrated the most horrid enormities, is itself a frightful despotism. But this leads at length to a more formal and permanent despotism. The disorders and miseries which result, gradually incline the minds of men to seek security and repose in the absolute power of an individual, and sooner or later the chief of some prevailing faction, more able or more fortunate than his competitors, turns this disposition to the purposes of his own elevation on the ruins of public liberty.

Without looking forward to an extremity of this kind (which nevertheless ought not to be entirely out of sight), the common and continual mischiefs of the spirit of party are sufficient to make it the interest and duty of a wise people to discourage and restrain it.

It serves always to distract the public councils and enfeeble the public administration. It agitates the community with ill-founded jealousies and false alarms; kindles the animosity of one part against another; foments occasionally riot and insurrection. It opens the door to foreign influence and corruption, which find a facilitated access to the government itself through the channels of party passion. Thus the policy and the will of one country are subjected to the policy and will of another.

There is an opinion that parties in free countries are useful checks upon the administration of the government and serve to keep alive the spirit of liberty. This within certain limits is probably true; and in governments of a monarchical cast patriotism may look with indulgence, if not with favor, upon the spirit of party. But in those of the popular character, in governments purely elective, it is a spirit not to be encouraged. From their natural tendency it is certain there will always be enough of that spirit for every salutary purpose. And there being constant danger of excess, the effort ought to be, by force of public opinion, to mitigate and assuage it. A fire not to be quenched, it demands a uniform vigilance to prevent its bursting into a flame, lest, instead of warming, it should consume.

It is important, likewise, that the habits of thinking in a free country should inspire caution in those entrusted with its administration, to confine themselves within their respective constitutional spheres, avoiding in the exercise of the powers of one department to encroach upon another. The spirit of encroachment tends to consolidate the powers of all the departments in one, and thus to create, whatever the form of government, a real despotism. A just estimate of that love of power, and proneness to abuse it, which predominates in the human heart is sufficient to satisfy us of the truth of this position.

The necessity of reciprocal checks in the exercise of political power, by dividing and distributing it into different depositories, and constituting each the guardian of the public weal against invasions by the others, has been evinced by experiments ancient and modern, some of them in our country and under our own eyes. To preserve them must be as necessary as to institute them.

If in the opinion of the people the distribution or modification of the constitutional powers be in any particular wrong, let it be corrected by an amendment in the way which the Constitution designates. But let there be no change by usurpation; for though this, in one instance, may be the instrument of good, it is the customary weapon by which free governments are destroyed. The precedent must always greatly overbalance in permanent evil any partial or transient benefit which the use can at any time yield.

Of all the dispositions and habits which lead to political prosperity, religion and morality are indispensable supports. In vain would that man claim the tribute of patriotism who should labor to subvert these great pillars of human happiness, these firmest props of the duties of men and citizens. The mere politician, equally with the pious man, ought to respect and to cherish them. A volume could not trace all their connections with private and public felicity. Let it simply be asked: Where is the security for property, for reputation, for life, if the sense of religious obligation desert the oaths which are the instruments of investigation in courts of justice? And let us with caution indulge the supposition that morality can be maintained without religion. Whatever may be conceded to the influence of refined education on minds of peculiar structure, reason and experience both forbid us to expect that national morality can prevail in exclusion of religious principle.

'Tis substantially true that virtue or morality is a necessary spring of popular government. The rule indeed extends with more or less force to every species of free government. Who that is a sincere friend to it, can look with indifference upon attempts to shake the foundation of the fabric? Promote, then, as an object of primary importance, institutions for the general diffusion of knowledge. In proportion as the structure of a government gives force to public opinion, it is essential that public opinion should be enlightened.

As a very important source of strength and security, cherish public credit. One method of preserving it is to use it as sparingly as possible, avoiding occasions of expense by cultivating peace, but remembering also that timely disbursements to prepare for danger frequently prevent much greater disbursements to repel it; avoiding likewise the accumulation of debt, not only by shunning occasions of expense, but by vigorous exertions in time of peace to discharge the debts which unavoidable wars have occasioned, not ungenerously throwing upon posterity the burthen which we ourselves ought to bear.

The execution of these maxims belongs to your representatives; but it is necessary that public opinion should cooperate. To facilitate to them the performance of their duty, it is essential that you should practically bear in mind that toward the payment of debts there must be revenue; that to have revenue there must be taxes; that no taxes can be devised which are not more or less inconvenient and unpleasant; that the intrinsic embarrassment inseparable from the selection of the proper objects (which is always a choice of difficulties) ought to be a decisive motive for a candid construction of the conduct of the government in making it, and for a spirit of acquiescence in the measures for obtaining revenue which the public exigencies may at any time dictate.

Observe good faith and justice toward all nations. Cultivate peace and harmony with all. Religion and morality enjoin this conduct; and can it be that good policy does not equally enjoin it? It will be worthy of a free, enlightened, and at no distant period, a great nation, to give to mankind the magnanimous and too novel example of a people always guided by an exalted justice and benevolence. Who can doubt that in the course of time and things the fruits of such a plan would richly repay any temporary advantages which might be lost by a steady adherence to it? Can it be that Providence has not connected the permanent felicity of a nation with its virtues? The experiment, at least, is recommended by every sentiment which ennobles human nature. Alas! is it rendered impossible by its vices?

In the execution of such a plan nothing is more essential than that permanent, inveterate antipathies against particular nations and passionate attachments for others should be excluded, and that in place of them just and amicable feelings toward all should be cultivated. The nation which indulges toward another an habitual hatred, or an habitual fondness, is in some degree a slave. It is a slave to its animosity or to its affection, either of which is sufficient to lead it astray from its duty and its interest. Antipathy in one nation against another disposes each more readily to offer insult and injury, to lay hold of slight causes of umbrage, and to be haughty and intractable when accidental or trifling occasions of dispute occur.

Hence frequent collisions, obstinate, envenomed, and bloody contests. The nation prompted by ill will and resentment sometimes impels to war the government, contrary to the best calculations of policy. The government sometimes participates in the national propensity, and adopts through passion what reason would reject; at other times it makes the animosity of the nation subservient to projects of hostility, instigated by pride, ambition, and other sinister and pernicious motives. The peace often, sometimes perhaps the liberty, of nations has been the victim.

So, likewise, a passionate attachment of one nation for another produces a variety of evils. Sympathy for the favorite nation, facilitating the illusion of an imaginary common interest in cases where no real common interest exists, and infusing into one the enmities of the other, betrays the former into a participation in the quarrels and wars of the latter, without adequate inducement or justification.

It leads also to concessions to the favorite nation of privileges denied to others, which is apt doubly to injure the nation making the concessions, by unnecessarily parting with what ought to have been retained; and by exciting jealousy, ill will, and a disposition to retaliate in the parties from whom equal privileges are withheld; and it gives to ambitious, corrupted, or deluded citizens (who devote themselves to the favorite nation) facility to betray or sacrifice the interests of their own country without odium, sometimes even with popularity, gilding with the appearances of a virtuous sense of obligation, a commendable deference for public opinion, or a laudable zeal for public good, the base or foolish compliances of ambition, corruption, or infatuation.

As avenues to foreign influence in innumerable ways, such attachments are particularly alarming to the truly enlightened and independent patriot. How many opportunities do they afford to tamper with domestic factions, to practice the arts of seduction, to mislead public opinion, to influence or awe the public councils! Such an attachment of a small or weak toward a great and powerful nation dooms the former to be the satellite of the latter. Against the insidious wiles of foreign influence (I conjure you to believe me, fellow-citizens) the jealousy of a free people ought to be constantly awake, since history and experience prove that foreign influence is one of the most baneful foes of republican government.

But that jealousy, to be useful, must be impartial, else it becomes the instrument of the very influence to be avoided, instead of a defense against it. Excessive partiality for one foreign nation and excessive dislike for another, cause those whom they actuate to see danger only on one side, and serve to veil and even second the arts of influence on the other. Real patriots, who may resist the intrigues of the favorite, are liable to become suspected and odious, while its tools and dupes usurp the applause and confidence of the people to surrender their interests.

The great rule of conduct for us in regard to foreign nations is, in extending our commercial relations, to have with them as little political connection as possible. So far as we have already formed engagements, let them be fulfilled with perfect good faith. Here let us stop.

Europe has a set of primary interests which to us have none, or a very remote relation. Hence she must be engaged in frequent controversies, the causes of which are essentially foreign to our concerns. Hence, therefore, it must be unwise in us to implicate ourselves by artificial ties in the ordinary vicissitudes of her politics, or the ordinary combinations and collisions of her friendships or enmities.

Our detached and distant situation invites and enables us to pursue a different course. If we remain one people, under an efficient government, the period is not far off when we may defy material injury from external annoyance; when we may take such an attitude as will cause the neutrality we may at any time resolve upon to be scrupulously respected; when belligerent nations, under the impossibility of making acquisitions upon us, will not lightly hazard the giving us provocation; when we may choose peace or war, as our interest, guided by justice, shall counsel.

Why forego the advantages of so peculiar a situation? Why quit our own to stand upon foreign ground? Why, by interweaving our destiny with that of any part of Europe, entangle our peace and prosperity in the toils of European ambition, rivalship, interest, humor, or caprice?

'Tis our true policy to steer clear of permanent alliances with any portion of the foreign world, so far, I mean, as we are now at liberty to do it; for let me not be understood as capable of patronizing infidelity to existing engagements. (I hold the maxim no less applicable to public than to private affairs, that honesty is always the best policy.) I repeat it, therefore, let those engagements be observed in their genuine sense. But in my opinion it is unnecessary and would be unwise to extend them.

Taking care always to keep ourselves by suitable establishments on a respectable defensive posture, we may safely trust to temporary alliances for extraordinary emergencies.

Harmony, liberal intercourse with all nations, are recommended by policy, humanity, and interest. But even our commercial policy should hold an equal and impartial hand, neither seeking nor granting exclusive favors or preferences; consulting the natural course of things; diffusing and diversifying by gentle means the streams of commerce, but forcing nothing; establishing with powers so disposed, in order to give to trade a stable course, to define the rights of our merchants, and to enable the government to support them, conventional rules of intercourse, the best that present circumstances and mutual opinion will permit, but temporary and liable to be from time to time abandoned or varied as experience and circumstances shall dictate; constantly keeping in view that 'tis folly in one nation to look for disinterested favors from another; that it must pay with a portion of its independence for whatever it may accept under that character; that by such acceptance it may place itself in the condition of having given equivalents for nominal favors, and yet of being reproached with ingratitude for not giving more. There can be no greater error than to expect or calculate upon real favors from nation to nation. 'Tis an illusion which experience must cure, which a just pride ought to discard.

In offering to you, my countrymen, these counsels of an old and affectionate friend, I dare not hope they will make the strong and lasting impression I could wish; that they will control the usual current of the passions or prevent our nation from running the course which has hitherto marked the destiny of nations. But if I may even flatter myself that they may be productive of some partial benefit, some occasional good; that they may now and then recur to moderate the fury of party spirit, to warn against the mischiefs of foreign intrigue, to guard against the impostures of pretended patriotism; this hope will be a full recompense for the solicitude for your welfare by which they have been dictated.

How far in the discharge of my official duties I have been guided by the principles which have been delineated, the public records and other evidences of my conduct must witness to you and to the world. To myself, the assurance of my own conscience is that I have at least believed myself to be guided by them.

In relation to the still subsisting war in Europe my proclamation of the twenty-second of April, 1793, is the index to my plan. Sanctioned by your approving voice and by that of your representatives in both Houses of Congress, the spirit of that measure has continually governed me, uninfluenced by any attempts to deter or divert me from it.

After deliberate examination, with the aid of the best lights I could obtain, I was well satisfied that our country, under all the circumstances of the case, had a right to take, and was bound in duty and interest to take, a neutral position. Having taken it, I determined, as far as should depend upon me, to maintain it with moderation, perseverance, and firmness.

The considerations which respect the right to hold this conduct, it is not necessary on this occasion to detail. I will only observe that, according to my understanding of the matter, that right, so far from being denied by any of the belligerent powers, has been virtually admitted by all.

The duty of holding a neutral conduct may be inferred, without anything more, from the obligation which justice and humanity impose on every nation, in cases in which it is free to act, to maintain inviolate the relations of peace and amity toward other nations.

The inducements of interest for observing that conduct will best be referred to your own reflections and experience. With me a predominant motive has been to endeavor to gain time to our country to settle and mature its yet recent institutions, and to progress without interruption to that degree of strength and consistency which is necessary to give it, humanly speaking, the command of its own fortunes.

Though in reviewing the incidents of my administration I am unconscious of intentional error, I am nevertheless too sensible of my defects not to think it probable that I may have committed many errors. Whatever they may be, I fervently beseech the Almighty to avert or mitigate the evils to which they may tend. I shall also carry with me the hope that my country will never cease to view them with indulgence, and that after forty-five years of my life dedicated to its service, with an upright zeal, the faults of incompetent abilities will be consigned to oblivion, as myself must soon be to the mansions of rest.

Relying on its kindness in this as in other things, and actuated by that fervent love toward it which is so natural to a man who views in it the native soil of himself and his progenitors for several generations, I anticipate with pleasing expectation that retreat in which I promise myself to realize, without alloy, the sweet enjoyment of partaking, in the midst of my fellow-citizens, the benign influence of good laws under a free government–the ever favorite object of my heart and the happy reward, as I trust, of our mutual cares, labors, and dangers.

JEFFERSON OUTLINES A BETTER DEMOCRACY

1801

March 4, 1801—the day of the first presidential inauguration to be held in the new capital of Washington—dawned to the accompaniment of an artillery salute. Thomas Jefferson, President-elect, kept to his rooms at Conrad's boardinghouse on Capitol Hill. Once during the morning companies of infantry and artillery paraded before the house to the delight of the curious and admiring group which had gathered there, but Jefferson remained inside. Not until noon did he emerge to walk the short distance that separated Conrad's from the Capitol.

In the company which surrounded him—worshiping citizens and members of Congress—only his height set him apart. His face, sun-reddened and freckled, his gray hair carelessly tended, the undistinguished clothes which seemed a little too tight for his loose and angular frame—all could have belonged as easily to a prosperous farmer as to a statesman. Yet this was the man who had written the

Declaration of Independence, served his country with honor in France, delighted savants everywhere with the breadth of his knowledge and the sharpness of his eager mind. And now he moved to take over the government of the United States in opposition to the policies of Washington, Hamilton, and Adams.

He had missed the Presidency in 1796 by only three electoral votes. In the next four years his Republican party[1] grew stronger with every month. Federalist measures building up the power of the central government at the expense of the states, that party's frank preference for "the wise and good and rich," the repercussions of the Jay Treaty, the administration's foolish attempt to suppress opposition through the Alien and Sedition Acts, and its horror of the French Revolution—all pointed surely to Republican victory in 1800. Even so, Jefferson almost missed the Presidency a second time.

[1] Not to be confused with the Republican party of the present time, first represented in the Presidency by Abraham Lincoln.

When the votes of the Electoral College were counted, he and Aaron Burr, the personable schemer from New York, were found to be tied, and it was not until the thirty-sixth ballot that the deadlock was broken in Jefferson's favor.

Now he walked to the Capitol, not in conscious protest against the "aristocratic" practices of the two previous administrations, but because he was a man who, by habit, did all things simply. Yet fanfare marked his entrance. As he stepped across the threshold, guns boomed a salute. In the Senate Chamber the members of both Houses rose and remained standing until he took his seat, flanked on one side by Aaron Burr, Vice-President, and on the other by John Marshall, Chief Justice. After a brief pause Jefferson stood, and in a voice barely audible, read his inaugural. That done, he turned to Marshall, who administered the oath. Outside, crowds cheered and the artillery roared again.

Jefferson's affirmation of the democratic faith, his wise counsel, the easy cadence of his style, make his first inaugural one of the most distinguished of presidential addresses.

Jefferson's First Inaugural Address

March 4, 1801

Friends and Fellow-Citizens: Called upon to undertake the duties of the first executive office of our country, I avail myself of the presence of that portion of my fellow-citizens which is here assembled to express my grateful thanks for the favor with which they have been pleased to look toward me, to declare a sincere consciousness that the task is above my talents, and that I approach it with those anxious and awful presentiments which the greatness of the charge and the weakness of my powers so justly inspire.

A rising nation, spread over a wide and fruitful land, traversing all the seas with the rich productions of their industry, engaged in commerce with nations who feel power and forget right, advancing rapidly to destinies beyond the reach of mortal eye—when I contemplate these transcendent objects and see the honor, the happiness, and the hopes of this beloved country committed to the issue and the auspices of this day, I shrink from the contemplation, and humble myself before the magnitude of the undertaking.

Utterly, indeed, should I despair did not the presence of many whom I here see remind me that in the other high authorities provided by our Constitution I shall find resources of wisdom, of virtue, and of zeal on which to rely under all difficulties. To you, then, gentlemen, who are charged with the sovereign functions of legislation, and to those associated with you, I look with encouragement for that guidance and support which may enable us to steer with safety the vessel in which we are all embarked amidst the conflicting elements of a troubled world.

During the contest of opinion through which we have passed, the animation of discussions and of exertions has sometimes worn an aspect which might impose on [deceive] strangers unused to think freely and to speak and to write what they think; but this being now decided by the voice of the nation, announced according to the rules of the Constitution, all will, of course, arrange themselves under the will of the law, and unite in common efforts for the common good. All, too, will bear in mind this sacred principle, that though the will of the majority is in all cases to prevail, that will to be rightful must be reasonable; that the minority possess their equal rights, which equal law must protect, and to violate would be oppression.

Let us, then, fellow-citizens, unite with one heart and one mind. Let us restore to social intercourse that harmony and affection without which liberty and even life itself are but dreary things. And let us reflect that, having banished from our land that religious intolerance under which mankind so long bled and suffered, we have yet gained little if we countenance a political intolerance as despotic, as wicked, and capable of as bitter and bloody persecutions.

During the throes and convulsions of the ancient world, during the agonizing spasms of infuriated man, seeking through blood and slaughter his long-lost liberty, it was not wonderful that the agitation of the billows should reach even this distant and peaceful shore; that this should be more felt and feared by some and less by others, and should divide opinions as to measures of safety. But every difference of opinion is not a difference of principle. We have called by different names brethren of the same principle. We are all Republicans, we are all Federalists. If there be any among us who would wish to dissolve this Union or to change its republican form, let them stand undisturbed as monuments of the safety with which error of opinion may be tolerated where reason is left free to combat it.

I know, indeed, that some honest men fear that a republican government cannot be strong, that this government is not strong enough; but would the honest patriot, in the full tide of successful experiment, abandon a government which has so far kept us free and firm on the theoretic and visionary fear that this government, the world's best hope, may by possibility want energy to preserve itself? I trust not. I believe this, on the contrary, the strongest government on earth. I believe it the only one where every man, at the call of the law, would fly to the standard of the law, and would meet invasions of the public order as his own personal concern. Sometimes it is said that man cannot be trusted with the government of himself. Can he, then, be trusted with the government of others? Or have we found angels in the forms of kings to govern him? Let history answer this question.

Let us, then, with courage and confidence pursue our own Federal and Republican principles, our attachment to union and representative government. Kindly separated by nature and a wide ocean from the exterminating havoc of one quarter of the globe; too high-minded to endure the degradations of the others; possessing a chosen country, with room enough for our descendants to the thousandth and thousandth generation; entertaining a due sense of our equal right to the use of our own faculties, to the acquisitions of our own industry, to honor and confidence from our fellow-citizens, resulting not from birth, but from our actions and their sense of them; enlightened by a benign religion, professed, indeed, and practiced in various forms, yet all of them inculcating honesty, truth, temperance, gratitude, and the love of man; acknowledging and adoring an overruling Providence, which by all its dispensations proves that it delights in the happiness of man here and his greater happiness hereafter—with all these blessings, what more is necessary to make us a happy and a prosperous people?

Still one thing more, fellow-citizens—a wise and frugal government, which shall restrain men from injuring one another, shall leave them otherwise free to regulate their own pursuits of industry and improvement, and shall not take from the mouth of labor the bread it has earned. This is the sum of good government, and this is necessary to close the circle of our felicities.

About to enter, fellow-citizens, on the exercise of duties which comprehend everything dear and valuable to you, it is proper you should understand what I deem the essential principles of our government, and consequently those which ought to shape its administration. I will compress them within the narrowest compass they will bear, stating the general principle, but not all its limitations:

Equal and exact justice to all men, of whatever state or persuasion, religious or political; peace, commerce, and honest friendship with all nations, entangling alliances with none; the support of the state governments in all their rights, as the most competent administrations for our domestic concerns and the surest bulwarks against antirepublican tendencies; the preservation of the general government in its whole constitutional vigor, as the sheet anchor of our peace at home and safety abroad; a jealous care of the right of election by the people—a mild and safe corrective of abuses which are lopped by the sword of revolution where peaceable remedies are unprovided; absolute acquiescence in the decisions of the majority, the vital principle of republics, from which is no appeal but to force, the vital principle and immediate parent of despotism; a well-disciplined militia, our best reliance in peace and for the first moments of war, till regulars may relieve them; the supremacy of the civil over the military authority; economy in the public expense, that labor may be lightly burthened; the honest payment of our debts and sacred preservation of the public faith; encouragement of agriculture, and of commerce as its handmaid; the diffusion of information and arraignment of all abuses at the bar of the public reason; freedom of religion; freedom of the press, and freedom of person under the protection of the habeas corpus, and trial by juries impartially selected.

These principles form the bright constellation which has gone before us and guided our steps through an age of revolution and reformation. The wisdom of our sages and blood of our heroes have been devoted to their attainment. They should be the creed of our political faith, the text of civic instruction, the touchstone by which to try the services of those we trust; and should we wander from them in moments of error or of alarm, let us hasten to retrace our steps and to regain the road which alone leads to peace, liberty, and safety.

I repair, then, fellow-citizens, to the post you have assigned me. With experience enough in subordinate offices to have seen the difficulties of this the greatest of all, I have learnt to expect that it will rarely fall to the lot of imperfect man to retire from this station with the reputation and the favor which bring him into it.

Without pretensions to that high confidence you reposed in our first and greatest revolutionary character, whose pre-eminent services had entitled him to the first place in his country's love and destined for him the fairest page in the volume of faithful history, I ask so much confidence only as may give firmness and effect to the legal administration of your affairs. I shall often go wrong through defect of judgment. When right, I shall often be thought wrong by those whose positions will not command a view of the whole ground. I ask your indulgence for my own errors, which will never be intentional, and your support against the errors of others, who may condemn what they would not if seen in all its parts. The approbation implied by your suffrage is a great consolation to me for the past, and my future solicitude will be to retain the good opinion of those who have bestowed it in advance, to conciliate that of others by doing them all good in my power, and to be instrumental to the happiness and freedom of all.

Relying, then, on the patronage of your good will, I advance with obedience to the work, ready to retire from it whenever you become sensible how much better choice it is in your power to make. And may that Infinite Power which rules the destinies of the universe lead our councils to what is best, and give them a favorable issue for your peace and prosperity.

MONROE ISSUES A FAMOUS WARNING

1823

James Monroe, President of the United States, was deeply worried. The attitude of foreign countries toward the nation which he headed seemed more ominous than at any time since the War of 1812. Russia had moved to exclude all but her own vessels from the northwest coast of America, and had indicated that she might press claims to territory as far south as the middle of California. In Europe a harmless alliance, formed by Russia, Prussia, and Austria for the laudable purpose of conducting relations with each other in the spirit of Christian forbearance, had added France to the combination and was turning toward the suppression of all movements against established monarchies. In 1822 it had authorized France to invade Spain in order to restore the absolute authority of a king who had been forced to accept a constitutional monarchy. Now, a year later, Monroe and such experienced observers as George Canning, British Foreign Secretary, feared that the four powers would undertake the reconquest of Spain's South American colonies. For thirteen years these colonies had been fighting for their independence with such success that the United States had recently recognized six of the most stable.

From the first days of its existence as a nation, the United States had stressed the concept of continental independence. Washington, Adams, Jefferson, and Clay had all urged their countrymen to hold aloof from European politics and to repel, as far as they could, European meddling in American affairs. Monroe, therefore, followed established policy when he decided to give notice to the powers that interference on their part in the concerns of the American continent would not be tolerated.

The President searched for the most effective means of asserting his country's position. From early November, 1823, until the end of the month his Cabinet struggled with the question. Some members favored direct communications to the ministers of the nations involved, while John Quincy Adams, Secretary of State, scoffed at the existence of a real threat. Monroe believed that the danger of foreign intervention was imminent, and finally decided that the position of the United States could best be declared in the annual message–his seventh–which he would send to Congress on December 2.

The Monroe Doctrine, therefore, consists simply of two widely separated passages in a presidential message–one referring to Russia, the other to South America. It has never received legislative confirmation, and even its content was more an epitome of American opinion than a creation of the man whose name it bears. The message, enthusiastically received at home, produced only irritation and contempt abroad. Fortunately, no European power was sufficiently interested to challenge it before the United States became strong enough to be reckoned with. Even today the Monroe Doctrine has no standing in international law, but no national principle is more deeply cherished by the American people, or less likely to be defied by a European nation.

The Monroe Doctrine

December 2, 1823

Fellow-Citizens of the Senate and House of Representatives: . . . At the proposal of the Russian Imperial Government, made through the minister of the Emperor residing here, a full power and instructions have been transmitted to the minister of the United States at St. Petersburg to arrange by amicable negotiation the respective rights and interests of the two nations on the northwest coast of this continent. A similar proposal had been made by His Imperial Majesty to the government of Great Britain, which has likewise been acceded to. The government of the United States has been desirous, by this friendly proceeding, of manifesting the great value which they have invariably attached to the friendship of the Emperor and their solicitude to cultivate the best understanding with his government. In the discussions to which this interest has given rise and in the arrangements by which they may terminate, the occasion has been judged proper for asserting, as a principle in which the rights and interests of the United States are involved, that the American continents, by the free and independent condition which they have assumed and maintain, are henceforth not to be considered as subjects for future colonization by any European powers. . . .

It was stated at the commencement of the last session that a great effort was then making in Spain and Portugal to improve the condition of the people of those countries, and that it appeared to be conducted with extraordinary moderation. It need scarcely be remarked that the result has been so far very different from what was then anticipated.

Of events in that quarter of the globe, with which we have so much intercourse and from which we derive our origin, we have always been anxious and interested spectators. The citizens of the United States cherish sentiments the most friendly in favor of the liberty and happiness of their fellow-men on that side of the Atlantic. In the wars of the European powers in matters relating to themselves we have never taken any part, nor does it comport with our policy so to do. It is only when our rights are invaded or seriously menaced that we resent injuries or make preparation for our defense.

With the movements in this hemisphere we are of necessity more immediately connected, and by causes which must be obvious to all enlightened and impartial observers. The political system of the allied powers is essentially different in this respect from that of America. This difference proceeds from that which exists in their respective governments; and to the defense of our own, which has been achieved by the loss of so much blood and treasure, and matured by the wisdom of their most enlightened citizens, and under which we have enjoyed unexampled felicity, this whole nation is devoted.

We owe it, therefore, to candor and to the amicable relations existing between the United States and those powers to declare that we should consider any attempt on their part to extend their system to any portion of this hemisphere as dangerous to our peace and safety. With the existing colonies or dependencies of any European power we have not interfered and shall not interfere. But with the governments who have declared their independence and maintained it, and whose independence we have, on great consideration and on just principles, acknowledged, we could not view any interposition for the purpose of oppressing them, or controlling in any other manner their destiny, by any European power in any other light than as the manifestation of an unfriendly disposition toward the United States. In the war between those new governments and Spain we declared our neutrality at the time of their recognition, and to this we have adhered, and shall continue to adhere, provided no change shall occur which, in the judgment of the competent authorities of this government, shall make a corresponding change on the part of the United States indispensable to their security.

The late events in Spain and Portugal show that Europe is still unsettled. Of this important fact no stronger proof can be adduced than that the allied powers should have thought it proper, on any principle satisfactory to themselves, to have interposed by force in the internal concerns of Spain. To what extent such interposition may be carried, on the same principle, is a question in which all independent powers whose governments differ from theirs are interested, even those most remote, and surely none more so than the United States. Our policy in regard to Europe, which was adopted at an early stage of the wars which have so long agitated that quarter of the globe, nevertheless remains the same, which is, not to interfere in the internal concerns of any of its powers; to consider the government de facto as the legitimate government for us; to cultivate friendly relations with it, and to preserve those relations by a frank, firm, and manly policy, meeting in all instances the just claims of every power, submitting to injuries from none.

But in regard to those [the American] continents circumstances are eminently and conspicuously different. It is impossible that the allied powers should extend their political system to any portion of either continent without endangering our peace and happiness; nor can anyone believe that our southern brethren, if left to themselves, would adopt it of their own accord. It is equally impossible, therefore, that we should behold such interposition in any form with indifference. If we look to the comparative strength and resources of Spain and those new governments, and their distance from each other, it must be obvious that she can never subdue them. It is still the true policy of the United States to leave the parties to themselves, in the hope that other powers will pursue the same course. . . .

JACKSON DENOUNCES THE THEORY OF SECESSION

1832

As the regular toasts progressed, the tense men at the long tables searched the face of the President. On this occasion, by studied prearrangement, the case for "nullification"—the right of a single state to annul a federal law—was being tested. For two years South Carolina had seethed with resentment against a tariff measure, passed in 1828, which she considered harmful to her interests. Despairing of changing the law, her statesmen—principally John C. Calhoun and Robert Y. Hayne—had resorted to the doctrine of nullification. A state, they contended, had the right to decide when federal legislation breached the Constitution, and to "nullify" a law which it considered a dangerous infraction. But for two years they had tried in vain to find out what course Andrew Jackson would take if they should try to put this divisive theory into practice. Now they would learn. After the regular toasts, volunteer toasts were in order, and the first would come from the President.

Old Hickory rose, his craglike face impassive until the cheers subsided. Facing Calhoun, he spoke six words:

"Our Union: It must be preserved."

In the silence that followed Jackson raised his glass. No one dared to remain seated, although several noted that Calhoun's hand trembled so much that the yellow wine trickled down the side of the glass as he brought it to his lips. The toast drunk, Hayne rushed up. Would the President consent to insert the word "Federal" before "Union" in his toast? Jackson readily agreed: he had written the toast in that form originally, and had inadvertently omitted the one word when he spoke from memory.

Calhoun came next. "The Union," he said, "next to our liberty, most dear." Then he added: "May we all remember that it can only be preserved by respecting the rights of the states and by distributing equally the benefits and burdens of the Union."

Though rebuffed, Calhoun and his followers had no intention of abandoning their program. They would wait, however, until Congress had a chance to amend or repeal the obnoxious tariff. Congress acted in 1832, reducing the schedule of import duties, but not enough to satisfy the objectors. Becoming ever bolder, the nullifiers talked of raising troops to defend South Carolina against the federal "aggressors." Jackson countered by changing the Charleston garrisons, by sending Major General Winfield Scott to command them in person, and by letting it be known that he would double any force the disunionists might decide to put under arms.

In the first week of November the President was triumphantly re-elected. South Carolina moved quickly. Delegates to a state convention, called to consider the tariff act of 1832, passed resolutions declaring this act, and its predecessor of 1828, "null, void, and no law"; outlawing any effort, after February 1, 1833, to collect the duties imposed by the acts; and barring any appeal to the Supreme Court of the United States should the legality of the convention's ordinances be questioned.

Jackson took his time. His annual message to Congress, read before that body on December 4, 1832, was conciliatory: in it he recommended further tariff reductions and said nothing about resisting nullification by force. But behind the scenes his Secretary of State, Edward Livingston, was working on a proclamation which the President had decided to issue as soon as he learned of the action of the South Carolina convention. "Let it receive your best flight of eloquence," he had admonished the Secretary. But Livingston was not to forget, Jackson added, that "the Union must be preserved, without blood if this be possible, but it must be preserved at all hazards and at any price."

The Proclamation was published on December 10, 1832. The nation responded with fervent approval, and soon made clear that if South Carolina persisted with nullification, she would act alone. Even so, it was probably the action of Congress in passing a new and more palatable tariff, rather than the logic of Jackson's Proclamation, that led her to repeal her Ordinance of Nullification. The Proclamation, nevertheless, loses nothing in stature by that fact. Twenty-eight years later, in an even more critical situation, Abraham Lincoln took Jackson's Proclamation as a guide, and to this day it stands as one of the greatest of presidential papers.

Proclamation against Nullification

December 10, 1832

Whereas, A convention assembled in the State of South Carolina have passed an ordinance by which they declare "that the several acts and parts of acts of the Congress of the United States purporting to be laws for the imposing of duties and imposts on the importation of foreign commodities . . . . are unauthorized by the Constitution of the United States, and violate the true meaning and intent thereof, and are null and void and no law," nor binding on the citizens of that state or its officers; and . . . .

Whereas, By the said ordinance it is further ordained that in no case of law or equity decided in the courts of said state wherein shall be drawn in question the validity of the said ordinance, or of the acts of the legislature that may be passed to give it effect, or of the said laws of the United States, no appeal shall be allowed to the Supreme Court of the United States, and . . . .

Whereas, The said ordinance prescribes to the people of South Carolina a course of conduct in direct violation of their duty as citizens of the United States, contrary to the laws of their country, subversive of its Constitution, and having for its object the destruction of the Union. . . . .

To preserve this bond of our political existence from destruction, to maintain inviolate this state of national honor and prosperity, and to justify the confidence my fellow-citizens have reposed in me, I, Andrew Jackson, President of the United States, have thought proper to issue this my proclamation. . . . .

Strict duty would require of me nothing more than the exercise of those powers with which I am now or may hereafter be invested for preserving the peace of the Union and for the execution of the laws; but the imposing aspect which opposition has assumed in this case, by clothing itself with state authority, and the deep interest which the people of the United States must all feel in preventing a resort to stronger measures while there is a hope that anything will be yielded to reasoning and remonstrance, perhaps demand, and will certainly justify, a full exposition to South Carolina and the nation of the views I entertain of this important question, as well as a distinct enunciation of the course which my sense of duty will require me to pursue.

The ordinance is founded, not on the indefeasible right of resisting acts which are plainly unconstitutional and too oppressive to be endured, but on the strange position that any one state may not only declare an act of Congress void, but prohibit its execution; that they may do this consistently with the Constitution; that the true construction of that instrument permits a state to retain its place in the Union and yet be bound by no other of its laws than those it may choose to consider as constitutional. . . .

Look for a moment to the consequence. If South Carolina considers the revenue laws unconstitutional and has a right to prevent their execution in the port of Charleston, there would be a clear constitutional objection to their collection in every other port; and no revenue could be collected anywhere, for all imposts must be equal. It is no answer to repeat that an unconstitutional law is no law so long as the question of its legality is to be decided by the state itself, for every law operating injuriously upon any local interest will be perhaps thought, and certainly represented, as unconstitutional, and, as has been shown, there is no appeal.

If this doctrine had been established at an earlier day, the Union would have been dissolved in its infancy. The excise law in Pennsylvania, the embargo and nonintercourse law in the eastern states, the carriage tax in Virginia, were all deemed unconstitutional, and were more unequal in their operation than any of the laws now complained of; but, fortunately, none of those states discovered that they had the right now claimed by South Carolina. The war into which we were forced to support the dignity of the nation and the rights of our citizens might have ended in defeat and disgrace, instead of victory and honor, if the states who supposed it a ruinous and unconstitutional measure had thought they possessed the right of nullifying the act by which it was declared and denying supplies for its prosecution. . . .

If the doctrine of a state veto upon the laws of the Union carries with it internal evidence of its impracticable absurdity, our constitutional history will also afford abundant proof that it would have been repudiated with indignation had it been proposed to form a feature in our government.

In our colonial state, although dependent on another power, we very early considered ourselves as connected by common interest with each other. Leagues were formed for the common defense, and before the Declaration of Independence we were known in our aggregate character as the United Colonies of America. That decisive and important step was taken jointly. We declared ourselves a nation by a joint, not by several acts; and when the terms of our confederation were reduced to form, it was in that of a solemn league of several states, by which they agreed that they would collectively form one nation for the purpose of conducting some certain domestic concerns and all foreign relations. In the instrument forming that union is found an article which declares that "every state shall abide by the determinations of Congress on all questions which by that Confederation should be submitted to them."

Under the Confederation, then, no state could legally annul a decision of the Congress or refuse to submit to its execution; but no provision was made to enforce these decisions. Congress made requisitions, but they were not complied with. The government could not operate on individuals. They had no judiciary, no means of collecting revenue.

But the defects of the Confederation need not be detailed. Under its operation we could scarcely be called a nation. We had neither prosperity at home nor consideration abroad. This state of things could not be endured, and our present happy Constitution was formed, but formed in vain if this fatal doctrine prevails. It was formed for important objects that are announced in the preamble, made in the name and by the authority of the people of the United States, whose delegates framed and whose conventions approved it. The most important among these objects—that which is placed first in rank, on which all the others rest—is "to form a more perfect union."

Now, is it possible that even if there were no express provision giving supremacy to the Constitution and laws of the United States over those of the states, can it be conceived that an instrument made for the purpose of "forming a more perfect union" than that of the Confederation could be so constructed by the assembled wisdom of our country as to substitute for that Confederation a form of government dependent for its existence on the local interest, the party spirit, of a state, or of a prevailing faction in a state? Every man of plain, unsophisticated understanding who hears the question will give such an answer as will preserve the Union. Metaphysical subtlety, in pursuit of an impracticable theory, could alone have devised one that is calculated to destroy it.

I consider, then, the power to annul a law of the United States, assumed by one state, incompatible with the existence of the Union, contradicted expressly by the letter of the Constitution, unauthorized by its spirit, inconsistent with every principle on which it was founded, and destructive of the great object for which it was formed.

After this general view of the leading principle, we must examine the particular application of it which is made in the ordinance.

The preamble rests its justification on these grounds: It assumes as a fact that the obnoxious laws, although they purport to be laws for raising revenue, were in reality intended for the protection of manufacturers, which purpose it asserts to be unconstitutional; that the operation of these laws is unequal; that the amount raised by them is greater than is required by the wants of the government; and, finally, that the proceeds are to be applied to objects unauthorized by the Constitution. These are the only causes alleged to justify an open opposition to the laws of the country and a threat of seceding from the Union if any attempt should be made to enforce them.

The first virtually acknowledges that the law in question was passed under a power expressly given by the Constitution to lay and collect imposts; but its constitutionality is drawn in question from the motives of those who passed it. However apparent this purpose may be in the present case, nothing can be more dangerous than to admit the position that an unconstitutional purpose entertained by the members who assent to a law enacted under a constitutional power shall make that law void. For how is that purpose to be ascertained? Who is to make the scrutiny? How often may bad purposes be falsely imputed, in how many cases are they concealed by false confessions, in how many is no declaration of motive made? Admit this doctrine, and you give to the states an uncontrolled right to decide, and every law may be annulled under this pretext. . . . .

The next objection is that the laws in question operate unequally. This objection may be made with truth to every law that has been or can be passed. The wisdom of man never yet contrived a system of taxation that would operate with perfect equality. If the unequal operation of a law makes it unconstitutional, and if all laws of that description may be abrogated by any state for that cause, then, indeed, is the federal Constitution unworthy of the slightest effort for its preservation.

We have hitherto relied on it as the perpetual bond of our Union; we have received it as the work of the assembled wisdom of the nation; we have trusted to it as to the sheet anchor of our safety in the stormy times of conflict with a foreign or domestic foe; we have looked to it with sacred awe as the palladium of our liberties, and with all the solemnities of religion have pledged to each other our lives and fortunes here and our hopes of happiness hereafter in its defense and support.

Were we mistaken, my countrymen, in attaching this importance to the Constitution of our country? Was our devotion paid to the wretched, inefficient, clumsy contrivance which this new doctrine would make it? Did we pledge ourselves to the support of an airy nothing—a bubble that must be blown away by the first breath of disaffection? Was this self-destroying, visionary theory the work of the profound statesmen, the exalted patriots, to whom the task of constitutional reform was entrusted? Did the name of Washington sanction, did the states deliberately ratify, such an anomaly in the history of fundamental legislation?

No; we were not mistaken. The letter of this great instrument is free from this radical fault. Its language directly contradicts the imputation; its spirit, its evident intent, contradicts it. No; we did not err. Our Constitution does not contain the absurdity of giving power to make laws and another to resist them. The sages whose memory will always be reverenced have given us a practical and, as they hoped, a permanent constitutional compact. The Father of His Country did not affix his revered name to so palpable an absurdity. Nor did the states, when they severally ratified it, do so under the impression that a veto on the laws of the United States was reserved to them or that they could exercise it by implication. . . . . The Constitution is still the object of our reverence, the bond of our Union, our defense in danger, the source of our prosperity in peace. . . . .

The two remaining objections made by the ordinance to these laws are that the sums intended to be raised by them are greater than are required and that the proceeds will be unconstitutionally employed.

The Constitution has given, expressly, to Congress the right of raising revenue and of determining the sum the public exigencies will require. The states have no control over the exercise of this right other than that which results from the power of changing the representatives who abuse it, and thus procure redress. Congress may undoubtedly abuse this discretionary power; but the same may be said of others with which they are vested. Yet the discretion must exist somewhere. The Constitution has given it to the representatives of all the people, checked by the representatives of the states and by the executive power. The South Carolina construction gives it to the legislature or the convention of a single state, where neither the people of the different states, nor the states in their separate capacity, nor the Chief Magistrate elected by the people have any representation.

Which is the most discreet disposition of the power? I do not ask you, fellow-citizens, which is the constitutional disposition; that instrument speaks a language not to be misunderstood. But if you were assembled in general convention, which would you think the safest depository of this discretionary power in the last resort? Would you add a clause giving it to each of the states, or would you sanction the wise provisions already made by your Constitution? . . . .

The ordinance, with the same knowledge of the future that characterizes a former objection, tells you that the proceeds of the tax will be unconstitutionally applied. If this could be ascertained with certainty, the objection would with more propriety be reserved for the law so applying the proceeds, but surely cannot be urged against the laws levying the duty.

These are the allegations contained in the ordinance. Examine them seriously, my fellow-citizens; judge for yourselves. I appeal to you to determine whether they are so clear, so convincing, as to leave no doubt of their correctness; and even if you should come to this conclusion, how far they justify the reckless, destructive course which you are directed to pursue.

Review these objections and the conclusions drawn from them once more. What are they? Every law, then, for raising revenue, according [illegible] the South Carolina ordinance, may be rightfully annulled, unless [illegible] so framed [illegible] no law ever will or can be framed. Congress have a right to pass laws for raising revenue and each state have a right to oppose their execution–two rights directly opposed to each other; and yet is this absurdity supposed to be contained in an instrument drawn for the express purpose of avoiding collisions between the states and the general government by an assembly of the most enlightened statesmen and purest patriots ever embodied for a similar purpose? . . . .

The people of the United States formed the Constitution, acting through the state legislatures in making the compact, to meet and discuss its provisions, and acting in separate conventions when they ratified those provisions; but the terms used in its construction show it to be a government in which the people of all the states, collectively, are represented. We are one people in the choice of President and Vice-President. . . . .

The Constitution of the United States, then, forms a government, not a league; and whether it be formed by compact between the states or in any other manner, its character is the same. It is a government in which all the people are represented, which operates directly on the people individually, not upon the states; they retained all the power they did not grant. But each state, having expressly parted with so many powers as to constitute, jointly with the other states, a single nation, cannot, from that period, possess any right to secede, because such secession does not break a league, but destroys the unity of a nation, and any injury to that unity is not only a breach which would result from the contravention of a compact, but it is an offense against the whole Union. To say that any state may at pleasure secede from the Union is to say that the United States are not a nation, because it would be a solecism to contend that any part of a nation might dissolve its connection with the other parts, to their injury or ruin, without committing any offense. . . . .

Because the Union was formed by a compact, it is said the parties to that compact may, when they feel themselves aggrieved, depart from it; but it is precisely because it is a compact that they cannot. A compact is an agreement or binding obligation. It may by its terms have a sanction or penalty for its breach, or it may not. If it contains no sanction, it may be broken with no other consequence than moral guilt; if it have a sanction, then the breach incurs the designated or implied penalty.

A league between independent nations generally has no sanction other than a moral one; or if it should contain a penalty, as there is no common superior it cannot be enforced. A government, on the contrary, always has a sanction, express or implied; and in our case it is both necessarily implied and expressly given. An attempt, by force of arms, to destroy a government is an offense, by whatever means the constitutional compact may have been formed; and such government has the right by the law of self-defense to pass acts for punishing the offender, unless that right is modified, restrained, or resumed by the constitutional act. . . .

Fellow-citizens of my native state, let me not only admonish you, as the First Magistrate of our common country, not to incur the penalty of its laws, but use the influence that a father would over his children whom he saw rushing to certain ruin. In that paternal language, with that paternal feeling, let me tell you, my countrymen, that you are deluded by men who are either deceived themselves or wish to deceive you. . . . They are not champions of liberty, emulating the fame of our revolutionary fathers, nor are you an oppressed people, contending, as they repeat to you, against worse than colonial vassalage. You are free members of a flourishing and happy Union. There is no settled design to oppress you. You have indeed felt the unequal operation of laws which may have been unwisely, not unconstitutionally, passed; but that inequality must necessarily be removed.

At the very moment when you were madly urged on to the unfortunate course you have begun, a change in public opinion had commenced. The nearly approaching payment of the public debt and the consequent necessity of a diminution of duties had already produced a considerable reduction, and that, too, on some articles of general consumption in your state. The importance of this change was underrated, and you were authoritatively told that no further alleviation of your burthens was to be expected as the very time when the condition of the country imperiously demanded such a modification of the duties as should reduce them to a just and equitable scale. But, as if apprehensive of the effect of this change in allaying your discontents, you were precipitated into the fearful state in which you now find yourselves.

I have urged you to look back to the means that were used to hurry you on to the position you have now assumed and forward to the consequences it will produce. Something more is necessary. Contemplate the condition of that country of which you still form an important part. Consider its government, uniting in one bond of common interest and general protection so many different states, giving to all their inhabitants the proud title of American citizen, protecting their commerce, securing their literature and their arts, facilitating their intercommunication, defending their frontiers, and making their name respected in the remotest parts of the earth. Consider the extent of its territory, its increasing and happy population, its advance in arts which render life agreeable, and the sciences which elevate the mind! See education spreading the lights of religion, morality, and general information into every cottage in this wide extent of our territories and states. Behold it as the asylum where the wretched and the oppressed find a refuge and support. Look on this picture of happiness and honor and say, "We too are

citizens of America." Carolina is one of these proud states; her arms have defended, her best blood has cemented, this happy Union.

And then add, if you can, without horror and remorse, "This happy Union we will dissolve; this picture of peace and prosperity we will deface; this free intercourse we will interrupt; these fertile fields we will deluge with blood; the protection of that glorious flag we renounce; the very name of Americans we discard."

And for what, mistaken men? For what do you throw away these inestimable blessings? For what would you exchange your share in the advantages and honor of the Union? For the dream of a separate independence–a dream interrupted by bloody conflicts with your neighbors and a vile dependence on a foreign power. If your leaders could succeed in establishing a separation, what would be your situation? Are you united at home? Are you free from the apprehension of civil discord, with all its fearful consequences? Do our neighboring republics, every day suffering some new revolution or contending with some new insurrection, do they excite your envy?

But the dictates of a high duty oblige me solemnly to announce that you cannot succeed. The laws of the United States must be executed. I have no discretionary power on the subject; my duty is emphatically pronounced in the Constitution. Those who told you that you might peaceably prevent their execution deceived you;

they could not have been deceived themselves. They know that a forcible opposition could alone prevent the execution of the laws, and they know that such opposition must be repelled. Their object is disunion. But be not deceived by names. Disunion by armed force is treason. Are you really ready to incur its guilt? If you are, on the heads of the instigators of the act be the dreadful consequences; on their heads be the dishonor, but on yours may fall the punishment.

On your unhappy state will inevitably fall all the evils of the conflict you force upon the government of your country. It cannot accede to the mad project of disunion, of which you would be the first victims. Its First Magistrate cannot, if he would, avoid the performance of his duty. The consequence must be fearful for you, distressing to your fellow-citizens here and to the friends of good government throughout the world. Its enemies have beheld our prosperity with a vexation they could not conceal; it was a standing refutation of their slavish doctrines, and they will point to our discord with the triumph of malignant joy.

It is yet in your power to disappoint them. There is yet time to show that the descendants of the Pinckneys, the Sumters, the Rutledges, and of the thousand other names which adorn the pages of your Revolutionary history, will not abandon that Union, to support which, so many of them fought and bled and died. I adjure you, as you honor their memory, as you love the cause of freedom, to which they dedicated their lives, as you prize the peace of your country, the lives of its best citizens, and your own fair fame, to retrace your steps.

Snatch from the archives of your state the disorganizing edict of its convention; bid its members to reassemble and promulgate the decided expressions of your will to remain in the path which alone can conduct you to safety, prosperity, and honor. Tell them that compared to disunion all other evils are light, because that brings with it an accumulation of all. Declare that you will never take the field unless the star-spangled banner of your country shall float over you; that you will not be stigmatized when dead, and dishonored and scorned while you live, as the authors of the first attack on the Constitution of your country. Its destroyers you cannot be. You may disturb its peace, you may interrupt the course of its prosperity, you may cloud its reputation for stability; but its tranquillity will be restored, its prosperity will return, and the stain upon its national character will be transferred and remain an eternal blot on the memory of those who caused the disorder.

Fellow-citizens of the United States, the threat of unhallowed disunion, the names of those once respected by whom it is uttered, the array of military force to support it, denote the approach of a crisis in our affairs on which the continuance of our unexampled prosperity, our political existence, and perhaps that of all free governments may depend. The conjuncture demanded a free, a full, and explicit enunciation, not only of my intentions, but of my principles of action; and as the claim was asserted of a right by a state to annul the laws of the Union, and even to secede from it at pleasure, a frank exposition of my opinions in relation to the origin and form of our government and the construction I give to the instrument by which it was created seemed to be proper.

Having the fullest confidence in the justness of the legal and constitutional opinion of my duties which has been expressed, I rely with equal confidence on your undivided support in my determination to execute the laws, to preserve the Union by all constitutional means, to arrest, if possible, by moderate and firm measures the necessity of a recourse to force; and if it be the will of Heaven that the recurrence of its primeval curse on man for the shedding of a brother's blood should fall upon our land, that it be not called down by any offensive act on the part of the United States.

Fellow-citizens, the momentous case is before you. On your undivided support of your government depends the decision of the great question it involves—whether your sacred Union will be preserved and the blessing it secures to us as one people shall be perpetuated. No one can doubt that the unanimity with which that decision will be expressed will be such as to inspire new confidence in republican institutions, and that the prudence, the wisdom, and the courage which it will bring to their defense will transmit them unimpaired and invigorated to our children.

May the Great Ruler of Nations grant that the signal blessings with which He has favored ours may not, by the madness of party or personal ambition, be disregarded and lost; and may His wise providence bring those who have produced this crisis to see the folly before they feel the misery of civil strife, and inspire a returning veneration for that Union which, if we may dare to penetrate His designs, He has chosen as the only means of attaining the high destinies to which we may reasonably aspire.

BOSTON'S CORDWAINERS WIN A BASIC LABOR RIGHT

1842

A cordwainer made shoes. And until a century and a quarter ago a cordwainer made shoes in a time-honored way. Either he had a little shop of his own—a "ten-footer" it was called—or he worked with a few other men for a shop owner who supplied leather and other materials and paid his journeymen on a piece-work basis. In either case the cordwainer was likely to be a high-grade craftsman—intelligent, respected, and independent. He made a decent living and was no slave to his bench. If he wanted to plow and plant his garden, or catch a mess of fish, he took a day off, or several days, and no one complained that he was lazy or irresponsible.

But in the 1830's the system changed. Enterprising men with capital began to establish factories in which many men, instead of a few, were employed; and power-driven machines took over some of the work of skilled hands. At first the cordwainer had little reason to complain. Early in the decade business boomed, and profits and wages were high. Then came the Panic of 1837, followed by years of depression. Jobs became scarce, wages skidded, hours of work grew longer. The cordwainers found themselves in serious straits.

They were not alone. Weavers, tailors, ironworkers, printers, and many other craftsmen faced economic forces that were slowly but surely pushing them into poverty. As individuals they were helpless: a man could accept the terms his employer offered, or he could starve. They saw, on the other hand, that if they would organize, and refuse to work unless they received a decent wage, they could regain their ancient status.

So workmen began to form "societies" and "associations"—organizations essentially the same as the modern trade union. Members bound themselves not to work for less than a minimum rate of pay, and not to work for an employer who hired men who did not belong to their group.

Employers, often hard pressed themselves, fought back. To them, and to the courts, combinations of workingmen violated the common law, which forbade conspiracies to injure others. In case after case brought in the 1830's, workingmen's societies were prosecuted as conspiracies, and while juries sometimes refused to convict, usually the verdict went against the workingmen. In the case of the Geneva shoemakers (1835) the court rendered a typical judgment when it said: "If the defendants cannot make coarse boots for less than one dollar a pair, let them refuse to do so; but let them not directly or indirectly undertake to say that others shall not do the work for a less price."

Thus the trend until 1842, when the case of the Boston cordwainers, known in the lawbooks as *Commonwealth* v. *Hunt*, was finally decided.

In 1835 the shoemakers of Boston had formed the Boston Society of Journeymen Bootmakers for the purpose of maintaining "that rate of wages which is necessary to insure us the necessaries of life." To that end the members sought to compel all journeymen bootmakers in Boston to join the organization, and to force masters to employ no one who did not belong to the society.

In 1840 seven members of the society were indicted for conspiracy. The case came on for trial at the October term of the Municipal Court of Boston. Counsel for both sides argued at length and with great learning. "The gist of conspiracy," the county attorney contended, "is the unlawful confederacy to do an unlawful act, or even a lawful act with an unlawful purpose. The offense is complete when the confederacy is made, and any act done in pursuance of it is no constituent part of the offense, but merely an aggravation of it." The defense countered with the argument that the acts alleged to have been committed–bringing pressure on journeymen and masters–were not unlawful or criminal.

The case was "as important in principle as any one which was ever tried in this court," the trial judge asserted when he asked for a verdict of guilty.

"I am of opinion," he said in his charge, "and it is my duty to instruct you, as matter of law, that this society of journeymen bootmakers . . . . is an unlawful conspiracy against the laws of this commonwealth. It is a new power in the state, unknown to its constitution and laws, and subversive of their equal spirit. If such associations should be organized and carried into operation through the varying grades, professions and pursuits of the people of this commonwealth, all industry and enterprise would be suspended, and all property would become insecure. It would involve in one common, fatal ruin, both laborer and employer, and the rich as well as the poor. It would tend directly to array them against each other, and to convulse the social system to its center. Nothing but the force of government can put down a general spirit of misrule. But what could be hoped from the interference of government, when every citizen would be engaged in this civil strife? A frightful despotism would soon be erected on the ruins of this free and happy commonwealth."

The jury found the defendants guilty. The defense asked for a bill of exceptions, which was allowed, and the case was argued before the Supreme Judicial Court of Massachusetts in the spring of 1841. The opinion of the court, written by Chief Justice Lemuel Shaw, was not announced until the March term, 1842.

Shaw's opinion reversed the lower court completely, holding not only that workingmen had a right to form unions, but also that they had a right to compel employers to hire none but union members. This second principle—the closed shop—is still in dispute, but the long-unquestioned right of labor unions to exist rests squarely on Shaw's opinion.

Commonwealth v. Hunt

March 1842

Shaw, C. J. . . . . We have no doubt that by the operation of the constitution of this commonwealth, the general rules of the common law, making conspiracy an indictable offense, are in force here, and that this is included in the description of laws which had, before the adoption of the constitution, been used and approved in the Province, Colony, or State of Massachusetts Bay, and usually practiced in the courts of law. . . . Still, it is proper in this connection to remark that although the common law in regard to conspiracy in this commonwealth is in force, yet it will not necessarily follow that every indictment at common law for this offense is a precedent for a similar indictment in this state.

The general rule of the common law is that it is a criminal and indictable offense for two or more to confederate and combine together, by concerted means, to do that which is unlawful or criminal, to the injury of the public, or portions or classes of the community, or even to the rights of an individual. This rule of law may be equally in force as a rule of the common law, in England and in this commonwealth; and yet it must depend upon the local laws of each country to determine, whether the purpose to be accomplished by the combination, or the concerted means of accomplishing it, be unlawful or criminal in the respective countries.

All those laws of the parent country, whether rules of the common law or early English statutes, which were made for the purpose of regulating the wages of laborers, the settlement of paupers, and making it penal for any one to use a trade or handicraft to which he had not served a full apprenticeship–not being adapted to the circumstances of our colonial condition–were not adopted, used, or approved, and therefore do not come within the description of the laws adopted and confirmed by the provision of the constitution already cited . . . .

But the rule of law that an illegal conspiracy, whatever may be the facts which constitute it, is an offense punishable by the laws of this commonwealth, is established as well by legislative as by judicial authority. Like many other cases, that of murder, for instance, it leaves the definition or description of the offense to the common law, and provides modes for its prosecution and punishment. . . . .

But the great difficulty is, in framing any definition or description, to be drawn from the decided cases, which shall specifically identify this offense–a description broad enough to include all cases punishable under this description, without including acts which are not punishable. Without attempting to review and reconcile all the cases, we are of opinion that as a general description, though perhaps not a precise and accurate definition, a conspiracy must be a combination of two or more persons, by some concerted action, to accomplish some criminal or unlawful purpose, or to accomplish some purpose, not in itself criminal or unlawful, by criminal or unlawful means. . . . .

From this view of the law respecting conspiracy, we think it an offense which especially demands the application of that wise and humane rule of the common law, that an indictment shall state, with as much certainty as the nature of the case will admit, the facts which constitute the crime intended to be charged. This is required to enable the defendant to meet the charge and prepare for his defense, and, in case of acquittal or conviction, to show by the record the identity of the charge, so that he may not be indicted a second time for the same offense. . . . .

The first count set forth, that the defendants, with divers others unknown, on the day and at the place named, being workmen, and journeymen, in the art and occupation of bootmakers, unlawfully, perniciously, and deceitfully designing and intending to continue, keep up, form, and unite themselves into an unlawful club, society, and combination, and make unlawful bylaws, rules, and orders among themselves, and thereby govern themselves and other workmen in the said art, and unlawfully and unjustly to extort great sums of money by means thereof, did unlawfully assemble and meet together; and being so assembled, did unjustly and corruptly conspire, combine, confederate, and agree together that none of them should thereafter, and that none of them would, work for any master or person whatsoever in the said art, mystery, and occupation, who should employ any workman or journeyman, or other person . . . . who was not a member of said club, society, or combination, after notice given him to discharge such workman from the employ of such master; to the great damage and oppression, etc.

Now it is to be considered that the preamble and introductory matter in the indictment—such as unlawfully and deceitfully designing and intending unjustly to extort great sums, etc.—is mere recital, and not traversable, and therefore cannot aid an imperfect averment of the facts constituting the description of the offense. The same may be said of the concluding matter, which follows the averment, as to the great damage and oppression not only of their said masters, employing them in said art and occupation, but also of divers other workmen in the same art, mystery and occupation, to the evil example, etc. If the facts averred constitute the crime, these are properly stated as the legal inferences to be drawn from them. If they do not constitute the charge of such an offense, they cannot be aided by these alleged consequences.

Stripped then of these introductory recitals and alleged injurious consequences, and of the qualifying epithets attached to the facts, the averment is this: that the defendants and others formed themselves into a society, and agreed not to work for any person who should employ any journeyman or other person, not a member of such society, after notice given him to discharge such workman.

The manifest intent of the association is, to induce all those engaged in the same occupation to become members of it. Such a purpose is not unlawful. It would give them a power which might be exerted for useful and honorable purposes, or for dangerous and pernicious ones. If the latter were the real and actual object, and susceptible of proof, it should have been specially charged. Such an association might be used to afford each other assistance in times of poverty, sickness, and distress; or to raise their intellectual, moral, and social condition; or to make improvement in their art; or for other proper purposes. Or the association might be designed for purposes of oppression and injustice. But in order to charge all those who become members of an association with the guilt of a criminal conspiracy, it must be averred and proved that the actual, if not the avowed object of the association, was criminal. An association may be formed, the declared objects of which are innocent and laudable, and yet they may have secret articles, or an agreement communicated only to the members, by which they are banded together for purposes injurious to the peace of society or the rights of its members. Such would undoubtedly be a criminal conspiracy, on proof of the fact, however meritorious and praiseworthy the declared objects might be.

The law is not to be hoodwinked by colorable pretenses. It looks at truth and reality through whatever disguise it may assume. But to make such an association, ostensibly innocent, the subject of prosecution as a criminal conspiracy, the secret agreement which makes it so, is to be averred and proved as the gist of the offense. But when an association is formed for purposes actually innocent, and afterward its powers are abused, by those who have the control and management of it, to purposes of oppression and injustice, it will be criminal in those who thus misuse it, or give consent thereto, but not in the other members of the association. In this case, no such secret agreement, varying the objects of the association from those avowed, is set forth in this count of the indictment.

Nor can we perceive that the objects of this association, whatever they may have been, were to be attained by criminal means. The means which they proposed to employ, as averred in this count, and which, as we are now to presume, were established by the proof, were that they would not work for a person who, after due notice, should employ a journeyman not a member of their society. Supposing the object of the association to be laudable and lawful, or at least not unlawful, are these means criminal? The case supposes that these persons are not bound by contract, but free to work for whom they please, or not to work, if they so prefer. In this state of things, we cannot perceive that it is criminal for men to agree together to exercise their own acknowledged rights in such a manner as best to subserve their own interests.

One way to test this is to consider the effect of such an agreement, where the object of the association is acknowledged on all hands to be a laudable one. Suppose a class of workmen, impressed with the manifold evils of intemperance, should agree with each other not to work in a shop in which ardent spirit was furnished, or not to work in a shop with any one who used it, or not to work for an employer, who should, after notice, employ a journeyman who habitually used it. The consequences might be the same. A workman, who should still persist in the use of ardent spirit, would find it more difficult to get employment; a master employing such an one might, at times, experience inconvenience in his work, in losing the services of a skillful but intemperate workman. Still it seems to us, that as the object would be lawful, and the means not unlawful, such an agreement could not be pronounced a criminal conspiracy. . . . .

The second count, omitting the recital of unlawful intent and evil disposition, and omitting the direct averment of an unlawful club or society, alleges that the defendants, with others unknown, did assemble, conspire, confederate, and agree together not to work for any master or person who should employ any workman not being a member of a certain club, society or combination, called the Boston Journeymen Bootmakers' Society. . . . So far as the averment of a conspiracy is concerned, all the remarks made in reference to the first count are equally applicable to this. It is simply an averment of an agreement amongst themselves not to work for a person who should employ any person not a member of a certain association. It sets forth no illegal or criminal purpose to be accomplished, nor any illegal or criminal means to be adopted for the accomplishment of any purpose. . . . .

We think, therefore, that associations may be entered into, the object of which is to adopt measures that may have a tendency to impoverish another, that is, to diminish his gains and profits, and yet so far from being criminal or unlawful, the object may be highly meritorious and public spirited. The legality of such an association will therefore depend upon the means to be used for its accomplishment. If it is to be carried into effect by fair or honorable and lawful means, it is, to say the least, innocent; if by falsehood or force, it may be stamped with the character of conspiracy. . . . .

It appears by the bill of exceptions that it was contended on the part of the defendants, that this indictment did not set forth any agreement to do a criminal act, or to do any lawful act by criminal means, and that the agreement therein set forth did not constitute a conspiracy indictable by the law of this state, and that the court was requested so to instruct the jury. This the court declined doing, but instructed the jury that the indictment did describe a confederacy among the defendants to do an unlawful act, and to effect the same by unlawful means—that the society, organized and associated for the purposes described in the indictment, was an unlawful conspiracy against the laws of this state, and that if the jury believed, from the evidence, that the defendants or any of them had engaged in such confederacy, they were bound to find such of them guilty.

In this opinion of the learned judge, this court, for the reasons stated, cannot concur. Whatever illegal purpose can be found in the constitution of the Bootmakers' Society, it not being clearly set forth in the indictment, cannot be relied upon to support this conviction. So if any facts were disclosed at the trial, which, if properly averred, would have given a different character to the indictment, they do not appear in the bill of exceptions, nor could they, after verdict, aid the indictment. But looking solely at the indictment, disregarding the qualifying epithets, recitals, and immaterial allegations, and confining ourselves to facts so averred as to be capable of being traversed and put in issue, we cannot perceive that it charges a criminal conspiracy punishable by law. The exceptions must, therefore, be sustained, and the judgment arrested.

Several other exceptions were taken and have been argued; but this decision on the main question has rendered it unnecessary to consider them.

HUMAN FREEDOM IS THE CAUSE OF GOD

1854

On January 4, 1854, Stephen A. Douglas, Senator from Illinois and chairman of the Committee on Territories, reported a bill to organize the Territory of Nebraska. On the most disturbing question of the day the bill provided simply that when states should be organized from the territory, they should come into the Union with or without slavery as their constitutions might prescribe. Douglas soon discovered that the bill fell far short of satisfying the extreme proslavery Senators, who would block its passage unless it were amended to fit their views.

In the next three weeks he yielded to the pressure the Southerners exerted. When the amended bill was reported on January 23, it explicitly repealed the Missouri Compromise, by which slavery had been prohibited north of the line of 36° 30′; created two territories—Kansas and Nebraska—instead of one; and provided that the inhabitants of the territories could decide the slavery question prior to statehood. By this time President Pierce had given the bill his blessing, thus requiring all loyal Democrats to vote for its passage.

The proposed repeal of the Missouri Compromise, which had been accepted by all parties since 1820, and reaffirmed as recently as 1850, shocked all except the proslavery extremists. But Whig objectors, being a minority, were impotent, while most Democrats were cowed by party discipline. Not so a small group of Free-Soilers, nominally Democratic, in both houses—Salmon P. Chase of Ohio and Charles Sumner of Massachusetts in the Senate; Joshua R. Giddings and Edward Wade of Ohio, Gerrit Smith of New York, and Alexander De Witt of Massachusetts in the House of Representatives. One day after the introduction of the Kansas-Nebraska Bill in its final form these six published the Appeal of the Independent Democrats in Congress to the People of the United States.

Drafted by Giddings, polished and elaborated by Chase, the Appeal was an impassioned plea to the North to resist the encroachments of the slave power. Reprinted by hundreds of Whig and Free-Soil newspapers, it aroused such opposition to the Kansas-Nebraska Bill that Douglas, heretofore a popular figure, was burned in effigy, even in Democratic communities. By parliamentary skill and the sheer power of the administration he forced the bill through Congress, but by that time the storm of antislavery feeling, aroused by the Appeal, had crystallized into opposition that was to give birth to the Republican party and, in seven short years, to lead to civil war.

The Appeal of the Independent Democrats

January 19, 1854

As Senators and Representatives in the Congress of the United States, it is our duty to warn our constituents whenever imminent danger menaces the freedom of our institutions or the permanency of the Union.

Such danger, as we firmly believe, now impends, and we earnestly solicit your prompt attention to it.

At the last session of Congress a bill for the organization of the Territory of Nebraska passed the House of Representatives by an overwhelming majority. That bill was based on the principle of excluding slavery from the new territory. It was not taken up for consideration in the Senate, and consequently failed to become a law.

At the present session a new Nebraska Bill has been reported by the Senate Committee on Territories, which, should it unhappily receive the sanction of Congress, will open all the unorganized territories of the Union to the ingress of slavery.

We arraign this bill as a gross violation of a sacred pledge; as a criminal betrayal of precious rights; as part and parcel of an atrocious plot to exclude from a vast unoccupied region immigrants from the Old World and free laborers from our own states, and convert it into a dreary region of despotism, inhabited by masters and slaves. . . . .

This immense region, occupying the very heart of the North American continent, and larger by thirty-three thousand square miles than all the existing free states–including California; this immense region, well watered and fertile, through which the middle and northern routes from the Atlantic to the Pacific must pass; this immense region, embracing all the unorganized territory of the nation, except the comparatively insignificant district of Indian Territory north of Red River and between Arkansas and Texas, and now for more than thirty years regarded by the common consent of the American people as consecrated to freedom by statute and by compact–this immense region the bill now before the Senate, without reason and without excuse, but in flagrant disregard of sound policy and sacred faith, purposes to open to slavery.

We beg your attention, fellow-citizens, to a few historical facts:

The original settled policy of the United States, clearly indicated by the Jefferson Proviso of 1784 and the Ordinance of 1787, was nonextension of slavery.

In 1803, Louisiana was acquired by purchase from France. At that time there were some twenty-five or thirty thousand slaves in the territory; most of them within what is now the State of Louisiana; a few only, farther north, on the west bank of the Mississippi. Congress, instead of providing for the abolition of slavery in this new Territory, permitted its continuance. In 1812 the State of Louisiana was organized and admitted into the Union with slavery.

In 1818, six years later, the inhabitants of the Territory of Missouri applied to Congress for authority to form a state constitution, and for admission into the Union. There were, at that time, in the whole territory acquired from France, outside of the State of Louisiana, not three thousand slaves.

There was no apology, in the circumstances of the country, for the continuance of slavery. The original national policy was against it, and not less the plain language of the treaty under which the territory had been acquired from France.

It was proposed, therefore, to incorporate in the bill authorizing the formation of a state government, a provision requiring that the constitution of the new state should contain an article providing for the abolition of existing slavery, and prohibiting the further introduction of slaves.

This provision was vehemently and pertinaciously opposed, but finally prevailed in the House of Representatives by a decided vote. In the Senate it was rejected, and–in consequence of the disagreement between the two Houses–the bill was lost.

At the next session of Congress, the controversy was renewed with increased violence. It was terminated at length by a compromise. Missouri was allowed to come into the Union with slavery; but a section was inserted in the act authorizing her admission, excluding slavery forever from all the territory acquired from France, not included in the new state, lying north of 36° 30′. . . .

The question of the constitutionality of this prohibition was submitted by President Monroe to his cabinet. John Quincy Adams was then Secretary of State; John C. Calhoun was Secretary of War; William H. Crawford was Secretary of the Treasury; and William Wirt was Attorney-General. Each of these eminent gentlemen–three of them being from the slave states–gave a written opinion, affirming its constitutionality, and thereupon the act received the sanction of the President himself, also from a slave state.

Nothing is more certain in history than the fact that Missouri could not have been admitted as a slave state had not certain members from the free states been reconciled to the measure by the incorporation of this prohibition into the act of admission. Nothing is more certain than that this prohibition has been regarded and accepted by the whole country as a solemn compact against the extension of slavery into any part of the territory acquired from France lying north of 36° 30′, and not included in the new State of Missouri.

The same act—let it be ever remembered—which authorized the formation of a constitution by the state, without a clause forbidding slavery, consecrated, beyond question and beyond honest recall, the whole remainder of the territory to freedom and free institutions forever. For more than thirty years—during more than half our national existence under our present Constitution—this compact has been universally regarded and acted upon as inviolable American law. In conformity with it, Iowa was admitted as a free state and Minnesota has been organized as a free territory.

It is a strange and ominous fact, well calculated to awaken the worst apprehensions and the most fearful forebodings of future calamities, that it is now deliberately proposed to repeal this prohibition, by implication or directly—the latter certainly the manlier way—and thus to subvert the compact, and allow slavery in all the yet unorganized territory.

We cannot, in this address, review the various pretenses under which it is attempted to cloak this monstrous wrong, but we must not altogether omit to notice one.

It is said that Nebraska sustains the same relations to slavery as did the territory acquired from Mexico prior to 1850, and that the proslavery clauses of the bill are necessary to carry into effect the compromise of that year. . . .

The Compromise Acts themselves refute this pretension. In the third article of the second section of the joint resolution for annexing Texas to the United States, it is expressly declared that "in such state or states as shall be formed out of such territory north of said Missouri Compromise line, slavery or involuntary servitude, except for crime, shall be prohibited"; and in the act for organizing New Mexico and settling the boundary of Texas, a proviso was incorporated, on motion of Mr. Mason, of Virginia, which distinctly preserves this prohibition, and flouts the barefaced pretension that all the territory of the United States, whether south or north of the Missouri Compromise line, is to be open to slavery. . . .

Here is proof beyond controversy that the principle of the Missouri act prohibiting slavery north of 36° 30′, far from being abrogated by the Compromise Acts, is expressly affirmed; and that the proposed repeal of this prohibition, instead of being an affirmation of the Compromise Acts, is a repeal of a very prominent provision of the most important act of the series. It is solemnly declared in the very Compromise Acts "that nothing herein contained shall be construed to impair or qualify" the prohibition of slavery north of 36° 30′; and yet, in the face of this declaration, that sacred prohibition is said to be overthrown. Can presumption further go? To all who, in any way, lean upon these compromises, we commend this exposition. . . . .

In 1820 the slave states said to the free states: "Admit Missouri with slavery, and refrain from positive exclusion south of 36° 30′, and we will join you in perpetual prohibition north of that line." The free states consented. In 1854 the slave states say to the free states: "Missouri is admitted; no prohibition south of 36° 30′ has been attempted; we have received the full consideration of our agreement; no more is to be gained by adherence to it on our part; we therefore propose to cancel the compact." If this is not Punic faith, what is? Not without the deepest dishonor and crime can the free states acquiesce in the demand.

We confess our total inability properly to delineate the character or describe the consequences of this measure. Language fails to express the sentiments of indignation and abhorrence which it inspires; and no vision less penetrating and comprehensive than that of the All-Seeing can reach its evil issues. . . . .

We appeal to the people. We warn you that the dearest interests of freedom and the Union are in imminent peril. Demagogues may tell you that the Union can be maintained only by submitting to the demands of slavery. We tell you that the Union can only be maintained by the full recognition of the just claims of freedom and man. The Union was formed to establish justice and secure the blessings of liberty. When it fails to accomplish these ends, it will be worthless, and when it becomes worthless, it cannot long endure.

We entreat you to be mindful of that fundamental maxim of democracy–*EQUAL RIGHTS AND EXACT JUSTICE FOR ALL MEN*. Do not submit to become agents in extending legalized oppression and systematized injustice over a vast territory yet exempt from these terrible evils.

We implore Christians and Christian ministers to interpose. Their divine religion requires them to behold in every man a brother, and to labor for the advancement and regeneration of the human race.

Whatever apologies may be offered for the toleration of slavery in the states, none can be offered for its extension into territories where it does not exist, and where that extension involves the repeal of ancient law and the violation of solemn compact. Let all protest, earnestly and emphatically, by correspondence, through the press, by memorials, by resolutions of public meetings and legislative bodies, and in whatever other mode may seem expedient, against this enormous crime.

For ourselves, we shall resist it by speech and vote, and with all the abilities which God has given us. Even if overcome in the impending struggle, we shall not submit. We shall go home to our constituents, erect anew the standard of freedom, and call on the people to come to the rescue of the country from the domination of slavery. We will not despair; for the cause of human freedom is the cause of God.

JOHN BROWN PLEADS FOR THE DOWNTRODDEN

1859

In the courtroom at Charlestown, Virginia (now West Virginia), the judge asked the convicted man if he wished to make a statement before sentence was passed. John Brown, weak from wounds, rose painfully. His heavy beard could not conceal his pallor and his eyes glittered with feverish brightness, but his voice carried to every listener in the room, and to millions beyond its walls.

Behind him lay a career of failure, grim zeal for reform, and madness. Always an Abolitionist, he had finally come to consider himself God's chosen instrument to free the slaves. As a man in his fifties, and the father of many children, he made his decision: he would lead the blacks in a revolt against their masters that would put an end to slavery in one bloody spasm. Meanwhile, he would strike such blows as he could against the system. In Kansas, only three years earlier, he and his sons had murdered proslavery settlers in cold blood. A year ago he had raided plantations in Missouri, carried off slaves, and escaped with them to Canada. He had returned to the United States with a price upon his head, yet no one molested him while he planned the stroke that was to lead to the Charlestown courtroom.

On the evening of October 16, 1859, Brown and seventeen followers swung down a lonely road to Harpers Ferry, the hill-shadowed village that stands at the junction of the Shenandoah and the Potomac. With a rush the little band assaulted and captured the United States armory and arsenal. While they waited in vain for the slaves of the countryside to rise and join them, the alarm spread. Volunteers and militia companies mustered, regulars and marines were ordered to the scene. Brown chose to make his stand in the engine house. Under the fire of the troops his men lost heavily; it was his fate to see two of his sons die in agony. On the early morning of the eighteenth the officer commanding the attacking force, a regular army brevet-colonel named Robert E. Lee, ordered an assault. It succeeded. Brown, wounded, was one of five prisoners. Two of his band escaped, ten lay dead or dying.

John Brown was indicted for murder, treason to the Commonwealth of Virginia, and conspiracy with Negroes to produce insurrection. After a trial marked by scrupulous fairness, a jury found him guilty of all three charges. As he rose to hear sentence pronounced on the morning of November 2, he knew that he faced death, yet he stood unafraid and unrepentant. And out of his warped mind came a plea for the oppressed of his country that still rings with the aspirations of humanity.

On December 2, 1859, John Brown died at the end of a hangman's rope. Yet the great marching song of the Civil War is evidence that of few men could it be asked more pertinently: "O death, where is thy sting? O grave, where is thy victory?"

John Brown's Last Speech

November 2, 1859

I have, may it please the court, a few words to say. In the first place, I deny everything but what I have all along admitted–of a design on my part to free slaves. I intended certainly to have made a clean thing of that matter, as I did last winter, when I went into Missouri and there took slaves without the snapping of a gun on either side, moving them through the country, and finally leaving them in Canada. I designed to have done the same thing again, on a larger scale. That was all I intended. I never did intend murder, or treason, or the destruction of property, or to excite or incite slaves to rebellion, or to make insurrection.

I have another objection, and that is that it is unjust that I should suffer such a penalty. Had I interfered in the manner which I admit, and which I admit has been fairly proved (for I admire the truthfulness and candor of the greater portion of the witnesses who have testified in this case)–had I so interfered in behalf of the rich, the powerful, the intelligent, the so-called great, or in behalf of any of their friends, either father, mother, brother, sister, wife, or children, or any of that class, and suffered and sacrificed what I have in this interference, it would have been all right. Every man in this court would have deemed it an act worthy of reward rather than punishment.

This court acknowledges, too, as I suppose, the validity of the law of God. I see a book kissed, which I suppose to be the Bible, or at least the New Testament, which teaches me that all things whatsoever I would that men should do to me, I should do even so to them. It teaches me, further, to remember them that are in bonds, as bound with them. I endeavored to act up to that instruction. I say, I am yet too young to understand that God is any respecter of persons. I believe that to have interfered as I have done, as I have always freely admitted I have done, in behalf of His despised poor, was no wrong, but right. Now if it is deemed necessary that I should forfeit my life for the furtherance of the ends of justice, and mingle my blood further with the blood of my children and with the blood of millions in this slave country whose rights are disregarded by wicked, cruel, and unjust enactments—I say, let it be done!

Let me say one word further.

I feel entirely satisfied with the treatment I have received on my trial. Considering all the circumstances, it has been more generous than I expected. But I feel no consciousness of guilt. I have stated from the first what was my intention and what was not. I never had any design against the liberty of any person, nor any disposition to commit treason, or excite slaves to rebel, or make any general insurrection. I never encouraged any man to do so, but always discouraged any idea of that kind.

Let me say, also, a word in regard to the statements made by some of those who were connected with me. I hear it has been stated by some of them that I have induced them to join me. But the contrary is true. I do not say this to injure them, but as regretting their weakness. No one but joined me of his own accord, and the greater part at their own expense. A number of them I never saw, and never had a word of conversation with, till the day they came to me, and that was for the purpose I have stated.

Now I have done.

SOUTH CAROLINA JUSTIFIES SECESSION

1860

The delegates to the South Carolina Convention, called to meet on December 17, 1860, found the city of Columbia infested with smallpox. They remained in session long enough to adopt a resolution declaring that "the State should forthwith secede from the Federal Union" and that a committee should be appointed "to draft an ordinance to be adopted by the convention in order to accomplish this purpose of secession." Then they resolved to reassemble the following day, but at Charleston rather than at the capital.

Charleston, reveling in the unexpected role of host, greeted the delegates as heralds of a brilliant future. Bunting and flags gave a festive air to the streets; excited men gathered in groups to congratulate each other on the coming of "independence." The convention, meeting in St. Andrew's Hall, soberly proceeded with routine business pending the report of the committee charged with preparing the ordinance.

Early in the afternoon of December 20, while tense and impatient crowds filled the approaches to the hall, Chancellor J. A. Inglis asked for the floor. His committee, he announced, believed that the ordinance should be brief and simple, containing nothing not necessary to effect the "solemn act of secession." Therefore they submitted the following:

AN ORDINANCE

To dissolve the Union between the State of South Carolina and other States united with her under the compact entitled "The Constitution of the United States of America."

We, the People of the State of South Carolina, in Convention assembled, do declare and ordain, and it is hereby declared and ordained,

That the Ordinance adopted by us in Convention, on the twenty-third day of May, in the year of our Lord one thousand seven hundred and eighty-eight, whereby the Constitution of the United States of America was ratified, and also, all Acts and parts of Acts of the General Assembly of this State, ratifying amendments of the said Constitution, are hereby repealed; and that the union now subsisting between South Carolina and other States, under the name of "The United States of America," is hereby dissolved.

The question was put at once. Result: 169 yeas, nays none. The convention then invited the governor and the members of the legislature to meet at seven that evening at Institute Hall, where the ordinance would be signed.

At the appointed time the delegates left St. Andrew's Hall in a body. As they moved through the streets of the lovely city, the cheers of thou[illegible] greeted their every step. When they entered Institute Hall, the ladies who packed the galleries waved hundreds of handkerchiefs and made the air crackle with handclapping. An engrossed copy of the ordinance, bearing the great seal of the state, was presented, and one by one the delegates came forward to affix their signatures. At the end of the ceremony the president of the convention announced:

"The Ordinance of Secession has been signed and ratified, and I proclaim the State of South Carolina an independent Commonwealth."

The audience broke into applause. Outside, church bells pealed, artillery at the Citadel roared in salute. Hundreds of citizens illuminated their homes, while on the streets military companies in gay uniforms marched and countermarched to the strains of martial music. In the words of one observer, "The whole heart of the people had spoken."

The convention spent the next several days in framing a Declaration of Causes, by which it explained and justified the act of secession. Though based on a determination to perpetuate human slavery, the Declaration's argument for states rights and the compact theory of government was in line with historic concepts of American democracy.

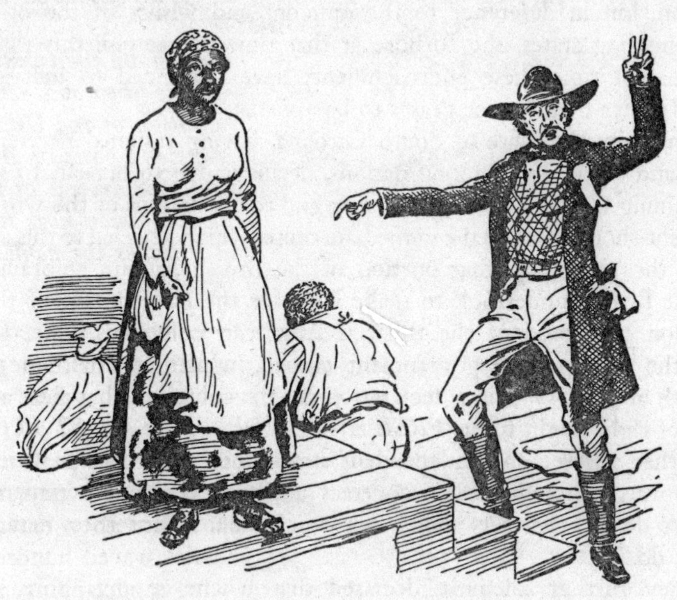

Declaration of Causes

December 24, 1860

The people of the State of South Carolina in convention assembled, on the second day of April, A.D. 1852, declared that the frequent violations of the Constitution of the United States by the federal government, and its encroachments upon the reserved rights of the states, fully justified this state in their withdrawal from the federal Union, but in deference to the opinions and wishes of the other slaveholding states, she forbore at that time to exercise this right. Since that time these encroachments have continued to increase, and further forbearance ceases to be a virtue.

And now the State of South Carolina, having resumed her separate and equal place among nations, deems it due to herself, to the remaining United States of America, and to the nations of the world, that she should declare the immediate causes which have led to this act.

In the year 1765, that portion of the British Empire embracing Great Britain undertook to make laws for the government of that portion composed of the thirteen American colonies. A struggle for the right of self-government ensued, which resulted, on the fourth of July, 1776, in a declaration, by the colonies, "that they are, and of right ought to be, *FREE AND INDEPENDENT STATES;* and that, as free and independent states, they have full power to levy war, conclude peace, contract alliances, establish commerce, and to do all other acts and things which independent states may of right do."

They further solemnly declared that whenever any "form of government becomes destructive of the ends for which it was established, it is the right of the people to alter or abolish it, and to institute a new government." Deeming the government of Great Britain to have become destructive of these ends, they declared that the colonies "are absolved from all allegiance to the British Crown, and that all political connection between them and the state of Great Britain is, and ought to be, totally dissolved."

In pursuance of this Declaration of Independence, each of the thirteen states proceeded to exercise its separate sovereignty; adopted for itself a constitution, and appointed officers for the administration of government in all its departments–legislative, executive, and judicial. For purposes of defense they united their arms and their counsels; and, in 1778, they entered into a league known as the Articles of Confederation, whereby they agreed to entrust the administration of their external relations to a common agent, known as the Congress of the United States, expressly declaring, in the first article, "that each state retains its sovereignty, freedom, and independence, and every power, jurisdiction, and right which is not, by this Confederation, expressly delegated to the United States in Congress assembled."

Under this Confederation the War of the Revolution was carried on; and on the third of September, 1783, the contest ended, and a

definite treaty was signed by Great Britain, in which she acknowledged the independence of the colonies. . . .

Thus were established the two great principles asserted by the colonies, namely, the right of a state to govern itself; and the right of a people to abolish a government when it becomes destructive of the ends for which it was instituted. And concurrent with the establishment of these principles, was the fact that each colony became and was recognized by the mother country as a *FREE, SOVEREIGN, AND INDEPENDENT STATE.*

In 1787, deputies were appointed by the states to revise the Articles of Confederation; and on [the] seventeenth [of] September, 1787, these deputies recommended, for the adoption of the states, the articles of union, known as the Constitution of the United States. . . . .

By this Constitution, certain duties were imposed upon the several states, and the exercise of certain of their powers was restrained,

which necessarily impelled their continued existence as sovereign states. But, to remove all doubt, an amendment was added, which declared that the powers not delegated to the United States by the Constitution, nor prohibited by it to the states, are reserved to the states respectively, or to the people. On the twenty-third [of] May, 1788, South Carolina, by a convention of her people, passed an ordinance assenting to this Constitution, and afterward altered her own Constitution to conform herself to the obligations she had undertaken.

Thus was established, by compact between the states, a government with defined objects and powers, limited to the express words of the grant. This limitation left the whole remaining mass of power subject to the clause reserving it to the states or the people, and rendered unnecessary any specification of reserved rights. We hold that the government thus established is subject to the two great principles asserted in the Declaration of Independence; and we hold further, that the mode of its formation subjects it to a third fundamental principle, namely, the law of compact. We maintain that in every compact between two or more parties, the obligation is mutual; that the failure of one of the contracting parties to perform a material part of the agreement entirely releases the obligation of the other; and that, where no arbiter is provided, each party is remitted to his own judgment to determine the fact of failure, with all its consequences.

In the present case that fact is established with certainty. We assert that fourteen of the states have deliberately refused for years past to fulfill their constitutional obligations, and we refer to their own statutes for the proof.

The Constitution of the United States, in its fourth article, provides as follows:

"No person held to service or labor in one state, under the laws thereof, escaping into another, shall, in consequence of any law or regulation therein, be discharged from such service or labor, but shall be delivered up on claim of the party to whom such service or labor may be due."

This stipulation was so material to the compact that without it that compact would not have been made. The greater number of the contracting parties held slaves, and they had previously evinced their estimate of the value of such a stipulation by making it a condition in the ordinance for the government of the territory ceded by Virginia, which obligations, and the laws of the general government, have ceased to effect the objects of the Constitution. The states of Maine, New Hampshire, Vermont, Massachusetts, Connecticut, Rhode Island, New York, Pennsylvania, Illinois, Indiana, Michigan, Wisconsin, and Iowa have enacted laws which either nullify the acts of Congress, or render useless any attempt to execute them.

The ends for which this Constitution was framed are declared by itself to be "to form a more perfect union, to establish justice, insure domestic tranquillity, provide for the common defense, promote the general welfare, and secure the blessings of liberty to ourselves and our posterity. . . . ."

We affirm that these ends for which this government was instituted have been defeated, and the government itself has been destructive of them by the action of the nonslaveholding states. Those states have assumed the right of deciding upon the propriety of our domestic institutions; and have denied the rights of property established in fifteen of the states and recognized by the Constitution; they have denounced as sinful the institution of slavery; they have permitted the open establishment among them of societies whose avowed object is to disturb the peace of and eloign [move away] the property of the citizens of other states. They have encouraged and assisted thousands of our slaves to leave their homes; and those who remain, have been incited by emissaries, books, and pictures to servile insurrection.

For twenty-five years this agitation has been steadily increasing until now it has secured to its aid the power of the common government. Observing the forms of the Constitution, a sectional party has found within that article establishing the executive department the means of subverting the Constitution itself. A geographical line has been drawn across the Union, and all the states north of that line have united in the election of a man to the high office of President of the United States, whose opinions and purposes are hostile to slavery. He is to be entrusted with the administration of the common government because he has declared that that "government cannot endure permanently half slave, half free," and that the public mind must rest in the belief that slavery is in the course of ultimate extinction. This sectional combination for the subversion of the Constitution has been aided, in some of the states, by elevating to citizenship persons who, by the supreme law of the land, are incapable of becoming citizens; and their votes have been used to inaugurate a new policy, hostile to the South, and destructive of its peace and safety.

On the fourth of March next this party will take possession of the government. It has announced that the South shall be excluded from the common territory, and that the judicial tribunal shall be made sectional, and that a war must be waged against slavery until it shall cease throughout the United States.

The guarantees of the Constitution will then no longer exist; the equal rights of the states will be lost. The slaveholding states will no longer have the power of self-government, or self-protection, and the federal government will have become their enemy.

Sectional interest and animosity will deepen the irritation; and all hope of remedy is rendered vain by the fact that the public opinion at the North has invested a great political error with the sanctions of a more erroneous religious belief.

We, therefore, the people of South Carolina, by our delegates in convention assembled, appealing to the Supreme Judge of the world for the rectitude of our intentions, have solemnly declared that the Union heretofore existing between this state and the other states of North America is dissolved, and that the State of South Carolina has resumed her position among the nations of the world, as [a] separate and independent state, with full power to levy war, conclude peace, contract alliances, establish commerce, and to do all other acts and things which independent states may of right do.

WE ARE NOT ENEMIES, BUT FRIENDS

1861

Abraham Lincoln, President-elect, was harassed by visitors. Time pressed, yet he had one duty to perform before leaving Springfield: he must write the address he would deliver when he would take the oath of office on March 4, 1861. First of all, he needed privacy. This he found in a vacant room over a store owned by his brother-in-law —a room bare and dusty and furnished only with an old desk and a chair or two. And he needed books. William H. Herndon, his law partner, expected the President-elect to ask for half the volumes in Herndon's extensive library. Instead, Lincoln requested only Clay's speech in favor of the Compromise of 1850, Jackson's Proclamation against Nullification, Webster's Reply to Hayne, and the Constitution. With these, and a quire of paper, he closeted himself.

Lincoln left Springfield on February 11, 1861, with several copies of his inaugural address, printed on proof sheets, in his valise. En route, and after his arrival in Washington, he showed the speech to a number of leading Republicans. At the suggestion of an old friend, Orville H. Browning, he modified his original declaration that he would "hold, occupy, and repossess" the property belonging to the federal government to the much more conciliatory form of "hold, occupy, and possess." William H. Seward, who was to be Secretary

of State, recommended numerous amendments, of which the most important was a closing paragraph stressing the historic bonds of affection and mutual confidence that had united all sections of the country for almost a century. With rare literary artistry Lincoln transmuted Seward's draft into a prose poem of unsurpassed beauty.

At noon on the fourth of March, 1861, President James Buchanan, with Senators E. D. Baker of Oregon and James A. Pearce of Maryland, drove to Willard's Hotel in an open carriage. Buchanan stepped down, entered the hotel, and soon afterward returned with the President-elect. The procession moved along Pennsylvania Avenue to the Capitol—a ragged column consisting of the diplomatic corps, members of Congress, governors of states, veterans of the Revolutionary War and the War of 1812, and a variety of military units.

At the Capitol, Buchanan and Lincoln were escorted to the Senate Chamber, where they occupied seats of honor while Hannibal Hamlin, the Vice-President, took the oath of office. Again a procession formed and moved through the corridors to the east portico, where thousands surrounded a wooden platform. As soon as the presidential party was seated, Senator Baker, a friend of Lincoln's since early days in Springfield, stepped forward. "Fellow-citizens," he announced, "I introduce to you Abraham Lincoln, the President-elect of the United States." To scattered applause Lincoln drew his address from the inside pocket of his long black coat and began to read in clear, deliberate tones.

When he finished, Chief Justice Taney, whom Lincoln had criticized caustically for his opinion in the Dred Scott case four years earlier, rose and received the Bible from the clerk of the Supreme Court. Lincoln placed his left hand on an open page, raised his right hand, and repeated the oath: "I do solemnly swear that I will faithfully execute the office of President of the United States, and will, to the best of my ability, preserve, protect, and defend the Constitution of the United States."

The artillery boomed a final salute, and the crowd drifted away.

Lincoln's First Inaugural Address

March 4, 1861

Fellow-Citizens of the United States: In compliance with a custom as old as the government itself, I appear before you to address you briefly, and to take, in your presence, the oath prescribed by the Constitution of the United States, to be taken by the President "before he enters on the execution of his office."

I do not consider it necessary, at present, for me to discuss those matters of administration about which there is no special anxiety, or excitement.

Apprehension seems to exist among the people of the Southern States, that by the accession of a Republican administration, their property, and their peace, and personal security, are to be endangered. There has never been any reasonable cause for such apprehension. Indeed, the most ample evidence to the contrary has all the while existed, and been open to their inspection. It is found in nearly all the published speeches of him who now addresses you. I do but quote from one of those speeches when I declare that "I have no purpose, directly or indirectly, to interfere with the institution of slavery in the states where it exists. I believe I have no lawful right to do so, and I have no inclination to do so."

Those who nominated and elected me did so with full knowledge that I had made this, and many similar declarations, and had never recanted them. And more than this, they placed in the platform, for my acceptance, and as a law to themselves, and to me, the clear and emphatic resolution which I now read:

"*Resolved*, That the maintenance inviolate of the rights of the states, and especially the right of each state to order and control its own domestic institutions according to its own judgment exclusively, is essential to that balance of power on which the perfection and endurance of our political fabric depend; and we denounce the lawless invasion by armed force of the soil of any state or territory, no matter under what pretext, as among the gravest of crimes."

I now reiterate these sentiments and, in doing so, I only press upon the public attention the most conclusive evidence of which the case is susceptible, that the property, peace, and security of no section are to be in any wise endangered by the now incoming administration. I add, too, that all the protection which, consistently with the Constitution and the laws, can be given, will be cheerfully given to all the states when lawfully demanded, for whatever cause—as cheerfully to one section as to another.

There is much controversy about the delivering up of fugitives from service or labor. The clause I now read is as plainly written in the Constitution as any other of its provisions:

"No person held to service or labor in one state, under the laws thereof, escaping into another, shall, in consequence of any law or regulation therein, be discharged from such service or labor, but shall be delivered up on claim of the party to whom such service or labor may be due."

It is scarcely questioned that this provision was intended by those who made it, for the reclaiming of what we call fugitive slaves; and the intention of the lawgiver is the law. All members of Congress swear their support to the whole Constitution—to this provision as much as to any other. To the proposition, then, that slaves whose cases come within the terms of this clause "shall be delivered up," their oaths are unanimous. Now, if they would make the effort in good temper, could they not, with nearly equal unanimity, frame and pass a law, by means of which to keep good that unanimous oath? There is some difference of opinion whether this clause should be enforced by national or by state authority; but surely that difference is not a very material one. If the slave is to be surrendered, it can be of but little consequence to him, or to others, by which authority it is done. And should anyone, in any case, be content that his oath shall go unkept, on a merely unsubstantial controversy as to how it shall be kept?

Again, in any law upon this subject, ought not all the safeguards of liberty known in civilized and humane jurisprudence to be introduced, so that a free man be not, in any case, surrendered as a slave? And might it not be well, at the same time, to provide by law for the enforcement of that clause in the Constitution which guarantees that "the citizens of each state shall be entitled to all privileges and immunities of citizens in the several states"?

I take the official oath today, with no mental reservations, and with no purpose to construe the Constitution or laws, by any hypercritical rules. And while I do not choose now to specify particular acts of Congress as proper to be enforced, I do suggest, that it will be much safer for all, both in official and private stations, to conform to, and abide by, all those acts which stand unrepealed, than to violate any of them, trusting to find impunity in having them held to be unconstitutional.

It is seventy-two years since the first inauguration of a President under our national Constitution. During that period fifteen different and greatly distinguished citizens have, in succession, administered the executive branch of the government. They have conducted it through many perils; and, generally, with great success. Yet, with all this scope for precedent, I now enter upon the same task for the brief constitutional term of four years, under great and peculiar difficulty. A disruption of the federal Union, heretofore only menaced, is now formidably attempted.

I hold, that in contemplation of universal law, and of the Constitution, the Union of these states is perpetual. Perpetuity is implied, if not expressed, in the fundamental law of all national governments. It is safe to assert that no government proper, ever had a provision in its organic law for its own termination. Continue to execute all the express provisions of our national Constitution, and the Union will endure forever–it being impossible to destroy it, except by some action not provided for in the instrument itself.

Again, if the United States be not a government proper, but an association of states in the nature of contract merely, can it, as a contract, be peaceably unmade, by less than all the parties who made it? One party to a contract may violate it–break it, so to speak; but does it not require all to lawfully rescind it?

Descending from these general principles, we find the proposition that, in legal contemplation, the Union is perpetual, confirmed by the history of the Union itself. The Union is much older than the Constitution. It was formed, in fact, by the Articles of Association in 1774. It was matured and continued by the Declaration of

Independence in 1776. It was further matured and the faith of all the then thirteen states expressly plighted and engaged that it should be perpetual, by the Articles of Confederation in 1778. And finally, in 1787, one of the declared objects for ordaining and establishing the Constitution, was "to form a more perfect Union."

But if destruction of the Union, by one, or by a part only, of the states, be lawfully possible, the Union is less perfect than before the Constitution, having lost the vital element of perpetuity.

It follows from these views that no state, upon its own mere motion, can lawfully get out of the Union, that resolves and ordinances to that effect are legally void; and that acts of violence, within any state or states, against the authority of the United States, are insurrectionary or revolutionary, according to circumstances.

I therefore consider that, in view of the Constitution and the laws, the Union is unbroken; and, to the extent of my ability, I shall take care, as the Constitution itself expressly enjoins upon me, that the laws of the Union be faithfully executed in all the states. Doing this I deem to be only a simple duty on my part; and I shall perform it, so far as practicable, unless my rightful masters, the American people, shall withhold the requisite means, or, in some authoritative manner, direct the contrary. I trust this will not be regarded as a menace, but only as the declared purpose of the Union that it will constitutionally defend, and maintain itself.

In doing this there needs to be no bloodshed or violence; and there shall be none, unless it be forced upon the national authority. The power confided to me, will be used to hold, occupy, and possess the property, and places belonging to the government, and to collect the duties and imposts; but beyond what may be necessary for these objects, there will be no invasion–no using of force against, or among the people anywhere. Where hostility to the United States, in any interior locality, shall be so great and universal, as to prevent competent resident citizens from holding the federal offices, there will be no attempt to force obnoxious strangers among the people for that object. While the strict legal right may exist in the government to enforce the exercise of these offices, the attempt to do so would be so irritating, and so nearly impracticable withal, that I deem it better to forego, for the time, the uses of such offices.

The mails, unless repelled, will continue to be furnished in all parts of the Union. So far as possible, the people everywhere shall have that sense of perfect security which is most favorable to calm thought and reflection. The course here indicated will be followed, unless current events, and experience, shall show a modification, or change, to be proper; and in every case and exigency, my best discretion will be exercised, according to circumstances actually existing, and with a view and a hope of a peaceful solution of the national troubles, and the restoration of fraternal sympathies and affections.

That there are persons in one section, or another who seek to destroy the Union at all events, and are glad of any pretext to do it, I will neither affirm nor deny; but if there be such, I need address no word to them. To those, however, who really love the Union, may I not speak?

Before entering upon so grave a matter as the destruction of our national fabric, with all its benefits, its memories, and its hopes, would it not be wise to ascertain precisely why we do it? Will you hazard so desperate a step, while there is any possibility that any portion of the ills you fly from, have no real existence? Will you, while the certain ills you fly to, are greater than all the real ones you fly from? Will you risk the commission of so fearful a mistake?

All profess to be content in the Union, if all constitutional rights can be maintained. Is it true, then, that any right, plainly written in the Constitution, has been denied? I think not. Happily the human mind is so constituted, that no party can reach to the audacity of doing this. Think, if you can, of a single instance in which a plainly written provision of the Constitution has ever been denied. If, by the mere force of numbers, a majority should deprive a minority of any clearly written constitutional right, it might, in a moral point of view, justify revolution—certainly would, if such right were a vital one.

But such is not our case. All the vital rights of minorities, and of individuals, are so plainly assured to them, by affirmations and negations, guarantees and prohibitions, in the Constitution, that controversies never arise concerning them. But no organic law can ever be framed with a provision specifically applicable to every question which may occur in practical administration. No foresight can anticipate, nor any document of reasonable length contain express provisions for all possible questions. Shall fugitives from labor be surrendered by national or by state authority? The Constitution does not expressly say. May Congress prohibit slavery in the territories? The Constitution does not expressly say. Must Congress protect slavery in the territories? The Constitution does not expressly say.

From questions of this class spring all our constitutional controversies, and we divide upon them into majorities and minorities. If the minority will not acquiesce, the majority must, or the government must cease. There is no other alternative; for continuing the government is acquiescence on one side or the other.

If a minority, in such case, will secede rather than acquiesce, they make a precedent which, in turn, will divide and ruin them; for a minority of their own will secede from them whenever a majority refuses to be controlled by such minority. For instance, why may not any portion of a new confederacy, a year or two hence, arbitrarily secede again, precisely as portions of the present Union now claim to secede from it? All who cherish disunion sentiments are now being educated to the exact temper of doing this.

Is there such perfect identity of interests among the states to compose a new union, as to produce harmony only, and prevent renewed secession?

Plainly, the central idea of secession is the essence of anarchy. A majority, held in restraint by constitutional checks and limitations, and always changing easily, with deliberate changes of popular opinions and sentiments, is the only true sovereign of a free people. Whoever rejects it does, of necessity, fly to anarchy or to despotism. Unanimity is impossible; the rule of a minority, as a permanent arrangement, is wholly inadmissible; so that, rejecting the majority principle, anarchy or despotism in some form, is all that is left.

I do not forget the position assumed by some, that constitutional questions are to be decided by the Supreme Court; nor do I deny that such decisions must be binding, in any case, upon the parties to a suit, as to the object of that suit, while they are also entitled to very high respect and consideration, in all parallel cases, by all other departments of the government. And while it is obviously possible that such decision may be erroneous in any given case, still the evil effect following it, being limited to that particular case, with the chance that it may be overruled, and never become a precedent for other cases, can better be borne than could the evils of a different practice.

At the same time the candid citizen must confess that if the policy of the government, upon vital questions affecting the whole people, is to be irrevocably fixed by decisions of the Supreme Court, the instant they are made, in ordinary litigation between parties, in personal actions, the people will have ceased to be their own rulers, having to that extent practically resigned their government into the hands of that eminent tribunal. Nor is there, in this view, any assault upon the court or the judges. It is a duty from which they may not shrink, to decide cases properly brought before them; and it is no fault of theirs, if others seek to turn their decisions to political purposes.

One section of our country believes slavery is right, and ought to be extended, while the other believes it is wrong, and ought not to be extended. This is the only substantial dispute. The fugitive-slave clause of the Constitution, and the law for the suppression of the foreign slave-trade, are each as well enforced, perhaps, as any law can ever be in a community where the moral sense of the people imperfectly supports the law itself. The great body of the people abide by the dry legal obligation in both cases, and a few break over in each. This, I think, cannot be perfectly cured; and it would be worse in both cases after the separation of the sections than before. The foreign slave-trade, now imperfectly suppressed, would be ultimately revived without restriction, in one section; while fugitive slaves, now only partially surrendered, would not be surrendered at all by the other.

Physically speaking, we cannot separate. We cannot remove our respective sections from each other, nor build an impassable wall between them. A husband and wife may be divorced, and go out of the presence, and beyond the reach of each other; but the different parts of our country cannot do this. They cannot but remain face to face; and intercourse, either amicable or hostile, must continue between them. Is it possible then to make that intercourse more advantageous, or more satisfactory, after separation than before? Can aliens make treaties easier than friends can make laws? Can treaties be more faithfully enforced between aliens, than laws can among friends? Suppose you go to war, you cannot fight always; and when, after much loss on both sides, and no gain on either, you cease fighting, the identical old questions, as to terms of intercourse, are again upon you.

This country, with its institutions, belongs to the people who inhabit it. Whenever they shall grow weary of the existing government, they can exercise their constitutional right of amending it, or their revolutionary right to dismember, or overthrow it. I cannot be ignorant of the fact that many worthy and patriotic citizens are desirous of having the national Constitution amended. While I make no recommendation of amendments, I fully recognize the rightful authority of the people over the whole subject, to be exercised in either of the modes prescribed in the instrument itself; and I should, under existing circumstances, favor rather than oppose a fair opportunity being afforded the people to act upon it.

I will venture to add that to me the convention mode seems preferable, in that it allows amendments to originate with the people themselves, instead of only permitting them to take, or reject, propositions originated by others, not especially chosen for the purpose, and which might not be precisely such, as they would wish to either accept or refuse. I understand a proposed amendment to the Constitution–which amendment, however, I have not seen–has passed Congress, to the effect that the federal government shall never interfere with the domestic institutions of the states, including that of persons held to service. To avoid misconstruction of what I have said, I depart from my purpose not to speak of particular amendments, so far as to say that, holding such a provision to now be implied constitutional law, I have no objection to its being made express and irrevocable.

The Chief Magistrate derives all his authority from the people, and they have conferred none upon him to fix terms for the separation of the states. The people themselves can do this also if they choose; but the Executive, as such, has nothing to do with it. His duty is to administer the present government, as it came to his hands, and to transmit it, unimpaired by him, to his successor.

Why should there not be a patient confidence in the ultimate justice of the people? Is there any better, or equal hope, in the world? In our present differences, is either party without faith of being in the right? If the Almighty Ruler of Nations, with His eternal truth and justice, be on your side of the North, or on yours of the South, that truth, and that justice, will surely prevail, by the judgment of this great tribunal, the American people.

By the frame of the government under which we live, this same people have wisely given their public servants but little power for mischief; and have, with equal wisdom, provided for the return of that little to their own hands at very short intervals. While the people retain their virtue and vigilance, no administration, by any extreme of wickedness or folly, can very seriously injure the government, in the short space of four years.

My countrymen, one and all, think calmly and well, upon this whole subject. Nothing valuable can be lost by taking time. If there be an object to hurry any of you, in hot haste, to a step which you would never take deliberately, that object will be frustrated by taking time; but no good object can be frustrated by it. Such of you as are now dissatisfied, still have the old Constitution unimpaired, and, on the sensitive point, the laws of your own framing under it; while the new administration will have no immediate power, if it would, to change either. If it were admitted that you who are dissatisfied, hold the right side in the dispute, there still is no single good reason for precipitate action. Intelligence, patriotism, Christianity, and a firm reliance on Him, who has never yet forsaken this favored land, are still competent to adjust, in the best way, all our present difficulty.

In your hands, my dissatisfied fellow-countrymen, and not in mine, is the momentous issue of civil war. The government will not assail you. You can have no conflict, without being yourselves the aggressors. You have no oath registered in Heaven to destroy the government, while I shall have the most solemn one to "preserve, protect, and defend it."

I am loath to close. We are not enemies, but friends. We must not be enemies. Though passion may have strained, it must not break our bonds of affection. The mystic chords of memory, stretching from every battlefield, and patriot grave, to every living heart and hearthstone, all over this broad land, will yet swell the chorus of the Union, when again touched, as surely they will be, by the better angels of our nature.

TANEY UPHOLDS A FUNDAMENTAL RIGHT

1861

At the door of his home in Baltimore, Roger Brooke Taney paused to say good-by to his son-in-law. "I think it not unlikely," he remarked quietly, "that before evening I shall be imprisoned in Fort McHenry, but I am going to court to do my duty."

For nearly twenty-six years Taney had presided with dignity and ability over the United States Supreme Court. He had long held the affection of his colleagues and the respect of the bar, but for the last four years the Republicans and Abolitionists of the North had roundly abused him for his opinion in the case of the ex-slave, Dred Scott. Nevertheless, he had won the admiration of thousands when he had administered the oath of office to Lincoln. His tall, frail figure bent with the weight of eighty-four years, his black silk gown accentuating the pallor of his face, he had seemed to be a living link with Andrew Jackson, whom he had served well, and with the spirit of Jackson's memorable toast, "Our Federal Union: It Must Be Preserved."

Now, less than three months after Lincoln's inauguration, Taney had come to an issue with the President. At two o'clock on the morning of May 25, military authorities arrested one John Merryman, a citizen of Baltimore with Southern sympathies, and imprisoned him in Fort McHenry. The following day Merryman's counsel appeared before Taney, in Washington, and petitioned for a writ of habeas corpus. Taney granted the petition, and directed that Merryman be brought before him in Baltimore on May 27.

This was the occasion to which the Chief Justice proceeded with the gravest apprehension. In the courtroom he found not Merryman but the military aide of General George Cadwalader, commander of the district. The aide, in full uniform, resplendent with sword and red sash, courteously but firmly informed the aged jurist that General Cadwalader had directed him to say that the President of the United States had suspended the writ of habeas corpus, and therefore the General could not produce John Merryman. Taney immediately ordered the clerk to issue a writ to bring General Cadwalader into court the next day.

At noon on May 28 the Chief Justice took his seat. The United States Marshal reported that he had gone to the fort the evening before but had been denied admittance. Taney began to speak in a low voice, consonant, somehow, with the gloom of the chill spring afternoon, and listeners crowded around the bench to hear his words. The President, he asserted, had no right to suspend the writ of habeas corpus or authorize a military officer to suspend it. John Merryman, therefore, was entitled to his liberty. The Chief Justice concluded by saying that in a short time he would file a written opinion and cause a copy to be placed in the hands of the President "so that that high officer may perform his constitutional duty of seeing that the laws are enforced."

Taney's opinion in *ex parte Merryman* was filed on June 1, and shortly afterward a copy, with the other proceedings in the case, was forwarded to Lincoln. The President ignored it. Merryman was released a few weeks later, but Lincoln never receded from his position that he had the right to suspend the writ of habeas corpus when circumstances required it, and military arrests continued throughout the war.

Taney, however, has won the sympathy of a later generation, if not a clear-cut verdict in favor of his position. Charles Warren, recognized authority on the history of the United States Supreme Court, states that while the basic legal controversy has never been officially decided, "the right and duty of the Chief Justice to issue the writ and to consider the legal question involved is now universally admitted." And many today agree with the assertion of William E. Mikell, one of Taney's biographers, that "there is no sublimer picture in our history than this of the aged Chief Justice, the fires of Civil War kindling around him, the President usurping the powers of Congress, and Congress itself a seething furnace of sectional animosities, serene and unafraid, while . . . . the storm of partisan fury broke over his devoted head, interposing the shield of the law in the defense of the liberty of the citizen."

Opinion in the Merryman Case

June 1, 1861

Taney, circuit justice. . . . . As the case comes before me . . . . I understand that the President not only claims the right to suspend the writ of habeas corpus himself, at his discretion, but to delegate that discretionary power to a military officer, and to leave it to him to determine whether he will or will not obey judicial process that may be served upon him.

No official notice has been given to the courts of justice, or to the public, by proclamation or otherwise, that the President claimed this power, and had exercised it in the manner stated in the return. And I certainly listened to it with some surprise, for I had supposed it to be one of those points of constitutional law upon which there was no difference of opinion, and that it was admitted on all hands, that the privilege of the writ could not be suspended, except by act of Congress.

When the conspiracy of which Aaron Burr was the head, became so formidable, and was so extensively ramified as to justify, in Mr. Jefferson's opinion, the suspension of the writ, he claimed, on his part, no power to suspend it, but communicated his opinion to Congress, with all the proofs in his possession, in order that Congress might exercise its discretion upon the subject, and determine whether the public safety required it. And in the debate which took place upon the subject, no one suggested that Mr. Jefferson might exercise the power himself if, in his opinion, the public safety demanded it.

Having, therefore, regarded the question as too plain and too well settled to be open to dispute, if the commanding officer had stated that, upon his own responsibility, and in the exercise of his own discretion, he refused obedience to the writ, I should have contented myself with referring to the clause in the Constitution, and to the construction it received from every jurist and statesman of that day, when the case of Burr was before them. But being thus officially notified that the privilege of the writ has been suspended, under the orders, and by the authority of the President, and believing, as I do, that the President has exercised a power which he does not possess under the Constitution, a proper respect for the high office he fills requires me to state plainly and fully the grounds of my opinion, in order to show that I have not ventured to question the legality of his act, without a careful and deliberate examination of the whole subject.

The clause of the Constitution, which authorizes the suspension of the privilege of the writ of habeas corpus, is in the ninth section of the first article.

This article is devoted to the legislative department of the United States, and has not the slightest reference to the executive department. It begins by providing "that all legislative powers therein granted, shall be vested in a Congress of the United States, which shall consist of a Senate and House of Representatives." And after prescribing the manner in which these two branches of the legislative department shall be chosen, it proceeds to enumerate specifically the legislative powers which it thereby grants; and, at the conclusion of this specification, a clause is inserted giving Congress "the power to make all laws which may be necessary and proper for carrying into execution the foregoing powers, and all other powers vested by this Constitution in the government of the United States, or in any department or officer thereof."

The power of legislation granted by this latter clause is, by its words, carefully confined to the specific objects before enumerated. But as this limitation was unavoidably somewhat indefinite, it was deemed necessary to guard more effectually certain great cardinal principles, essential to the liberty of the citizen, and to the rights and equality of the states, by denying to Congress, in express terms, any power of legislation over them.

It was apprehended, it seems, that such legislation might be attempted under the pretext that it was necessary and proper to carry into execution the powers granted; and it was determined, that there should be no room to doubt, where rights of such vital importance were concerned, and accordingly, this clause is immediately followed by an enumeration of certain subjects, to which the powers of legislation shall not extend. The great importance which the framers of the Constitution attached to the privilege of the writ of habeas corpus, to protect the liberty of the citizen, is proved by the fact that its suspension, except in cases of invasion and rebellion, is first in the list of prohibited powers—and even in these cases the power is denied, and its exercise prohibited, unless the public safety shall require it.

It is true that in the cases mentioned, Congress is of necessity the judge of whether the public safety does or does not require it; and their judgment is conclusive. But the introduction of these words is a standing admonition to the legislative body of the danger of suspending it, and of the extreme caution they should exercise before they give the government of the United States such power over the liberty of a citizen.

It is the second article of the Constitution that provides for the organization of the executive department, and enumerates the powers conferred on it, and prescribes its duties. And if the high power over the liberty of the citizen now claimed, was intended to be conferred on the President, it would undoubtedly be found in plain words in this article. But there is not a word in it that can furnish the slightest ground to justify the exercise of the power.

The article begins by declaring that the executive power shall be vested in a President of the United States of America, to hold his office during the term of four years; and then proceeds to prescribe the mode of election, and to specify in precise and plain words, the powers delegated to him, and the duties imposed upon him. The short term for which he is elected, and the narrow limits to which his power is confined, show the jealousy and apprehension of future danger which the framers of the Constitution felt in relation to that department of the government, and how carefully they withheld from it many of the powers belonging to the executive branch of the English government, which were considered as dangerous to the liberty of the subject; and conferred (and that in clear and specific terms) those powers only which were deemed essential to secure the successful operation of the government.

He is elected, as I have already said, for the brief term of four years, and is made personally responsible, by impeachment, for malfeasance in office. He is, from necessity, and the nature of his duties, the commander-in-chief of the army and navy, and of the militia, when called into actual service; but no appropriation for the support of the army can be made by Congress for a longer term than two years, so that it is in the power of the succeeding House of Representatives to withhold the appropriation for its support, and thus disband it, if, in their judgment, the President used or designed to use it for improper purposes. And although the militia, when in actual service, are under his command, yet the appointment of the officers is reserved to the states, as a security against the use of military power for purposes dangerous to the liberties of the people, or the rights of the states.

So, too, his powers in relation to the civil duties and authority necessarily conferred on him are carefully restricted as well as those belonging to his military character. He cannot appoint the ordinary officers of government, nor make a treaty with a foreign nation or tribe, without the advice and consent of the Senate; and cannot appoint even inferior officers, unless he is authorized by an act of Congress to do so. He is not empowered to arrest any one charged with an offense against the United States, and whom he may, from the evidence before him, believe to be guilty; nor can he authorize any officer, civil or military, to exercise this power, for the fifth article of the Amendments to the Constitution expressly provides that no person "shall be deprived of life, liberty, or property without due process of law"—that is, judicial process.

Even if the privilege of the writ of habeas corpus were suspended by act of Congress, and a party not subject to the rules and articles of war were afterward arrested and imprisoned by regular judicial process, he could not be detained in prison, or brought to trial before a military tribunal, for the article in the Amendments to the Constitution immediately following the one above referred to—that is, the sixth article—provides that "in all criminal prosecutions, the accused shall enjoy the right to a speedy and public trial by an impartial jury of the state and district wherein the crime shall have been committed, which district shall have been previously ascertained by law; and to be informed of the nature and cause of the accusation; to be confronted with the witnesses against him; to have compulsory process for obtaining witnesses in his favor; and to have the assistance of counsel for his defense."

The only power, therefore, which the President possesses, where the "life, liberty, or property" of a private citizen is concerned, is the power and duty prescribed in the third section of the second article, which requires "that he shall take care that the laws shall be faithfully executed." He is not authorized to execute them himself, or through agents or officers, civil or military, appointed by himself, but he is to take care that they be faithfully carried into execution, as they are expounded and adjudged by the co-ordinate branch of the government to which that duty is assigned by the Constitution. It is thus made his duty to come in aid of the judicial authority, if it shall be resisted by a force too strong to be overcome without the assistance of the executive arm; but in exercising this power, he acts in subordination to judicial authority, assisting it to execute its process and enforce its judgments.

With such provisions in the Constitution, expressed in language too clear to be misunderstood by any one, I can see no ground whatever for supposing that the President, in any emergency or in any state of things, can authorize the suspension of the privileges of the writ of habeas corpus, or arrest a citizen, except in aid of the judicial power. He certainly does not faithfully execute the laws, if he takes upon himself legislative power, by suspending the writ of habeas corpus, and the judicial power also, by arresting and imprisoning a person without due process of law. Nor can any argument be drawn from the nature of sovereignty, or the necessity of government, for self-defense in times of tumult and danger. The government of the United States is one of delegated and limited powers; it derives its existence and authority altogether from the Constitution; and neither of its branches, executive, legislative, or judicial, can exercise any of the powers of government beyond those specified and granted; for the tenth article of the Amendments to the Constitution in express terms provides that "the powers not delegated to the United States by the Constitution, nor prohibited by it to the states, are reserved to the states, respectively, or to the people."

Indeed, the security against imprisonment by executive authority, provided for in the fifth article of the Amendments to the Constitution, which I have before quoted, is nothing more than a copy of the like provision in the English constitution, which had been firmly established before the Declaration of Independence. . . . .

But I am not left to form my judgment upon this great question, from analogies between the English government and our own, or the commentaries of English jurists, or the decisions of English courts, although upon this subject they are entitled to the highest respect, and are justly regarded and received as authoritative by our courts of justice. To guide me to a right conclusion, I have the commentaries on the Constitution of the United States of the late Mr. Justice Story, not only one of the most eminent jurists of the age, but for a long time one of the brightest ornaments of the Supreme Court of the United States; and also the clear and authoritative decision of that court itself, given more than half a century since, and conclusively establishing the principles I have above stated.

Mr. Justice Story, speaking in his commentaries of the habeas corpus clause in the Constitution, says:

"It is obvious that cases of a peculiar emergency may arise, which may justify, nay, even require, the temporary suspension of any right to the writ. But as it has frequently happened in foreign countries, and even in England, that the writ has, upon various pretexts and occasions, been suspended, whereby persons apprehended upon suspicion have suffered a long imprisonment, sometimes from design, and sometimes because they were forgotten, the right to suspend it is expressly confined to cases of rebellion or invasion, where the public safety may require it. A very just and wholesome restraint, which cuts down at a blow a fruitful means of oppression, capable of being abused, in bad times, to the worst of purposes. Hitherto no suspension of the writ has ever been authorized by Congress, since the establishment of the Constitution. It would seem, as the power is given to Congress to suspend the writ of habeas corpus, in cases of rebellion or invasion, that the right to judge whether the exigency had arisen must exclusively belong to that body." 3 Story's Comm. on Constitution, section 1336.

And Chief Justice Marshall, in delivering the opinion of the Supreme Court in the case of *ex parte Bollman and Swartwout*, uses this decisive language in 4 Cranch, 95:

"It may be worthy of remark that this act (speaking of the one under which I am proceeding) was passed by the first Congress of the United States, sitting under a Constitution which had declared 'that the privilege of the writ of habeas corpus should not be suspended, unless when, in cases of rebellion or invasion, the public safety might require it.' Acting under the immediate influence of this injunction, they must have felt, with peculiar force, the obligation of providing efficient means, by which this great constitutional privilege should receive life and activity; for if the means be not in existence, the privilege itself would be lost, although no law for its suspension should be enacted. Under the impression of this obligation, they give to all the courts the power of awarding writs of habeas corpus."

. . . . I can add nothing to these clear and emphatic words of my great predecessor.

But the documents before me show, that the military authority in this case has gone far beyond the mere suspension of the privilege of the writ of habeas corpus. It has, by force of arms, thrust aside the judicial authorities and officers to whom the Constitution has confided the power and duty of interpreting and administering the laws, and substituted a military government in its place, to be administered and executed by military officers.

For, at the time these proceedings were had against John Merryman, the district judge of Maryland, the commissioner appointed under the act of Congress, the district attorney, and the marshal, all resided in the city of Baltimore, a few miles only from the home of the prisoner. Up to that time, there had never been the slightest resistance or obstruction to the process of any court or judicial officer of the United States, in Maryland, except by the military authority. And if a military officer, or any other person, had reason to believe that the prisoner had committed any offense against the laws of the United States, it was his duty to give information of the fact, and the evidence to support it, to the district attorney; it would then have become the duty of that officer to bring the matter before the district judge or commissioner, and if there was sufficient legal evidence to justify his arrest, the judge or commissioner would have issued his warrant to the marshal to arrest him; and upon the hearing of the case would have held him to bail, or committed him for trial, according to the character of the offense as it appeared in the testimony, or would have discharged him immediately, if there was not sufficient evidence to support the accusation. There was no danger of any obstruction or resistance to the action of the civil authorities, and therefore no reason whatever for the interposition of the military.

Yet, under these circumstances, a military officer stationed in Pennsylvania, without giving any information to the district attorney,

and without any application to the judicial authorities, assumes to himself the judicial power in the District of Maryland; undertakes to decide what constitutes the crime of treason or rebellion; what evidence (if, indeed, he required any) is sufficient to support the accusation and justify the commitment; and commits the party, without a hearing, even before himself, to close custody in a strongly garrisoned fort, to be there held, it would seem, during the pleasure of those who committed him.

The Constitution provides, as I have before said, that "no person shall be deprived of life, liberty, or property without due process of law." It declares that "the right of the people to be secure in their persons, houses, papers, and effects, against unreasonable searches and seizures, shall not be violated; and no warrant shall issue, but upon probable cause, supported by oath or affirmation, and particularly describing the place to be searched, and the persons or things to be seized." It provides that the party accused shall be entitled to a speedy trial in a court of justice.

These great and fundamental laws, which Congress itself could not suspend, have been disregarded and suspended, like the writ of habeas corpus, by a military order, supported by force of arms. Such is the case now before me, and I can only say that if the authority which the Constitution has confided to the judiciary department and judicial officers, may thus, upon any pretext or under any circumstances, be usurped by the military power, at its discretion, the people of the United States are no longer living under a government of laws, but every citizen holds life, liberty, and property at the will and pleasure of the army officer in whose military district he may happen to be found.

In such a case, my duty was too plain to be mistaken. I have exercised all the power which the Constitution and laws confer upon me, but that power has been resisted by a force too strong for me to overcome. It is possible that the officer who has incurred this grave responsibility may have misunderstood his instructions, and exceeded the authority intended to be given him. I shall, therefore, order all the proceedings in this case, with my opinion, to be filed and recorded in the Circuit Court of the United States for the District of Maryland, and direct the clerk to transmit a copy, under seal, to the President of the United States. It will then remain for that high officer, in fulfillment of his constitutional obligation, to "take care that the laws be faithfully executed," to determine what measures he will take to cause the civil process of the United States to be respected and enforced.

LINCOLN PRESENTS THE CASE FOR THE UNION

1861

At 4:30 A.M. on April 12, 1861, a mortar behind the parapet of Fort Johnson in Charleston Harbor fired a single shot in the direction of Fort Sumter. On Morris Island, Edmund Ruffin, who had grown old and gray in the advocacy of secession, pulled a lanyard, and a second shell, forerunner of hundreds that would scream through the air in the next thirty hours, arched toward the Union-held stronghold. The Civil War had begun.

In the White House, Abraham Lincoln directed that a proclamation be prepared in time to be issued on April 15. In it he called on the states of the Union to furnish militia to the number of 75,000, and summoned Congress to assemble in extraordinary session at twelve noon on the Fourth of July.

On the evening of the third of July, Orville H. Browning, who had taken Stephen A. Douglas' place in the Senate, called at the White House. The President, he learned, was finishing his message to Congress. Not wishing to intrude, Browning stopped to pay his respects to Mrs. Lincoln. In a few minutes a secretary appeared. The President had heard Browning's voice: would he step into the office? "I went to his room," Browning confided to his diary later that evening, "and as he had just finished his message, he said he wished to read it to me, and did so. It is a most admirable history of our present difficulties, and a conclusive and unanswerable argument against the abominable heresy of secession."

Browning's appraisal was correct, although one would not have known it from the scant attention that was given to the message when a clerk read it before Congress on July 5. Years were to pass before it was accorded general recognition as a great presidential paper.

Message to Congress

July 5, 1861

Fellow-Citizens of the Senate and House of Representatives: Having been convened on an extraordinary occasion, as authorized by the Constitution, your attention is not called to any ordinary subject of legislation.

At the beginning of the present presidential term, four months ago, the functions of the federal government were found to be generally suspended within the several states of South Carolina, Georgia, Alabama, Mississippi, Louisiana, and Florida, excepting only those of the Post Office Department.

Within these states all the forts, arsenals, dockyards, customhouses, and the like, including the movable and stationary property in and about them, had been seized, and were held in open hostility to this government, excepting only Forts Pickens, Taylor, and Jefferson, on and near the Florida coast, and Fort Sumter, in Charleston Harbor, South Carolina. The forts thus seized had been put in improved condition; new ones had been built; and armed forces had been organized, and were organizing, all avowedly with the same hostile purpose.

The forts remaining in the possession of the federal government in, and near, these states, were either besieged or menaced by warlike preparations; and especially Fort Sumter was nearly surrounded by well-protected hostile batteries, with guns equal in quality to the best of its own, and outnumbering the latter as perhaps ten to one. A disproportionate share of the federal muskets and rifles had somehow found their way into these states, and had been seized to be used against the government. Accumulations of the public revenue, lying within them, had been seized for the same object. The navy was scattered in distant seas, leaving but a very small part of it within the immediate reach of the government. Officers of the federal army and navy had resigned in great numbers; and, of those resigning, a large proportion had taken up arms against the government.

Simultaneously, and in connection with all this, the purpose to sever the federal Union was openly avowed. In accordance with this purpose, an ordinance had been adopted in each of these states, declaring the states respectively to be separated from the national Union. A formula for instituting a combined government of these states had been promulgated; and this illegal organization, in the character of confederate states, was already invoking recognition, aid, and intervention from foreign powers.

Finding this condition of things, and believing it to be an imperative duty upon the incoming Executive to prevent, if possible, the consummation of such attempt to destroy the federal Union, a choice of means to that end became indispensable. This choice was made; and was declared in the inaugural address. The policy chosen looked to the exhaustion of all peaceful measures, before a resort to any stronger ones. It sought only to hold the public places and property, not already wrested from the government, and to collect the revenue; relying for the rest on time, discussion, and the ballot box. It promised a continuance of the mails, at government expense, to the very people who were resisting the government; and it gave repeated pledges against any disturbance to any of the people, or any of their rights. Of all that which a President might constitutionally, and justifiably, do in such a case, everything was forborne without which it was believed possible to keep the government on foot.

On the fifth of March (the present incumbent's first full day in office), a letter of Major Anderson, commanding at Fort Sumter, written on the twenty-eighth of February, and received at the War Department on the fourth of March, was, by that department, placed in his hands. This letter expressed the professional opinion of the writer, that reinforcements could not be thrown into that fort within the time for his relief, rendered necessary by the limited supply of provisions, and with a view of holding possession of the same, with a force of less than twenty thousand good and well-disciplined men. This opinion was concurred in by all the officers of his command; and their memoranda on the subject, were made enclosures of Major Anderson's letter.

The whole was immediately laid before Lieutenant General Scott, who at once concurred with Major Anderson in opinion. On reflection, however, he took full time, consulting with other officers, both of the army and the navy; and at the end of four days, came reluctantly, but decidedly, to the same conclusion as before. He also stated at the same time that no such sufficient force was then at the control of the government, or could be raised, and brought to the ground, within the time when the provisions in the fort would be exhausted. In a purely military point of view, this reduced the duty of the administration, in the case, to the mere matter of getting the garrison safely out of the fort.

It was believed, however, that to so abandon that position, under the circumstances, would be utterly ruinous; that the necessity under which it was to be done, would not be fully understood; that by many it would be construed as a part of a voluntary policy; that at home it would discourage the friends of the Union, embolden its adversaries, and go far to ensure to the latter a recognition abroad; that, in fact, it would be our national destruction consummated. This could not be allowed. Starvation was not yet upon the garrison; and ere it would be reached, Fort Pickens might be reinforced. This last would be a clear indication of policy, and would better enable the country to accept the evacuation of Fort Sumter as a military necessity.

An order was at once directed to be sent for the landing of the troops from the steamship *Brooklyn* into Fort Pickens. This order could not go by land, but must take the longer and slower route by sea. The first return news from the order was received just one week before the fall of Fort Sumter. The news itself was that the officer commanding the *Sabine*, to which vessel the troops had been transferred from the *Brooklyn*, acting upon some quasi armistice of the late administration (and of the existence of which, the present administration, up to the time the order was dispatched, had only too vague and uncertain rumors to fix attention), had refused to land the troops. To now reinforce Fort Pickens before a crisis would be reached at Fort Sumter was impossible–rendered so by the near-exhaustion of provisions in the latter-named fort.

In precaution against such a conjuncture, the government had, a few days before, commenced preparing an expedition, as well adapted as might be, to relieve Fort Sumter, which expedition was intended to be ultimately used, or not, according to circumstances.

The strongest anticipated case for using it was now presented, and it was resolved to send it forward. As had been intended in this contingency, it was also resolved to notify the governor of South Carolina, that he might expect an attempt would be made to provision the fort; and that, if the attempt should not be resisted, there would be no effort to throw in men, arms, or ammunition, without further notice, or in case of an attack upon the fort. This notice was accordingly given; whereupon the fort was attacked and bombarded to its fall, without even awaiting the arrival of the provisioning expedition.

It is thus seen that the assault upon, and reduction of, Fort Sumter was, in no sense, a matter of self-defense on the part of the assailants. They well knew that the garrison in the fort could, by no possibility, commit aggression upon them. They knew—they were expressly notified—that the giving of bread to the few brave and hungry men of the garrison, was all which would on that occasion be attempted, unless themselves, by resisting so much, should provoke more. They knew that this government desired to keep the garrison in the fort, not to assail them, but merely to maintain visible possession, and thus to preserve the Union from actual and immediate dissolution—trusting, as hereinbefore stated, to time, discussion, and the ballot box for final adjustment; and they assailed and reduced the fort for precisely the reverse object—to drive out the visible authority of the federal Union, and thus force it to immediate dissolution.

That this was their object the Executive well understood; and having said to them in the inaugural address, "You can have no conflict without being yourselves the aggressors," he took pains, not only to keep this declaration good, but also to keep the case so free from the power of ingenious sophistry, as that the world should not be able to misunderstand it. By the affair at Fort Sumter, with its surrounding circumstances, that point was reached. Then and thereby the assailants of the government began the conflict of arms, without a gun in sight, or in expectancy, to return their fire, save only the few in the fort, sent to that harbor years before, for their own protection, and still ready to give that protection in whatever was lawful. In this act, discarding all else, they have forced upon the country the distinct issue: "Immediate dissolution or blood."

And this issue embraces more than the fate of these United States. It presents to the whole family of man the question, whether a constitutional republic, or a democracy—a government of the people, by the same people—can or cannot maintain its territorial integrity against its own domestic foes. It presents the question whether discontented individuals, too few in numbers to control administration, according to organic law, in any case, can always, upon the pretenses made in this case, or on any other pretenses, or arbitrarily, without any pretense, break up their government, and thus practically put an end to free government upon the earth. It forces us to ask: "Is there, in all republics, this inherent and fatal weakness?" "Must a government, of necessity, be too strong for the liberties of its own people, or too weak to maintain its own existence?"

So viewing the issue, no choice was left but to call out the war power of the government; and so to resist force, employed for its destruction, by force for its preservation. . . . .

Soon after the first call for militia, it was considered a duty to authorize the commanding general in proper cases, according to his discretion, to suspend the privilege of the writ of habeas corpus, or, in other words, to arrest and detain, without resort to the ordinary processes and forms of law, such individuals as he might deem dangerous to the public safety. This authority has purposely been exercised but very sparingly. Nevertheless, the legality and propriety of what has been done under it are questioned, and the attention of the country has been called to the proposition that one who has sworn to "take care that the laws be faithfully executed" should not himself violate them. Of course, some consideration was given to the questions of power and propriety before this matter was acted upon.

The whole of the laws which were required to be faithfully executed were being resisted, and failing of execution in nearly one-third of the states. Must they be allowed to finally fail of execution, even had it been perfectly clear that by the use of the means necessary to their execution some single law, made in such extreme tenderness of the citizen's liberty that, practically, it relieves more of the guilty than of the innocent, should, to a very limited extent, be violated? To state the question more directly, are all the laws but one to go unexecuted, and the government itself go to pieces, lest that one be violated? Even in such a case, would not the official oath be broken if the government should be overthrown, when it was believed that disregarding the single law would tend to preserve it?

But it was not believed that this question was presented. It was not believed that any law was violated. The provision of the Constitution that "the privilege of the writ of habeas corpus, shall not be suspended, unless when, in cases of rebellion or invasion, the public safety may require it" is equivalent to a provision—is a provision—that such privilege may be suspended when, in cases of rebellion or invasion, the public safety does require it. It was decided that we have a case of rebellion, and that the public safety does re-

quire the qualified suspension of the privilege of the writ which was authorized to be made.

Now it is insisted that Congress, and not the Executive, is vested with this power. But the Constitution is silent as to which, or who, is to exercise the power; and as the provision was plainly made for a dangerous emergency, it cannot be believed the framers of the instrument intended that in every case the danger should run its course until Congress could be called together, the very assembling of which might be prevented, as was intended in this case, by the rebellion. . . .

It might seem, at first thought, to be of little difference whether the present movement at the South be called "secession" or "rebellion." The movers, however, well understand the difference. At the beginning, they knew they could never raise their treason to any respectable magnitude, by any name which implies violation of law. They knew their people possessed as much of moral sense, as much of devotion to law and order, and as much pride in and reverence for the history and government of their common country, as any other civilized and patriotic people. They knew they could make no advancement directly in the teeth of these strong and noble sentiments. Accordingly, they commenced by an insidious debauching of the public mind. They invented an ingenious sophism which, if conceded, was followed by perfectly logical steps, through all the incidents, to the complete destruction of the Union.

The sophism itself is that any state of the Union may, consistently with the national Constitution, and therefore lawfully and peacefully, withdraw from the Union, without the consent of the Union, or of any other state. The little disguise that the supposed right is to be exercised only for just cause, themselves to be the sole judge of its justice, is too thin to merit any notice.

With rebellion thus sugar-coated, they have been drugging the public mind of their section for more than thirty years; and until at length they have brought many good men to a willingness to take up arms against the government the day after some assemblage of men have enacted the farcical pretense of taking their state out of the Union, who could have been brought to no such thing the day before.

This sophism derives much–perhaps the whole–of its currency from the assumption that there is some omnipotent and sacred supremacy pertaining to a state–to each state of our federal Union. Our states have neither more nor less power than that reserved to them, in the Union, by the Constitution–no one of them ever having been a state out of the Union. The original ones passed into the Union even before they cast off their British colonial independence; and the new ones each came into the Union directly from a condition of dependence, excepting Texas. And even Texas, in its temporary independence, was never designated a state.

The new ones only took the designation of states on coming into the Union, while that name was first adopted for the old ones in and by the Declaration of Independence. Therein the "United Colonies" were declared to be "free and independent states"; but even then, the object plainly was not to declare their independence of one another, or of the Union, but directly the contrary, as their mutual pledge and their mutual action before, at the time, and afterward, abundantly show. The express plighting of faith, by each and all of the original thirteen, in the Articles of Confederation, two years later, that the Union shall be perpetual, is most conclusive.

Having never been states, either in substance or in name, outside of the Union, whence this magical omnipotence of "states' rights," asserting a claim of power to lawfully destroy the Union itself? Much is said about the "sovereignty" of the states; but the word, even, is not in the national Constitution, nor, as is believed, in any of the state constitutions. What is a "sovereignty" in the political sense of the term? Would it be far wrong to define it "a political community without a political superior"? Tested by this, no one of our states except Texas ever was a sovereignty. And even Texas gave up the character on coming into the Union; by which act she acknowledged the Constitution of the United States, and the laws and treaties of the United States made in pursuance of the Constitution, to be for her the supreme law of the land.

The states have their status in the Union, and they have no other legal status. If they break from this, they can only do so against law, and by revolution. The Union, and not themselves separately, procured their independence and their liberty. By conquest or purchase the Union gave each of them whatever of liberty or independence it has. The Union is older than any of the states, and, in fact, it created them as states. Originally some dependent colonies made the Union, and, in turn, the Union threw off their old dependence for them, and made them states, such as they are. Not one of them ever had a state constitution independent of the Union. Of course, it is not forgotten that all the new states framed their constitutions before they entered the Union; nevertheless, dependent upon and preparatory to coming into the Union.

Unquestionably the states have the powers and rights reserved to them in and by the national Constitution; but among these, surely, are not included all conceivable powers, however mischievous or destructive, but, at most, such only as were known in the world at the time as governmental powers; and certainly, a power to destroy the government itself had never been known as a governmental, as a merely administrative power. This relative matter of national power and states' rights, as a principle, is no other than the principle of generality, and locality. Whatever concerns the whole, should be confided to the whole—to the general government; while whatever concerns only the state, should be left exclusively to the state. This is all there is of original principle about it. Whether the national Constitution, in defining boundaries between the two, has applied the principle with exact accuracy, is not to be questioned. We are all bound by that defining, without question.

What is now combated, is the position that secession is consistent with the Constitution—is lawful and peaceful. It is not contended that there is any express law for it; and nothing should ever be implied as law, which leads to unjust or absurd consequences. . . . .

The seceders insist that our Constitution admits of secession. They have assumed to make a national constitution of their own, in which, of necessity, they have either discarded or retained the right of secession, as they insist it exists in ours. If they have discarded it, they thereby admit that on principle it ought not to be in ours. If they have retained it, by their own construction of ours they show that to be consistent they must secede from one another, whenever they shall find it the easiest way of settling their debts, or effecting any other selfish or unjust object. The principle itself is one of disintegration, and upon which no government can possibly endure. . . . .

It may be affirmed without extravagance that the free institutions we enjoy have developed the powers and improved the condition of our whole people beyond any example in the world. Of this we now have a striking and an impressive illustration. So large an army as the government has now on foot was never before known, without a soldier in it but who has taken his place there of his own free choice. But more than this: there are many single regiments whose members, one and another, possess full practical knowledge of all the arts, sciences, professions, and whatever else, whether useful or elegant, is known in the world; and there is scarcely one from which there could not be selected a president, a cabinet, a congress, and perhaps a court, abundantly competent to administer the government itself.

Nor do I say this is not true, also, in the army of our late friends, now adversaries in this contest; but if it is, so much better the

reason why the government which has conferred such benefits on both them and us should not be broken up. Whoever in any section proposes to abandon such a government would do well to consider in deference to what principle it is that he does it—what better he is likely to get in its stead—whether the substitute will give, or be intended to give, so much of good to the people?

There are some foreshadowings on this subject. Our adversaries have adopted some declarations of independence in which, unlike the good old one, penned by Jefferson, they omit the words "all men are created equal." Why? They have adopted a temporary national constitution, in the preamble of which, unlike our good old one, signed by Washington, they omit "We, the people," and substitute, "We, the deputies of the sovereign and independent states." Why? Why this deliberate pressing out of view the rights of men and the authority of the people?

This is essentially a people's contest. On the side of the Union, it is a struggle for maintaining in the world that form and substance of government whose leading object is to elevate the condition of men—to lift artificial weights from all shoulders—to clear the paths of laudable pursuit for all—to afford all an unfettered start, and a fair chance, in the race of life. Yielding to partial and temporary departures, from necessity, this is the leading object of the government for whose existence we contend.

I am most happy to believe that the plain people understand and appreciate this. It is worthy of note that while in this, the government's hour of trial, large numbers of those in the army and navy who have been favored with the offices have resigned and proved false to the hand which had pampered them, not one common soldier or common sailor is known to have deserted his flag.

Great honor is due to those officers who remained true, despite the example of their treacherous associates; but the greatest honor, and most important fact of all, is the unanimous firmness of the common soldiers and the common sailors. To the last man, so far as known, they have successfully resisted the traitorous efforts of those whose commands, but an hour before, they obeyed as absolute law. This is the patriotic instinct of the plain people. They understand, without an argument, that destroying the government which was made by Washington means no good to them.

Our popular government has often been called an experiment. Two points in it our people have already settled—the successful establishing, and the successful administering of it. One still remains—its successful maintenance against a formidable internal attempt to overthrow it. It is now for them to demonstrate to the world that those who can fairly carry an election can also suppress a rebellion—that ballots are the rightful and peaceful successors of bullets; and that when ballots have fairly and constitutionally decided, there can be no successful appeal back to bullets; that there can be no successful appeal, except to ballots themselves, at succeeding elections. Such will be a great lesson of peace: teaching men that what they cannot take by an election, neither can they take it by a war—teaching all the folly of being the beginners of a war.

Lest there be some uneasiness in the minds of candid men as to what is to be the course of the government toward the Southern States after the rebellion shall have been suppressed, the Executive deems it proper to say that it will be his purpose then, as ever, to be guided by the Constitution and the laws; and that he probably will have no different understanding of the powers and duties of the federal government, relative to the rights of the states and the people, under the Constitution, than that expressed in the inaugural address.

He desires to preserve the government that it may be administered for all, as it was administered by the men who made it. Loyal citizens everywhere have the right to claim this of their government, and the government has no right to withhold or neglect it. It is not perceived that in giving it there is any coercion, any conquest, or any subjugation, in any just sense of those terms.

The Constitution provides, and all the states have accepted the provision, that "the United States shall guarantee to every state in this Union a republican form of government." But if a state may lawfully go out of the Union, having done so, it may also discard the republican form of goverment; so that to prevent its going out is an indispensable means to the end of maintaining the guarantee mentioned; and when an end is lawful and obligatory, the indispensable means to it are also lawful and obligatory.

It was with the deepest regret that the Executive found the duty of employing the war power, in defense of the government, forced upon him. He could but perform this duty or surrender the existence of the government. No compromise by public servants could, in this case, be a cure; not that compromises are not often proper, but that no popular government can long survive a marked precedent, that those who carry an election, can only save the government from immediate destruction, by giving up the main point upon which the people gave the election. The people themselves, and not their servants, can safely reverse their own deliberate decisions.

As a private citizen, the Executive could not have consented that these institutions shall perish; much less could he, in betrayal of so vast and so sacred a trust as the free people have confided to him. He felt that he had no moral right to shrink, not even to count the chances of his own life, in what might follow. In full view of his great responsibility he has, so far, done what he has deemed his duty. You will now, according to your own judgment, perform yours. He sincerely hopes that your views, and your action, may so accord with his as to assure all faithful citizens, who have been disturbed in their rights, of a certain and speedy restoration to them under the Constitution and the laws.

And having thus chosen our course, without guile, and with pure purpose, let us renew our trust in God, and go forward without fear, and with manly hearts.

DAVIS PRESENTS THE CASE FOR THE CONFEDERACY

1862

By February 1, 1861, six states had followed the lead of South Carolina and seceded from the Union. Although they claimed to be independent nations, they looked forward to a union of their own with a central government. There was need of speed, for it behooved the South to set up a strong organization before Abraham Lincoln would take over the federal government on the fourth of March. Accordingly, six of the seven states in secession sent delegates to meet at Montgomery, Alabama, on February 4. They quickly adopted a provisional constitution, resolved themselves into a provisional legislature, and chose Jefferson Davis of Mississippi and Alexander H. Stephens of Georgia, President and Vice-President of the Confederate States of America.

A messenger found Davis in the rose garden of his plantation near Vicksburg. The President-elect started for Montgomery at once.

Ovation after ovation greeted him as he changed from one train to another on the roundabout route he was compelled to follow. On February 18, with bright sun and soft winds foreshadowing spring, he took the oath of office on the portico of the Alabama capitol. In the hearing of thousands he delivered his inaugural address. He hoped for peace, but the South had determined upon independence, and if war must come, she would not shrink from it.

A few weeks after Davis' inauguration the Congress of the seceded states adopted a permanent constitution. Under its provisions he was elected President a year later, this time by popular vote. In February, 1862, he prepared to take the oath of office a second time. The place was Richmond, Virginia; the day—the twenty-second—an anniversary cherished by every patriot. Perversely, rain fell steadily from a steely sky as a procession of officials, accompanied by an immense crowd, escorted Davis and Stephens, who had also been re-elected, to the statue of Washington in Capitol Square. There, on a platform covered with an awning, the ceremonies began.

After a prayer, the President stepped forward—tall, thin, frail, but erect, his thin lips and sharp features conveying sure signs of character and will power even through the enveloping murk. With dignity, grace, and emotion he delivered his inaugural address while thousands, shivering beneath umbrellas, listened in respectful silence. With his hand on a Bible printed in the Confederacy, he took the oath and heard himself, above resounding cheers, proclaimed President of the Confederate States of America for a term of six years. Stumbling through the mud of the square, with the rain still dripping in their faces, the crowd went its way.

Could there have been a portent in the contrast between the warm sunshine of the year before and Richmond's chilling gloom? One could not have found it in the unshaken confidence, resolution, and sense of rectitude with which Jefferson Davis resumed office.

Jefferson Davis' Inaugural Address

February 22, 1862

Fellow-Citizens: On this the birthday of the man most identified with the establishment of American independence, and beneath the monument erected to commemorate his heroic virtues and those of his compatriots, we have assembled to usher into existence the permanent government of the Confederate States. Through this instrumentality, under the favor of Divine Providence, we hope to perpetuate the principles of our Revolutionary fathers. The day, the memory, and the purpose seem fitly associated.

It is with mingled feelings of humility and pride that I appear to take, in the presence of the people and before High Heaven, the oath prescribed as a qualification for the exalted station to which the unanimous voice of the people has called me. Deeply sensible of all that is implied by this manifestation of the people's confidence, I am yet more profoundly impressed by the vast responsibility of the office, and humbly feel my own unworthiness.

In return for their kindness I can offer assurances of the gratitude with which it is received, and can but pledge a zealous devotion of every faculty to the service of those who have chosen me as their Chief Magistrate.

When a long course of class legislation, directed not to the general welfare but to the aggrandizement of the Northern section of the Union, culminated in a warfare on the domestic institutions of the Southern States—when the dogmas of a sectional party, substituted for the provisions of the constitutional compact, threatened to destroy the sovereign rights of the states—six of those states, withdrawing from the Union, confederated together to exercise the right and perform the duty of instituting a government which would better secure the liberties for the preservation of which that Union was established.

Whatever of hope some may have entertained that a returning sense of justice would remove the danger with which our rights were threatened, and render it possible to preserve the Union of the Constitution, must have been dispelled by the malignity and barbarity of the Northern States in the prosecution of the existing war. The confidence of the most hopeful among us must have been destroyed by the disregard they have recently exhibited for all the time-honored bulwarks of civil and religious liberty.

Bastilles filled with prisoners, arrested without civil process or indictment duly found; the writ of habeas corpus suspended by executive mandate; a state legislature controlled by the imprisonment of members whose avowed principles suggested to the federal Executive that there might be another added to the list of seceded states; elections held under threats of a military power; civil officers, peaceful citizens, and gentlewomen incarcerated for opinion's sake —[all] proclaimed the incapacity of our late associates to administer a government as free, liberal, and humane as that established for our common use.

For proof of the sincerity of our purpose to maintain our ancient institutions, we may point to the Constitution of the Confederacy and the laws enacted under it, as well as to the fact that through all the necessities of an unequal struggle there has been no act on our part to impair personal liberty or the freedom of speech, of thought, or of the press. The courts have been open, the judicial functions fully executed, and every right of the peaceful citizen maintained as securely as if a war of invasion had not disturbed the land.

The people of the states now confederated became convinced the government of the United States had fallen into the hands of a sectional majority, who would pervert that most sacred of all trusts to the destruction of the rights which it was pledged to protect. They believed that to remain longer in the Union would subject them to a continuance of a disparaging discrimination, submission to which would be inconsistent with their welfare and intolerable to a proud people. They therefore determined to sever its bonds and establish a new confederacy for themselves.

The experiment instituted by our Revolutionary fathers, of a voluntary union of sovereign states for purposes specified in a solemn compact, had been perverted by those who, feeling power and forgetting right, were determined to respect no law but their own will. The government had ceased to answer the ends for which it was ordained and established. To save ourselves from a revolution which, in its silent but rapid progress, was about to place us under the despotism of numbers, and to preserve in spirit, as well as in form, a system of government we believed to be peculiarly fitted to our condition, and full of promise for mankind, we determined to make a new association, composed of states homogeneous in interest, in policy, and in feeling.

True to our traditions of peace and our love of justice, we sent commissioners to the United States to propose a fair and amicable settlement of all questions of public debt or property which might be in dispute. But the government at Washington, denying our right to self-government, refused even to listen to any proposals for a peaceful separation. Nothing was then left to do but to prepare for war.

The first year in our history has been the most eventful in the annals of this continent. A new government has been established, and its machinery put in operation over an area exceeding seven hundred thousand square miles. The great principles upon which we have been willing to hazard everything that is dear to man have made conquests for us which could never have been achieved by the sword. Our Confederacy has grown from six to thirteen states; and Maryland, already united to us by hallowed memories and material interests, will, I believe, when able to speak with unstifled voice, connect her destiny with the South.

Our people have rallied with unexampled unanimity to the support of the great principles of constitutional government, with firm resolve to perpetuate by arms the right which they could not peacefully secure. A million of men, it is estimated, are now standing in hostile array and waging war along a frontier of thousands of miles. Battles have been fought, sieges have been conducted, and although the contest is not ended, and the tide for the moment is against us, the final result in our favor is not doubtful.

The period is near at hand when our foes must sink under the immense load of debt which they have incurred, a debt which in their effort to subjugate us has already attained such fearful dimensions as will subject them to burthens which must continue to oppress them for generations to come.

We, too, have had our trials and difficulties. That we are to escape them in future is not to be hoped. It was to be expected when we entered upon this war that it would expose our people to sacrifices and cost them much, both of money and blood. But we knew the value of the object for which we struggled, and understood the nature of the war in which we were engaged. Nothing could be so bad as failure, and any sacrifice would be cheap as the price of success in such a contest.

But the picture has its lights as well as its shadows. This great strife has awakened in the people the highest emotions and qualities of the human soul. It is cultivating feelings of patriotism, virtue, and courage. Instances of self-sacrifice and of generous devotion to the noble cause for which we are contending are rife throughout the land. Never has a people evinced a more determined spirit than that now animating men, women, and children in every part of our country. Upon the first call, the men fly to arms; and wives and mothers send their husbands and sons to battle without a murmur of regret.

It was, perhaps, in the ordination of Providence that we were to be taught the value of our liberties by the price which we pay for them.

The recollections of this great contest, with all its common traditions of glory, of sacrifice, and of blood, will be the bond of harmony and enduring affection amongst the people, producing unity in policy, fraternity in sentiment, and joint effort in war.

Nor have the material sacrifices of the past year been made without some corresponding benefits. If the acquiescence of foreign nations in a pretended blockade has deprived us of our commerce with them, it is fast making us a self-supporting and an independent people. The blockade, if effectual and permanent, could only serve to divert our industry from the production of articles for export, and employ it in supplying commodities for domestic use.

It is a satisfaction that we have maintained the war by our unaided exertions. We have neither asked nor received assistance from any quarter. Yet the interest involved is not wholly our own. The world at large is concerned in opening our markets to its commerce. When the independence of the Confederate States is recognized by the nations of the earth, and we are free to follow our interests and inclinations by cultivating foreign trade, the Southern States will offer to manufacturing nations the most favorable markets which ever invited their commerce. Cotton, sugar, rice, tobacco, provisions, timber, and naval stores will furnish attractive exchanges. Nor would the constancy of these supplies be likely to be disturbed by war. Our confederate strength will be too great to tempt aggression; and never was there a people whose interests and principles committed them so fully to a peaceful policy as those of the Confederate States.

By the character of their productions they are too deeply interested in foreign commerce wantonly to disturb it. War of conquest they cannot wage because the constitution of their confederacy admits of no coerced association. Civil war there cannot be between states held together by their volition only. The rule of voluntary association, which cannot fail to be conservative, by securing just and impartial government at home, does not diminish the security of the obligations by which the Confederate States may be bound to foreign nations. In proof of this, it is to be remembered that at the first moment of asserting their right of secession these states proposed a settlement on the basis of a common liability for the obligations of the general government.

Fellow-citizens, after the struggle of ages had consecrated the right of the Englishman to constitutional representative government, our colonial ancestors were forced to vindicate that birthright by an appeal to arms. Success crowned their efforts, and they provided for their posterity a peaceful remedy against future aggression.

The tyranny of an unbridled majority, the most odious and least responsible form of despotism, has denied us both the rights and the remedy. Therefore we are in arms to renew such sacrifices as our fathers made to the holy cause of constitutional liberty. At the darkest hour of our struggle the provisional gives place to the permanent government. After a series of successes and victories, which covered our arms with glory, we have recently met with serious disasters. But in the heart of a people resolved to be free, these disasters tend but to stimulate to increased resistance.

To show ourselves worthy of the inheritance bequeathed to us by the patriots of the Revolution, we must emulate that heroic devotion which made reverse to them but the crucible in which their patriotism was refined.

With confidence in the wisdom and virtue of those who will share with me the responsibility, and aid me in the conduct of public affairs; securely relying on the patriotism and courage of the people, of which the present war has furnished so many examples, I deeply feel the weight of the responsibilities I now, with unaffected diffidence, am about to assume; and fully realizing the inequality of human power to guide and to sustain, my hope is reverently fixed on Him whose favor is ever vouchsafed to the cause which is just.

With humble gratitude and adoration, acknowledging the Providence which has so visibly protected the Confederacy during its brief but eventful career, to Thee, O God! I trustingly commit myself, and prayerfully invoke Thy blessing on my country and its cause.

LINCOLN DOOMS SLAVERY

1863

On a hot Sunday in July, 1862, Abraham Lincoln set out to attend a funeral. Three men accompanied him—Gideon Welles, Secretary of the Navy, William H. Seward, Secretary of State, and Seward's son. On the way to the cemetery, some miles distant, the men talked. Suddenly they realized that the President was making a momentous announcement—he had concluded, he said, that a proclamation freeing the slaves was an absolute necessity if the Union were to be saved. The war had been going badly—McClellan had just been driven back from the outskirts of Richmond—and the Southern Confederacy appeared to be impregnable. The slaves, he believed, were a great element in its strength. As field hands, they helped to keep the enemy in food, and thousands served with the opposing armies as teamsters and laborers.

He had given much thought to the matter, Lincoln continued, but this was the first time he had spoken of it to anyone. What, he asked, did Welles and Seward think of the proposal? Both men replied that they were inclined to favor it, but asked for time to reflect before committing themselves.

A few weeks later, in a full Cabinet meeting, Lincoln informed his heads of departments that he had prepared a proclamation of emancipation, and that he wished to read it to them. After he finished, several made suggestions. Then Seward asked to be heard. He approved of the proclamation, but he questioned the wisdom of issuing it after a series of disastrous defeats. Too many people, he feared, would consider it as a desperate expedient of an exhausted government, as the "last shriek on the retreat."

"I suggest, sir," he said, "that you postpone its issue, until you can give it to the country supported by military success, instead of issuing it, as would be the case now, upon the greatest disasters of the war!"

Lincoln laid the document away.

On September 17, 1862, McClellan's Army of the Potomac and Lee's Army of Northern Virginia lunged at each other on the banks of Antietam Creek in northwestern Maryland. After a day of bloody but inconclusive fighting, Lee turned back to Virginia. The North claimed a victory.

Five days later Lincoln called the Cabinet together. Instead of proceeding to business, he reached for a book which Artemus Ward, the most popular humorist of the day, had just sent him—*High-handed Outrage at Utica.* With obvious relish the President read a chapter. Then his mood changed.

"Gentlemen," he said, "I have, as you are aware, thought a great deal about the relation of this war to slavery, and you all remember that, several weeks ago, I read to you an order I had prepared on this subject, which, on account of objections made by some of you, was not issued. Ever since then, my mind has been much occupied by this subject, and I have thought all along that the time for acting on it might very probably come. I think the time has come now. I wish it were a better time. . . . .

"The action of the army against the rebels has not been quite what I should have best liked. But they have been driven out of Maryland, and Pennsylvania is no longer in danger of invasion. When the rebel army was at Frederick, I determined, as soon as it should be driven out of Maryland, to issue a proclamation of emancipation such as I thought most likely to be useful. I said nothing to anyone; but I made the promise to myself, and"—he hesitated a little—"to my

Maker. The rebel army is now driven out, and I am going to fulfill that promise.

"I have got you together to hear what I have written down. I do not wish your advice about the main matter—for that I have determined for myself. . . . . If there is anything in the expressions I use, or in any other minor matter, which any one of you thinks had best be changed, I shall be glad to receive the suggestions. One other observation I will make. I know very well that many others might, in this matter, as in others, do better than I can; and if I were satisfied that the public confidence was more fully possessed by any one of them than by me, and knew of any constitutional way in which he could be put in my place, he should have it. . . . . But though I believe that I have not so much of the confidence of the people as I had some time since, I do not know that, all things considered, any other person has more; and, however this may be, there is no way in which I can have any other man put where I am. I am here. I must do the best I can, and bear the responsibility of taking the course which I feel I ought to take."

That same day—September 22, 1862—Abraham Lincoln, as President of the United States and Commander-in-Chief of the Army and Navy, issued the proclamation which he had read to the Cabinet. The war, he promised, would be prosecuted in the future, as in the past, for the purpose of restoring the Union, and he gave notice that he would again urge upon the Congress a program of compensating the people of the loyal slave states who would voluntarily adopt measures of emancipation. But with the promise went a warning: On January 1, 1863, the slaves in all the states which were still in rebellion would be declared "then, thenceforward, and forever free," and the military and naval forces of the United States would enforce the edict.

The war continued, with the states of the Confederacy unmoved by Lincoln's threat.

On January 1, 1863, thousands crowded the White House for the annual public reception. For three hours Lincoln stood in line, greeting bemedaled diplomats, army officers in dress uniforms, and the rank and file of his fellow-countrymen. Late in the afternoon he slipped away to his office, accompanied only by a few officials and friends. The Proclamation of Emancipation lay before him. As he sat at his desk, he worked the fingers of his right hand, cramped from thousands of handclasps: he wanted no tremor to mar the signature he was about to write. Then he took the pen and without ceremony signed his name.

"That will do," he said to the group around him, and smiled with satisfaction.

Contrary to widespread belief, the Proclamation of Emancipation did not bring about the immediate end of human bondage in the United States. It left slavery untouched in Tennessee and in the border states which had remained loyal to the Union, while in those parts of the Confederacy to which it did apply, it could not be enforced. Lincoln himself looked upon it primarily as a military measure. Nevertheless, it stirred the enthusiasm of the opponents of slavery, gave a new direction to the war, and made the Thirteenth Amendment, which did free the slaves, inevitable.

Proclamation of Emancipation

January 1, 1863

By the President of the United States of America

A Proclamation

Whereas, On the twenty-second day of September, in the year of our Lord one thousand eight hundred and sixty-two, a proclamation was issued by the President of the United States, containing, among other things, the following, to wit:

"That on the first day of January, in the year of our Lord one thousand eight hundred and sixty-three, all persons held as slaves within any state or designated part of a state, the people whereof shall then be in rebellion against the United States, shall be then, thenceforward, and forever free; and the executive government of the United States, including the military and naval authority thereof, will recognize and maintain the freedom of such persons, and will do no act or acts to repress such persons, or any of them, in any efforts they may make for their actual freedom.

"That the Executive will, on the first day of January aforesaid, by proclamation, designate the states and parts of states, if any, in which the people thereof, respectively, shall then be in rebellion against the United States; and the fact that any state, or the people thereof, shall on that day be, in good faith, represented in the Congress of the United States by members chosen thereto at elections wherein a majority of the qualified voters of such state shall have participated, shall, in the absence of strong countervailing testimony, be deemed conclusive evidence that such state, and the people thereof, are not then in rebellion against the United States."

Now, therefore I, Abraham Lincoln, President of the United States, by virtue of the power in me vested as Commander-in-Chief, of the Army and Navy of the United States in time of actual armed rebellion against authority and government of the United States, and as a fit and necessary war measure for suppressing said rebellion, do, on this first day of January, in the year of our Lord one thousand eight hundred and sixty-three, and in accordance with my purpose so to do publicly proclaimed for the full period of one hundred days, from the day first above mentioned, order and designate as the states and parts of states wherein the people thereof respectively, are this day in rebellion against the United States, the following, to wit:

Arkansas, Texas, Louisiana, (except the parishes of St. Bernard, Plaquemines, Jefferson, St. Johns, St. Charles, St. James, Ascension, Assumption, Terrebonne, Lafourche, St. Mary, St. Martin, and Orleans, including the City of New Orleans), Mississippi, Alabama, Florida, Georgia, South Carolina, North Carolina, and Virginia, (except the forty-eight counties designated as West Virginia, and also the counties of Berkeley, Accomac, Northampton, Elizabeth City, York, Princess Ann, and Norfolk, including the cities of Norfolk and Portsmouth); and which excepted parts are, for the present, left precisely as if this proclamation were not issued.

And by virtue of the power, and for the purpose aforesaid, I do order and declare that all persons held as slaves within said designated states, and parts of states, are, and henceforward shall be free; and that the executive government of the United States, including the military and naval authorities thereof, will recognize and maintain the freedom of said persons.

And I hereby enjoin upon the people so declared to be free to abstain from all violence, unless in necessary self-defense; and I recommend to them that, in all cases when allowed, they labor faithfully for reasonable wages.

And I further declare and make known, that such persons of suitable condition, will be received into the armed service of the United States to garrison forts, positions, stations, and other places, and to man vessels of all sorts in said service.

And upon this act, sincerely believed to be an act of justice, warranted by the Constitution, upon military necessity, I invoke the considerate judgment of mankind, and the gracious favor of Almighty God.

In witness whereof, I have hereunto set my hand and caused the seal of the United States to be affixed.

[L.S.] Done at the City of Washington, this first day of January, in the year of our Lord one thousand eight hundred and sixty-three, and of the Independence of the United States of America the eighty-seventh.

ABRAHAM LINCOLN

By the President:
WILLIAM H. SEWARD, *Secretary of State*

LINCOLN DEDICATES A PEOPLE

1863

The invitation came so tardily that it was almost a slight. The commission which had undertaken to establish a cemetery for the burial of those who had died at Gettysburg had been planning dedicatory ceremonies for weeks before its members asked the President to speak. Even then they invited him only to set apart the grounds by "a few appropriate remarks" after Edward Everett, orator of the day, had concluded.

If Lincoln felt any resentment at the commission's lack of consideration, characteristically he kept his feeling to himself. Fully aware of the solemnity of the occasion, he made his preparations well in advance. At least ten days before November 19, the date finally settled upon for the dedication, he had committed to paper what he intended to say. Nor would he take any chance on arriving late. When the Secretary of War proposed that the presidential party travel from Washington to Gettysburg on the day of the ceremonies, Lincoln interposed a veto. "I do not like this arrangement," he commented. "I do not wish to so go that by the slightest accident we fail entirely, and, at the best, the whole to be a mere breathless running of the gauntlet." So the special train carrying the President and his party left Washington on the eighteenth and reached its destination on the afternoon of the same day.

At noon on the nineteenth—a day warmed by a wan sun—a ragged procession formed and started for the cemetery. There were troops, a band, and dignitaries—with the President, in a long coat and tall silk hat, an ungainly figure astride a horse. After a long prayer and dedicatory ode, Edward Everett took the stand and for two hours delivered a polished oration. Then Lincoln rose, a sheet of paper in one hand. Before the jaded crowd could come to full attention, he had finished. "The music wailed," wrote young John Hay, the President's secretary, "and we went home through crowded and cheering streets."

With no more fanfare than this were immortal words spoken and heard.

The Gettysburg Address

November 19, 1863

Fourscore and seven years ago our fathers brought forth on this continent, a new nation, conceived in liberty, and dedicated to the proposition that all men are created equal.

Now we are engaged in a great civil war, testing whether that nation, or any nation so conceived and so dedicated, can long endure. We are met on a great battlefield of that war. We have come to dedicate a portion of that field, as a final resting-place for those who here gave their lives that that nation might live. It is altogether fitting and proper that we should do this.

But, in a larger sense, we cannot dedicate–we cannot consecrate –we cannot hallow–this ground. The brave men, living and dead, who struggled here, have consecrated it, far above our poor power to add or detract. The world will little note, nor long remember what we say here, but it can never forget what they did here. It is for us the living, rather, to be dedicated here to the unfinished work which they who fought here have thus far so nobly advanced. It is rather for us to be here dedicated to the great task remaining before us–that from these honored dead we take increased devotion to that cause for which they gave the last full measure of devotion–that we here highly resolve that these dead shall not have died in vain –that this nation, under God, shall have a new birth of freedom–and that government of the people, by the people, for the people. shall not perish from the earth.

WITH MALICE TOWARD NONE

1865

Rain dripped relentlessly from a soggy sky, while underfoot the unpaved streets and walks of Washington turned into mud that sucked at shoes and spattered skirts and pantaloons. Yet thousands braved the weather to converge on the Capitol, where Abraham Lincoln was to take the oath of office a second time. In the galleries of the Senate Chamber fashionably dressed women whispered and twittered in spite of the presiding officer's attempts to preserve order. The muted hubbub swelled whenever eminent personages arrived—General Hooker, resplendent in full-dress uniform; the weather-beaten Admiral Farragut; Mrs. Lincoln on the arm of Senator Anthony of Rhode Island; the Justices of the Supreme Court in their black gowns; the members of the Cabinet with Seward at their head. Lincoln took a seat in the front row to the left of the chair.

While the clock struck twelve, Andrew Johnson, Vice-President-elect, and Hannibal Hamlin, the retiring Vice-President, entered the chamber arm in arm. Hamlin spoke briefly, and Johnson stepped forward to launch into a speech that was obviously affected by the liquor with which he had hoped to overcome the debilitating effect of a recent illness. Some of his auditors sat impassively, some writhed in mortification. Finally bringing his harangue to a close, he mumbled the oath of office and proclaimed, with a sweeping gesture, "I kiss this Book in the face of my nation of the United States!"

The Secretary of the Senate proceeded to read the President's proclamation convoking an extra session. Newly elected Senators took the oath, and then a procession formed and headed for the east front of the Capitol, where a temporary platform had been erected. A tremendous shout greeted the President. The sergeant-at-arms of the Senate stood before the crowd in a silent appeal for quiet. The noise died away, and Lincoln, his inaugural address in hand, walked to the rostrum. Applause ebbed and surged again and again. With the last handclap the sun broke through the clouds. In a voice clear and audible to the limits of the huge hushed throng, Abraham Lincoln began to speak.

Lincoln's Second Inaugural Address

March 4, 1865

Fellow-Countrymen: At this second appearing to take the oath of the presidential office, there is less occasion for an extended address than there was at the first. Then a statement, somewhat in detail, of a course to be pursued, seemed fitting and proper. Now, at the expiration of four years, during which public declarations have been constantly called forth on every point and phase of the great contest which still absorbs the attention, and engrosses the energies of the nation, little that is new could be presented. The progress of our arms, upon which all else chiefly depends, is as well known to the public as to myself; and it is, I trust, reasonably satisfactory and encouraging to all. With high hope for the future, no prediction in regard to it is ventured.

On the occasion corresponding to this four years ago, all thoughts were anxiously directed to an impending civil war. All dreaded it—all sought to avert it. While the inaugural address was being delivered from this place, devoted altogether to saving the Union without war, insurgent agents were in the city seeking to destroy it without war—seeking to dissolve the Union, and divide effects, by negotiation. Both parties deprecated war; but one of them would make war rather than let the nation survive; and the other would accept war rather than let it perish. And the war came.

One-eighth of the whole population were colored slaves, not distributed generally over the Union, but localized in the southern part of it. These slaves constituted a peculiar and powerful interest. All knew that this interest was, somehow, the cause of the war. To strengthen, perpetuate, and extend this interest was the object for which the insurgents would rend the Union, even by war; while the government claimed no right to do more than to restrict the territorial enlargement of it. Neither party expected for the war, the magnitude, or the duration, which it has already attained. Neither anticipated that the cause of the conflict might cease with, or even before, the conflict itself should cease. Each looked for an easier triumph, and a result less fundamental and astounding.

Both read the same Bible, and pray to the same God; and each invokes His aid against the other. It may seem strange that any men should dare to ask a just God's assistance in wringing their bread from the sweat of other men's faces; but let us judge not that we be not judged. The prayers of both could not be answered; that of neither has been answered fully.

The Almighty has His own purposes. "Woe unto the world because of offenses! for it must needs be that offenses come; but woe to that man by whom the offense cometh!" If we shall suppose that American slavery is one of those offenses which, in the providence of God, must needs come, but which, having continued through His appointed time, He now wills to remove, and that He gives to both North and South, this terrible war, as the woe due to those by whom the offense came, shall we discern therein any departure from those divine attributes which the believers in a living

God always ascribe to Him? Fondly do we hope—fervently do we pray—that this mighty scourge of war may speedily pass away. Yet, if God wills that it continue, until all the wealth piled by the bond-man's two hundred and fifty years of unrequited toil shall be sunk, and until every drop of blood drawn with the lash, shall be paid by another drawn with the sword, as was said three thousand years ago, so still it must be said "the judgments of the Lord, are true and righteous altogether."

With malice toward none; with charity for all; with firmness in the right, as God gives us to see the right, let us strive on to finish the work we are in; to bind up the nation's wounds; to care for him who shall have borne the battle, and for his widow, and his orphan—to do all which may achieve and cherish a just, and a lasting peace, among ourselves, and with all nations.

LEE SAYS FAREWELL TO A BRAVE ARMY

1865

For the first time in four years the guns were silent. Along the line of the Army of Northern Virginia gaunt veterans lounged beside stacked arms and unshotted cannon; cavalry horses, their ribs pitifully plain, munched the spring grass. It was good to know that there would be no more killing, but an army takes no pleasure in defeat. Still, when the commanding general came in sight, riding slowly to his own lines from the farmhouse where he had just signed articles of surrender, the troops instinctively shouted their welcome. Then, suddenly realizing that the end had come, they fell silent. Hats came off, and tears rolled down weather-beaten faces. Men in tattered uniforms pressed forward to take Lee's hand, or even to touch the white horse he had ridden through victory and defeat. Controlling himself, the General spoke a few words.

"Men, we have fought through the war together; I have done my best for you; my heart is too full to say more."

The next day he issued his last order.

Lee's Farewell to the Army of Northern Virginia

April 10, 1865

After four years of arduous service, marked by unsurpassed courage and fortitude, the Army of Northern Virginia has been compelled to yield to overwhelming numbers and resources. I need not tell the survivors of so many hard-fought battles, who have remained steadfast to the last, that I have consented to this result from no distrust of them; but, feeling that valor and devotion could accomplish nothing that could compensate for the loss that would have attended the continuation of the contest, I have determined to avoid the useless sacrifice of those whose past services have endeared them to their countrymen. By the terms of the agreement, officers and men can return to their homes and remain there until exchanged. You will take with you the satisfaction that proceeds from the consciousness of duty faithfully performed; and I earnestly pray that a merciful God will extend to you His blessing and protection. With an increasing admiration of your constancy and devotion to your country, and a grateful remembrance of your kind and generous consideration of myself, I bid you an affectionate farewell.

DAVID DAVIS STRIKES AT USURPATION

1866

Loyal citizens wasted little sympathy on men like Lambdin P. Milligan. If this lawyer of Huntington, Indiana, and his fellow-members of the Sons of Liberty—the strongest "copperhead" order in the North—had had their way, the Civil War would have been brought to a premature end, and the South might well have won. There were few protests, therefore, when Milligan and several associates were arrested in the fall of 1864 and convicted, by a military commission, of conspiracy against the government of the United States, of affording aid and comfort to the enemy, inciting insurrection, and violating the laws of war. And if young farm boys in uniform were to be shot merely for sleeping on sentry duty, Milligan's sentence—to be hanged by the neck until dead—seemed just.

But a few days before the date set for the hanging, Milligan came before the United States Circuit Court at Indianapolis on a petition for habeas corpus. His counsel contended that the military commission had no jurisdiction over the prisoner, and that if he were to be tried at all, it should be by a jury of his peers after an indictment by a grand jury. Since he had not been indicted, he should have his freedom.

David Davis, the Supreme Court Justice assigned to the Indiana circuit, and the district judge could not agree, and certified the questions involved to the United States Supreme Court. The case, heard at the March term in 1866, presented legal questions of the utmost importance. If a military commission had had no right to try Lambdin P. Milligan, a similar commission had had no jurisdiction over the Lincoln conspirators, and judicial murder had been committed. Military commissions were functioning even then in the conquered South: were they, too, unconstitutional? Illustrious counsel—as able lawyers as could be found in the country—represented both Milligan and the government.

The court, through Chief Justice Chase, announced its decision without delay. The military commission, it held, had had no jurisdiction, the writ should issue, and the prisoner should be discharged. Opinions, Chase promised, would be read at the next term.

On December 17, 1866, the justices, attired as usual in their black silk gowns, filed into the courtroom. Lawyers and members of Congress occupied every seat. They had come not only to learn at firsthand the reasoning of the court, but also to be present for the last scene of a drama. David Davis was to read the opinion—and David Davis was linked inseparably with the memory of Abraham

Lincoln. For years the two men had traveled the old eighth judicial circuit in Illinois, Davis the presiding judge, Lincoln the leading lawyer. To Davis, the astute politician, Lincoln owed his nomination for the Presidency; to Lincoln, Davis owed his appointment to the Supreme Court. And now Davis was to charge, in effect, his friend with exceeding his constitutional powers, for Lincoln had taken full responsibility for the policy of military arrests and trial by military commissions.

Small wonder, then, that no eye left the face of the corpulent Justice as he read the opinion that has long been considered one of the stoutest bulwarks of American liberty—the opinion which, in the words of the closest student of the case,[1] affirmed that "the civil liberties guaranteed by the Constitution are to be safeguarded not less in the fever of civil war than in time of peace," and proclaimed "the power of the civil courts to call to account other tribunals of every nature and pretension."

Opinion in the Milligan Case

December 17, 1866

Mr. Justice Davis delivered the opinion of the Court. . . . The controlling question in the case is this: Upon the facts stated in Milligan's petition, and the exhibits filed, had the military commission mentioned in it jurisdiction, legally, to try and sentence him? Milligan, not a resident of one of the rebellious states or a prisoner of war, but a citizen of Indiana for twenty years past, and never in the military or naval service, is, while at his home, arrested by the military power of the United States, imprisoned, and, on certain criminal charges preferred against him, tried, convicted, and sentenced to be hanged by a military commission, organized under the direction of the military commander of the military district of

[1] S. Klaus, *The Milligan Case* (New York: Alfred A. Knopf, 1929), Foreword.

Indiana. Had this tribunal the legal power and authority to try and punish this man?

No graver question was ever considered by this court, nor one which more nearly concerns the rights of the whole people; for it is the birthright of every American citizen, when charged with crime, to be tried and punished according to law. The power of punishment is alone through the means which the laws have provided for that purpose; and if they are ineffectual, there is an immunity from punishment, no matter how great an offender the individual may be, or how much his crimes may have shocked the sense of justice of the country, or endangered its safety. By the protection of the law human rights are secured; withdraw that protection, and they are at the mercy of wicked rulers, or the clamor of an excited people.

If there was law to justify this military trial, it is not our province to interfere; if there was not, it is our duty to declare the nullity of the whole proceedings. The decision of this question does not depend on argument or judicial precedents, numerous and highly illustrative as they are. These precedents inform us of the extent of the struggle to preserve liberty and to relieve those in civil life from military trials. The founders of our government were familiar with the history of that struggle; and secured in a written constitution every right which the people had wrested from power during a contest of ages. By that Constitution and the laws authorized by it this question must be determined.

The provisions of that instrument on the administration of criminal justice are too plain and direct to leave room for misconstruction or doubt of their true meaning. Those applicable to this case are found in that clause of the original Constitution which says, "That the trial of all crimes, except in case of impeachment, shall be by jury"; and in the fourth, fifth, and sixth articles of the amendments. The fourth proclaims the right to be secure in person and effects against unreasonable search and seizure; and directs that a judicial warrant shall not issue "without proof of probable cause supported by oath or affirmation." The fifth declares "that no person shall be held to answer for a capital or otherwise infamous crime unless on presentment by a grand jury, except in cases arising in the land or naval forces, or in the militia, when in actual service in time of war or public danger, nor be deprived of life, liberty, or property, without due process of law." And the sixth guarantees the right of trial by jury, in such manner and with such regulations that with upright judges, impartial juries, and an able bar the innocent will be saved and the guilty punished. . . . .

These securities for personal liberty thus embodied, were such as wisdom and experience had demonstrated to be necessary for the protection of those accused of crime. And so strong was the sense of the country of their importance, and so jealous were the people that these rights, highly prized, might be denied them by implication, that when the original Constitution was proposed for adoption, it encountered severe opposition; and, but for the belief that it would be so amended as to embrace them, it would never have been ratified.

Time has proven the discernment of our ancestors; for even these provisions, expressed in such plain English words that it would seem the ingenuity of man could not evade them, are now, after the lapse of more than seventy years, sought to be avoided. Those great and good men foresaw that troublous times would arise, when rulers and people would become restive under restraint, and seek by sharp and decisive measures to accomplish ends deemed just and proper; and that the principles of constitutional liberty would be in peril, unless established by irrepealable law. The history of the world had taught them that what was done in the past might be attempted in the future.

The Constitution of the United States is a law for rulers and people, equally in war and in peace, and covers with the shield of its protection all classes of men, at all times, and under all circumstances. No doctrine involving more pernicious consequences was ever invented by the wit of man than that any of its provisions can be suspended during any of the great exigencies of government. Such a doctrine leads directly to anarchy or despotism, but the theory of necessity on which it is based is false; for the government, within the Constitution, has all the powers granted to it, which are necessary to preserve its existence; as has been happily proved by the result of the great effort to throw off its just authority.

Have any of the rights guaranteed by the Constitution been violated in the case of Milligan? And if so, what are they?

Every trial involves the exercise of judicial power; and from what source did the military commission that tried him derive their authority? Certainly no part of the judicial power of the country was conferred on them; because the Constitution expressly vests it "in one Supreme Court and such inferior courts as the Congress may from time to time ordain and establish," and it is not pretended

that the commission was a court ordained and established by Congress. They cannot justify on the mandate of the President; because he is controlled by law, and has his appropriate sphere of duty, which is to execute, not to make, the laws; and there is "no unwritten criminal code to which resort can be had as a source of jurisdiction."

But it is said that the jurisdiction is complete under the "laws and usages of war."

It can serve no useful purpose to inquire what those laws and usages are, whence they originated, where found, and on whom they operate; they can never be applied to citizens in states which have upheld the authority of the government, and where the courts are open and their process unobstructed. This court has judicial knowledge that in Indiana the federal authority was always unopposed, and its courts always open to hear criminal accusations and redress grievances; and no usage of war could sanction a military trial there for any offense whatever of a citizen in civil life, in no wise connected with the military service. Congress could grant no such power; and to the honor of our national legislature be it said, it has never been provoked by the state of the country even to attempt its exercise. One of the plainest constitutional provisions was, therefore, infringed when Milligan was tried by a court not ordained and established by Congress, and not composed of judges appointed during good behavior.

Why was he not delivered to the Circuit Court of Indiana to be proceeded against according to law? No reason of necessity could be urged against it; because Congress had declared penalties against the offenses charged, provided for their punishment, and directed that court to hear and determine them. And soon after this military tribunal was ended, the Circuit Court met, peacefully transacted its business, and adjoined. It needed no bayonets to protect it, and required no military aid to execute its judgments. It was held in a state eminently distinguished for patriotism, by judges commissioned during the rebellion, who were provided with juries, upright, intelligent, and selected by a marshal appointed by the President. The government had no right to conclude that Milligan, if guilty, would not receive in that court merited punishment; for its records disclose that it was constantly engaged in the trial of similar offenses, and was never interrupted in its administration of criminal justice.

If it was dangerous, in the distracted condition of affairs, to leave Milligan unrestrained of his liberty, because he "conspired against the government, afforded aid and comfort to rebels, and incited the people to insurrection," the law said arrest him, confine him closely, render him powerless to do further mischief; and then present his case to the grand jury of the district, with proofs of his guilt, and, if indicted, try him according to the course of the common law. If this had been done, the Constitution would have been vindicated, the law of 1863 enforced, and the securities for personal liberty preserved and defended.

Another guarantee of freedom was broken when Milligan was denied a trial by jury. The great minds of the country have differed on the correct interpretation to be given to various provisions of the federal Constitution; and judicial decision has been often invoked to settle their true meaning; but until recently no one ever doubted

that the right of trial by jury was fortified in the organic law against the power of attack. It is now assailed; but if ideas can be expressed in words, and language has any meaning, this right–one of the most valuable in a free country–is preserved to every one accused of crime who is not attached to the army, or navy, or militia in actual service.

The Sixth Amendment affirms that "in all criminal prosecutions the accused shall enjoy the right to a speedy and public trial by an impartial jury," language broad enough to embrace all persons and cases; but the Fifth, recognizing the necessity of an indictment, or presentment, before any one can be held to answer for high crimes "except cases arising in the land or naval forces, or in the militia, when in actual service, in time of war or public danger," and the framers of the Constitution, doubtless, meant to limit the right of trial by jury, in the Sixth Amendment, to those persons who were subject to indictment or presentment in the Fifth.

The discipline necessary to the efficiency of the army and navy required other and swifter modes of trial than are furnished by the common law courts; and, in pursuance of the power conferred by the Constitution, Congress has declared the kinds of trial, and the manner in which they shall be conducted, for offenses committed while the party is in the military or naval service. Everyone connected with these branches of the public service is amenable to the jurisdiction which Congress has created for their government, and, while thus serving, surrenders his right to be tried by the civil courts. All other persons, citizens of states where the courts are open, if charged with crime, are guaranteed the inestimable privilege of trial by jury.

This privilege is a vital principle, underlying the whole administration of criminal justice; it is not held by sufferance, and cannot be frittered away on any plea of state or political necessity. When peace prevails and the authority of the government is undisputed, there is no difficulty of preserving the safeguards of liberty; for the ordinary modes of trial are never neglected, and no one wishes it otherwise; but if society is disturbed by civil commotion–if the passions of men are aroused and the restraints of law weakened, if not disregarded–these safeguards need, and should receive, the watchful care of those entrusted with the guardianship of the Constitution and laws. In no other way can we transmit to posterity unimpaired the blessings of liberty, consecrated by the sacrifices of the Revolution.

It is claimed that martial law covers with its broad mantle the proceedings of this military commission. The proposition is this: that in a time of war the commander of an armed force (if in his opinion the exigencies of the country demand it, and of which he is to judge) has the power, within the lines of his military district, to suspend all civil rights and their remedies, and subject citizens as well as soldiers to the rule of his will; and in the exercise of his lawful authority cannot be restrained, except by his superior officer or the President of the United States.

If this position is sound to the extent claimed, then when war exists, foreign or domestic, and the country is subdivided into military departments for mere convenience, the commander of one of them can, if he chooses, within his limits, on the plea of necessity, with the approval of the Executive, substitute military force for and to the exclusion of the laws, and punish all persons, as he thinks right and proper, without fixed or certain rules.

The statement of this proposition shows its importance; for, if true, republican government is a failure, and there is an end of liberty regulated by law. Martial law, established on such a basis, destroys every guarantee of the Constitution and effectually renders the "military independent of and superior to the civil power"—the attempt to do which by the King of Great Britain was deemed by our fathers such an offense, that they assigned it to the world as one of the causes which impelled them to declare their independence. Civil liberty and this kind of martial law cannot endure together; the antagonism is irreconcilable; and, in the conflict, one or the other must perish.

This nation, as experience has proved, cannot always remain at peace, and has no right to expect that it will always have wise and humane rulers, sincerely attached to the principles of the Constitution. Wicked men, ambitious of power, with hatred of liberty and contempt of law, may fill the place once occupied by Washington and Lincoln; and if this right is conceded, and the calamities of war again befall us, the dangers to human liberty are frightful to contemplate.

If our fathers had failed to provide for just such a contingency, they would have been false to the trust reposed in them. They knew—the history of the world told them—the nation they were founding, be its existence short or long, would be involved in war; how often or how long continued, human foresight could not tell; and that unlimited power, wherever lodged at such a time, was especially hazardous to freemen. For this, and other equally weighty reasons, they secured the inheritance they had fought to maintain, by incorporating in a written constitution the safeguards which time had proved were essential to its preservation. Not one of these safeguards can the President, or Congress, or the Judiciary disturb, except the one concerning the writ of habeas corpus. . . .

It will be borne in mind that this is not a question of the power to proclaim martial law when war exists in a community and the courts and civil authorities are overthrown. Nor is it a question what rule a military commander, at the head of his army, can impose on states in rebellion to cripple their resources and quell the insurrection. The jurisdiction claimed is much more extensive.

The necessities of the service, during the late rebellion, required that the loyal states should be placed within the limits of certain military districts and commanders appointed in them; and, it is urged, that this, in a military sense, constituted them the theater of military operations; and, as in this case, Indiana had been and was again threatened with invasion by the enemy, the occasion was furnished to establish martial law. The conclusion does not follow from the premises. If armies were collected in Indiana, they were to be employed in another locality, where the laws were obstructed and the national authority disputed. On her soil there was no hostile foot; if once invaded, that invasion was at an end, and with it all pretext for martial law. Martial law cannot arise from a threatened invasion. The necessity must be actual and present; the invasion real, such as effectually closes the courts and deposes the civil administration.

It is difficult to see how the safety of the country required martial law in Indiana. If any of her citizens were plotting treason, the power of arrest could secure them, until the government was prepared for their trial, when the courts were open and ready to try them. It was as easy to protect witnesses before a civil as a military tribunal; and as there could be no wish to convict, except on sufficient legal evidence, surely an ordained and established court was better able to judge of this than a military tribunal composed of gentlemen not trained to the profession of the law. . . . .

JOHNSON PLEADS FOR REUNION WITHOUT VENGEANCE

1866

Andrew Johnson, precipitated into the Presidency by the bullet of John Wilkes Booth, quickly underwent a change of heart. Taking office as a Radical Republican, he appeared at first to be bent on reducing the states of the South to the status of conquered provinces. But he soon made his own the lenient and tolerant policy that Lincoln had formulated in the last months of his administration.

Had the states of the former Confederacy, the Civil War President asked four days before his death, been in the Union or out of it? A useless, even pernicious, abstraction, he had answered. "Finding themselves safely at home, it would be utterly immaterial whether they had ever been abroad." Let everyone, he had pleaded, join in doing whatever was necessary to bring the erring states into a "proper practical relation" with the states which had remained loyal. Let there be no revenge or repression on account of the past. And let no one be disappointed if miracles should not happen overnight: the South had been shattered into "disorganized and discordant elements," and even the North differed as to the "mode, manner, and measure of reconstruction."

In the spirit of his predecessor, thus expressed, Johnson attacked the problem of reconstruction during the months that intervened between his succession to the Presidency and December, 1865, when Congress convened. By that time, under his direction, every one of the seceded states except Texas had formed governments and had elected Representatives and Senators who stood ready to take their seats as soon as congressional recognition should be extended. Large classes of former Confederates were pardoned by presidential proclamation; thousands excepted from the general amnesty were pardoned individually.

In the main, the President's course won the approval of the North. Many who remembered, with apprehension, his unfortunate condition when he took the oath as Vice-President came to admire his moderation, the obvious honesty of his convictions, and the stubborn courage with which he adhered to his beliefs. But in Congress the Radical Republicans smoldered with anger. Determined to punish the Southern States for bringing on the Civil War, and equally determined to enfranchise the Negroes and through their votes assure the rule of the Republican party, the Radicals would seize any chance to discredit the President and trim his power. Aided, often, by the President's own follies and lack of tact, they succeeded. By the end of 1866 it was clear that reconstruction would follow the Radical pattern—that native Southerners would be disfranchised while newly freed slaves would be allowed to vote, that the Southern States would be without real representation in Congress, and that the Republican party would be kept in power by the bayonets of federal troops.

But the former tailor who occupied the White House—a man who had lifted himself from poverty and ignorance through sheer will power—could never concede defeat. To a Congress hopelessly hostile he sent a message pleading again, as he had a year earlier, for measures that would have gone far toward healing the lingering wounds of civil war. The message was received, as Johnson knew it would be, with contempt, but it stands on the nation's record as a noble exposition of democratic principles.

Johnson's Annual Message to Congress

December 3, 1866

Fellow-Citizens of the Senate and House of Representatives: After a brief interval the Congress of the United States resumes its annual legislative labors. . . . . Peace, order, tranquillity, and civil authority have been formally declared to exist throughout the whole of the United States. In all the states civil authority has superseded

the coercion of arms, and the people, by their voluntary action, are maintaining their governments in full activity and complete operation. The enforcement of the laws is no longer "obstructed in any state by combinations too powerful to be suppressed by the ordinary course of judicial proceedings," and the animosities engendered by the war are rapidly yielding to the beneficent influences of our free institutions, and to the kindly effects of unrestricted social and commercial intercourse. An entire restoration of fraternal feeling must be the earnest wish of every patriotic heart; and we will have accomplished our grandest national achievement when, forgetting the sad events of the past, and remembering only their instructive lessons, we resume our onward career as a free, prosperous, and united people.

In my message of the fourth of December, 1865, Congress was informed of the measures which had been instituted by the Executive with a view to the gradual restoration of the states in which the insurrection occurred to their relations with the general government. Provisional governors had been appointed, conventions called, governors elected, legislatures assembled, and Senators and Representatives chosen to the Congress of the United States. Courts had been opened for the enforcement of laws long in abeyance. The blockade had been removed, customhouses re-established, and the internal revenue laws put in force, in order that the people might contribute to the national income. Postal operations had been renewed, and efforts were being made to restore them to their former condition of efficiency. The states themselves had been asked to take part in the high function of amending the Constitution, and of thus sanctioning the extinction of African slavery as one of the legitimate results of our internecine struggle.

Having progressed thus far, the executive department found that it had accomplished nearly all that was within the scope of its constitutional authority. One thing, however, yet remained to be done before the work of restoration could be completed, and that was the admission to Congress of loyal Senators and Representatives from the states whose people had rebelled against the lawful authority of the general government. This question devolved upon the respective Houses, which, by the Constitution, are made the judges of the elections, returns, and qualifications of their own members; and its consideration at once engaged the attention of Congress.

In the meantime, the executive department—no other plan having been proposed by Congress—continued its efforts to perfect, as far as was practicable, the restoration of the proper relations between the citizens of the respective states, the states, and the federal government, extending, from time to time, as the public interests seemed to require, the judicial, revenue, and postal systems of the country. With the advice and consent of the Senate, the necessary officers were appointed, and appropriations made by Congress for the payment of their salaries. The proposition to amend the federal Constitution, so as to prevent the existence of slavery within the United States or any place subject to their jurisdiction, was ratified by the requisite number of states; and on the eighteenth day of December, 1865, it was officially declared to have become valid as a part of the Constitution of the United States.

All of the states in which the insurrection had existed promptly amended their constitutions, so as to make them conform to the great change thus effected in the organic law of the land; declared null and void all ordinances and laws of secession; repudiated all pretended debts and obligations created for the revolutionary purposes of the insurrection, and proceeded, in good faith, to the enactment of measures for the protection and amelioration of the condition of the colored race. Congress, however, yet hesitated to admit any of these states to representation; and it was not until toward the close of the eighth month of the session that an exception was made in favor of Tennessee, by the admission of her Senators and Representatives.

I deem it a subject of profound regret that Congress has thus far failed to admit to seats loyal Senators and Representatives from the other states whose inhabitants, with those of Tennessee, had engaged in the rebellion. Ten states—more than one-fourth of the whole number—remain without representation; the seats of fifty members in the House of Representatives and of twenty members in the Senate are yet vacant—not by their own consent, not by a failure of election, but by the refusal of Congress to accept their credentials.

Their admission, it is believed, would have accomplished much toward the renewal and strengthening of our relations as one people, and removed serious cause for discontent on the part of the inhabitants of those states. It would have accorded with the great principle enunciated in the Declaration of American Independence, that no people ought to bear the burden of taxation, and yet be denied the right of representation. It would have been in consonance with the express provisions of the Constitution, that "each state shall have at least one Representative," and "that no state, without its consent, shall be deprived of its equal suffrage in the Senate." These provisions were intended to secure to every state, and to the people of every state, the right of representation in each House of Congress; and so important was it deemed by the framers of the Constitution that the equality of the states in the Senate should be preserved, that not even by an amendment of the Constitution can any state, without its consent, be denied a voice in that branch of the national legislature. . . . .

In the admission of Senators and Representatives from any and all of the states, there can be no just ground of apprehension that persons who are disloyal will be clothed with the powers of legislation, for this could not happen when the Constitution and the laws are enforced by a vigilant and faithful Congress. Each House is made the "judge of the elections, returns, and qualifications of its own members," and may, "with the concurrence of two-thirds, expel a member."

When a Senator or Representative presents his certificate of election, he may at once be admitted or rejected; or, should there be any question as to his eligibility, his credentials may be referred for investigation to the appropriate committee. If admitted to a seat, it must be upon evidence satisfactory to the House of which he thus becomes a member, that he possesses the requisite constitutional and legal qualifications. If refused admission as a member for want of due allegiance to the government, and returned to his constituents, they are admonished that none but persons loyal to the United States will be allowed a voice in the legislative councils of the nation, and the political power and moral influence of Congress are thus effectively exerted in the interests of loyalty to the government and fidelity to the Union.

Upon this question, so vitally affecting the restoration of the Union and the permanency of our present form of government, my convictions, heretofore expressed, have undergone no change; but, on the contrary, their correctness has been confirmed by reflection and time. If the admission of loyal members to seats in the respective Houses of Congress was wise and expedient a year ago, it is no less wise and expedient now. If this anomalous condition is right now—if, in the exact condition of these states at the present time, it is lawful to exclude them from representation—I do not see that the question will be changed by the efflux of time. Ten years hence, if these states remain as they are, the right of representation will be no stronger—the right of exclusion will be no weaker.

The Constitution of the United States makes it the duty of the President to recommend to the consideration of Congress "such measures as he shall judge necessary and expedient." I know of no measure more imperatively demanded by every consideration of

national interest, sound policy, and equal justice than the admission of loyal members from the now unrepresented states. This would consummate the work of restoration, and exert a most salutary influence in the re-establishment of peace, harmony, and fraternal feeling. It would tend greatly to renew the confidence of the American people in the vigor and stability of their institutions. It would bind us more closely together as a nation, and enable us to show to the world the inherent and recuperative power of a government founded upon the will of the people, and established upon the principles of liberty, justice, and intelligence.

Our increased strength and enhanced prosperity would irrefragably demonstrate the fallacy of the arguments against free institutions, drawn from our recent national disorders by the enemies of republican government. The admission of loyal members from the states now excluded from Congress, by allaying doubt and apprehension, would turn capital, now awaiting an opportunity for investment, into the channels of trade and industry. It would alleviate the present troubled condition of those states, and, by inducing immigration, aid in the settlement of fertile regions now uncultivated, and lead to an increased production of those staples which have added so greatly to the wealth of the nation and the commerce of the world. New fields of enterprise would be opened to our progressive people, and soon the devastations of war would be repaired, and all traces of our domestic differences effaced from the minds of our countrymen.

In our efforts to preserve "the unity of government which constitutes us one people," by restoring the states to the condition which they held prior to the rebellion, we should be cautious, lest, having rescued our nation from perils of threatened disintegration, we resort to consolidation, and in the end absolute despotism, as a remedy for the recurrence of similar troubles. The war having terminated, and with it all occasion for the exercise of powers of doubtful constitutionality, we should hasten to bring legislation within the boundaries prescribed by the Constitution, and to return to the ancient landmarks established by our fathers for the guidance of succeeding generations.

"The Constitution which at any time exists, until changed by an explicit and authentic act of the whole people, is sacredly obligatory upon all. . . . . If, in the opinion of the people, the distribution or modification of the constitutional powers be, in any particular, wrong, let it be corrected by an amendment in the way in which the Constitution designates, but let there be no change by usurpation; for . . . . it is the customary weapon by which free governments are destroyed." Washington spoke these words to his countrymen, when, followed by their love and gratitude, he voluntarily retired from the cares of public life.

"To keep in all things within the pale of our constitutional powers, and cherish the federal Union as the only rock of safety," were prescribed by Jefferson as rules of action to endear to his "countrymen the true principles of their Constitution, and promote a union of sentiment and action equally auspicious to their happiness and safety."

Jackson held that the action of the general government should always be strictly confined to the sphere of its appropriate duties, and justly and forcibly urged that our government is not to be maintained nor our Union preserved "by invasions of the rights and powers of the several states. In thus attempting to make our general government strong, we make it weak. Its true strength consists in leaving individuals and states as much as possible to themselves; in making itself felt, not in its power, but in its beneficence; not in its control, but in its protection; not in binding the states more closely to the center, but leaving each to move unobstructed in its proper constitutional orbit."

These are the teachings of men whose deeds and services have made them illustrious, and who, long since withdrawn from the scenes of life, have left to their country the rich legacy of their example, their wisdom, and their patriotism. Drawing fresh inspiration from their lessons, let us emulate them in love of country and respect for the Constitution and the laws. . . .

A GOVERNOR REBUKES A PRESIDENT

1894

John Peter Altgeld, Governor of Illinois, bristled with anger. He had just learned that Grover Cleveland, President of the United States and, like himself, a stalwart Democrat, had sent federal troops into Chicago to maintain order during the course of the railroad strike then in progress. This the President had done without an appeal from the state authorities, without consulting them, without even a formal notice of his intention. Altgeld knew nothing of Cleveland's decision until word came, on the Fourth of July, that soldiers from Fort Sheridan were pitching their tents on the lake front.

The situation in Chicago did give cause for apprehension. Toward the end of June a new union of railroad workers, the American Railway Union, had thrown its support to the workers of the Pullman Palace Car Company, who had been on strike since early May. The railroad men refused to handle Pullman cars, and moved no trains in which they were included. The railroads, not unwilling to come to grips with the union, began hauling Pullmans on trains that would not have carried them normally. Thus, what started as a boycott to help the striking employees of a single company quickly turned into a general railroad strike.

Rioting and the destruction of property would come in Chicago, if anywhere. Then as now, the city was the railroad center of the nation. The Pullman Company stood near its southern limits. There was, in fact, some disorder in the last days of June, but the local authorities were confident in their ability to keep the peace, and did not even ask the Governor for aid from the state militia.

But in Washington, Grover Cleveland and Richard Olney, his Attorney General, saw a greater menace than was apparent to those on the ground. Given a legal justification by an injunction which the United States court directed against the strikers, and by an appeal from federal officials in Chicago, the President sent in the Regulars.

Altgeld shot a sharp telegram to the White House. The State of Illinois, he informed the President, "is not only able to take care of itself, but it stands ready to furnish the federal government any assistance it may need elsewhere." No one in Cook County, either official or private citizen, had even intimated that the presence of troops was necessary. To be sure, the railroads were paralyzed in many places, but the Governor contended that the stoppages resulted from the refusal of men to operate the trains rather than from violence. Then he turned to the constitutional argument that lifted his communication to a high level:

"I repeat that you have been imposed upon in this matter, but even if by a forced construction it were held that the conditions here came within the letter of the statute, then I submit that local self-government is a fundamental principle of our Constitution. Each community shall govern itself so long as it can and is ready and able to enforce the law, and it is in harmony with this fundamental principle that the statute authorizing the President to send troops into states must be construed; especially is this so in matters relating to the exercise of the police power and the preservation of law and order.

"To absolutely ignore a local government in matters of this kind, when the local government is ready to furnish assistance needed, and is amply able to enforce the law, not only insults the people of this state by imputing to them an inability to govern themselves, or an unwillingness to enforce the law, but is in violation of a basic principle of our institutions. The question of federal supremacy is in no way involved. No one disputes it for a moment, but, under our Constitution, federal supremacy and local self-government must go hand in hand, and to ignore the latter is to do violence to the Constitution."

The Governor concluded by protesting, "with all due deference, against this uncalled-for reflection upon our people," and by asking that the federal troops be withdrawn immediately.

Altgeld's telegram was dated July 5. Cleveland replied on the same date. His answer was curt: Federal troops had been sent to Chicago "in strict accordance with the Constitution and laws of the United States." The post-office authorities had demanded that obstruction of the mails be removed, and judicial officers of the United States had represented that the process of the federal courts could not be executed through ordinary means. Under the circumstances, the presence of federal troops was both proper and necessary.

The Illinois Governor stood his ground. The following day he sent a second and final telegram to the President, stating the case for local self-government as trenchantly as it has ever been presented. Cleveland's reply, dated July 6, consisted of one sentence: "While I am still persuaded that I have neither transcended my authority nor duty in the emergency that confronts us, it seems to me that in this hour of danger and public distress, discussion may well give way to active efforts on the part of all in authority to restore obedience to law and to protect life and property."

The fact that large-scale violence did break out in Chicago soon after Altgeld registered his second protest seemed at the time to justify Cleveland's action, and Altgeld's position was not strengthened by the resentment he had incurred, a year earlier, by pardoning the surviving Haymarket anarchists. Contemporaries condemned the Illinois Governor as a radical and doctrinaire. Many present-day scholars see him as a stanch defender of the long-cherished right of local self-government.

Altgeld's Protest to Cleveland

July 6, 1894

EXECUTIVE OFFICE, STATE OF ILLINOIS
Springfield, Ill., July 6, 1894

Hon. Grover Cleveland, President of the United States, SIR:—Your answer to my protest involves some startling conclusions and ignores and evades the question at issue—that is, that the principle of local self-government is just as fundamental in our institutions as is that of federal supremacy.

First—You calmly assume that the Executive has the legal right to order federal troops into any community of the United States, in the first instance, whenever there is the slightest disturbance, and that he can do this without any regard to the question as to whether that community is able to and ready to enforce the law itself. Inasmuch as the Executive is the sole judge of the question as to whether any disturbance exists or not in any part of the country, this assumption means that the Executive can send federal troops into any community in the United States at his pleasure, and keep them there as long as he chooses.

If this is the law, then the principle of self-government either never did exist in this country or else has been destroyed, for no community can be said to possess local self-government if the Executive can, at his pleasure, send military forces to patrol its streets under pretense of enforcing some law. The kind of local self-government that could exist under these circumstances can be found in any of the monarchies of Europe, and it is not in harmony with the spirit of our institutions.

Second–It is also a fundamental principle in our government that except in times of war the military shall be subordinate to the civil authority. In harmony with this provision, the state troops are ordered out to act under and with the civil authorities. The troops you have ordered to Chicago are not under civil authorities, and are in no way responsible to them for their conduct. They are not even acting under the United States Marshal or any federal officer of the state, but are acting directly under military orders issued from military headquarters at Washington; and in so far as these troops act at all, it is military government.

Third–The statute authorizing federal troops to be sent into states in certain cases contemplates that the state troops shall be taken first. This provision has been ignored, and it is assumed that the Executive is not bound by it. Federal interference with industrial disturbances in the various states is certainly a new departure, and it opens up so large a field that it will require a very little stretch of authority to absorb to itself all the details of local government.

Fourth–You say that troops were ordered into Illinois upon the demand of the Post Office Department, and upon representations of the judicial officers of the United States that process of the courts could not be served, and upon proof that conspiracies existed. We will not discuss the facts, but look for a moment at the principle involved in your statement.

All of these officers are appointed by the Executive. Most of them can be removed by him at will. They are not only obliged to do his bidding, but they are in fact a part of the Executive. If several of them can apply for troops, one alone can; so that under the law, as you assume it to be, an Executive, through any one of his appointees, can apply to himself to have the military sent into any city or number of cities, and base his application on such representations as he sees fit to make. In fact, it will be immaterial whether he makes any showing or not, for the Executive is the sole judge, and nobody else has any right to interfere or even inquire about it.

Then the Executive can pass on his own application, his will being the sole guide—he can hold the application to be sufficient, and order troops to as many places as he wishes and put them in command of anyone he chooses, and have them act, not under the civil officers, either federal or state, but directly under military orders from Washington, and there is not in the Constitution or laws, whether written or unwritten, any limitation or restraint upon his power. His judgment—that is, his will—is the sole guide; and it being purely a matter of discretion, his decision can never be examined or questioned.

This assumption as to the power of the Executive is certainly new, and I respectfully submit that it is not the law of the land. The jurists have told us that this is a government of law, and not a government by the caprice of an individual; and further, instead of being autocratic, it is a government of limited power. Yet the autocrat of Russia could certainly not possess, or claim to possess, greater power than is possessed by the Executive of the United States, if your assumption is correct.

Fifth—The Executive has the command not only of the regular forces of all the United States, but of the military forces of all the states, and can order them to any place he sees fit; and as there are always more or less local disturbances over the country, it will be an easy matter under your construction of the law for an ambitious Executive to order out the military forces of all of the states, and establish at once a military government. The only chance of failure in such a movement could come from rebellion, and with such a vast military power at command this could readily be crushed, for, as a rule, soldiers will obey orders.

As for the situation in Illinois, that is of no consequence now compared with the far-reaching principle involved. True, according to my advices, federal troops have now been on duty for over two days, and although the men were brave and the officers valiant and able, yet their very presence proved to be an irritant because it aroused the indignation of a large class of people who, while upholding law and order, had been taught to believe in local self-government, and therefore resented what they regarded as unwarranted interference.

Inasmuch as the federal troops can do nothing but what the state troops can do there, and believing that the state is amply able to take care of the situation and to enforce the law, and believing that the ordering out of the federal troops was unwarranted, I again ask their withdrawal.

JOHN P. ALTGELD

McKINLEY OFFERS OPPORTUNITY

1900

No one would rank William McKinley among our very great Presidents. A devout Republican, he carried his loyalty to party so far that he allowed himself and his country to be led into a war which he abhorred, and afterward, into a colonial policy which ran counter to his instincts of right and wrong.

But McKinley subscribed to the ethics of Christianity as sincerely as he held to the doctrines of the Republican party. He was also a kindly gentleman, and with all his conservatism, a democrat at heart. With his approval, the United States had taken Puerto Rico and the Philippines, but that was no reason, in his opinion, for holding the peoples of those islands in permanent subjection. They might be of different color, different race, and different religion from the majority of the inhabitants of the United States, but they were still entitled to the benefits of democratic government. Therefore, when McKinley came to define the duties of the Philippine

Commission, charged with inaugurating civil government in the islands, he readily adopted as his own the wise and progressive instructions drafted by his Secretary of War, Elihu Root—instructions notable for their liberal spirit and for their recognition of the principle that the people of American dependencies were entitled to a life as full and unfettered as the American people themselves.

Although Philippine independence was nowhere promised, it was a natural corollary of the McKinley-Root instructions. As time passed, many American statesmen came to this conclusion. In pursuance of a succession of laws enacted by the Congress of the United States, the Philippine Islands became an independent nation on July 4, 1946. No one can quarrel, except on the ground of understatement, with the assertion of an American historian: "The role of the United States in the Philippines has not been without honor."

Instructions to the Philippine Commission

April 7, 1900

The commissioners named will meet and act as a board, and the Hon. William H. Taft is designated as president of the board. It is probable that the transfer of authority from military commanders to civil officers will be gradual and will occupy a considerable period. Its successful accomplishment and the maintenance of peace and order in the meantime will require the most perfect co-operation between the civil and military authorities in the island, and both should be directed during the transition period by the same executive department. The commission will therefore report to the Secretary of War, and all their action will be subject to your approval and control.

You will instruct the commission to proceed to the city of Manila, where they will make their principal office, and to communicate with the military governor of the Philippine Islands, whom you will at the same time direct to render to them every assistance within his power in the performance of their duties. Without hampering them by too specific instructions, they should in general be enjoined, after making themselves familiar with the conditions and needs of the country, to devote their attention in the first instance to the establishment of municipal governments in which the natives of the islands, both in the cities and in the rural communities, shall be afforded the opportunity to manage their own local affairs to the fullest extent of which they are capable and subject to the least degree of supervision and control which a careful study of their capacities and observation of the workings of native control show to be consistent with the maintenance of law, order, and loyalty.

The next subject in order of importance should be the organization of government in the larger administrative divisions corresponding to counties, departments, or provinces, in which the common interests of many or several municipalities falling within the same tribal lines, or the same natural geographical limits, may best be subserved by a common administration. Whenever the commission is of the opinion that the condition of affairs in the islands is such that the central administration may safely be transferred from military to civil control, they will report that conclusion to you with their recommendations as to the form of central government to be established for the purpose of taking over the control. . . .

In the distribution of powers among the governments organized by the commission, the presumption is always to be in favor of the smaller subdivision, so that all the powers which can properly be exercised by the municipal government shall be vested in that government, and all the powers of a more general character which can be exercised by the departmental government shall be vested in that government; and so that in the governmental system, which is the result of the process, the central government of the islands, following the example of the distribution of the powers between the states and the national government of the United States, shall have no direct administration except of matters of purely general concern, and shall have only such supervision and control over local governments as may be necessary to secure and enforce faithful and efficient administration by local officers.

The many different degrees of civilization and varieties of custom and capacity among the people of the different islands preclude very definite instruction as to the part which the people shall take in the selection of their own officers; but these general rules are to be observed: That in all cases the municipal officers, who administer the local affairs of the people, are to be selected by the people; and that wherever officers of more extended jurisdiction are to be selected in any way, natives of the islands are to be preferred, and if they can be found competent and willing to perform the duties, they are to receive the offices in preference to any others.

It will be necessary to fill some offices for the present with Americans, which after a time may well be filled by natives of the islands. As soon as practicable a system for ascertaining the merit and fitness of candidates for civil office should be put in force. An indispensable qualification for all offices and positions of trust and authority in the islands must be absolute and unconditional loyalty to the United States; and absolute and unhampered authority and power to remove and punish any officer deviating from that standard must at all times be retained in the hands of the central authority of the islands.

In all the forms of government and administrative provisions which they are authorized to prescribe, the commission should bear in mind that the government which they are establishing is designed not for our satisfaction, or for the expression of our theoretical views, but for the happiness, peace, and prosperity of the people of the Philippine Islands; and the measures adopted should be made to conform to their customs, their habits, and even their prejudices, to the fullest extent consistent with the accomplishment of the indispensable requisites of just and effective government.

At the same time the commission should bear in mind, and the people of the islands should be made plainly to understand, that there are certain great principles of government which have been made the basis of our governmental system, which we deem essential to the rule of law and the maintenance of individual freedom, and of which they have, unfortunately, been denied the experience possessed by us; that there are also certain practical rules of government which we have found to be essential to the preservation of these great principles of liberty and law, and that these principles and these rules of government must be established and maintained in their islands for the sake of their liberty and happiness, however much they may conflict with the customs or laws of procedure with which they are familiar.

It is evident that the most enlightened thought of the Philippine Islands fully appreciates the importance of these principles and rules, and they will inevitably within a short time command universal assent. Upon every division and branch of the government of the Philippines, therefore, must be imposed these inviolable rules:

That no person shall be deprived of life, liberty, or property without due process of law; that private property shall not be taken for public use without just compensation; that in all criminal prosecutions the accused shall enjoy the right to a speedy and public trial, to be informed of the nature and cause of the accusation, to be confronted with the witnesses against him, to have compulsory process for obtaining witnesses in his favor, and to have the assistance of counsel for his defense; that excessive bail shall not be required, nor excessive fines imposed, nor cruel and unusual punishment inflicted; that no person shall be put twice in jeopardy for the same offense, or be compelled in any criminal case to be a witness against himself; that the right to be secure against unreasonable searches and seizures shall not be violated; that neither slavery nor involun-

tary servitude shall exist except as a punishment for crime; that no bill of attainder or ex post facto law shall be passed; that no law shall be passed abridging the freedom of speech or of the press, or the rights of the people to peaceably assemble and petition the government for a redress of grievances; that no law shall be made respecting an establishment of religion, or prohibiting the free exercise thereof, and that the free exercise and enjoyment of religious profession and worship without discrimination or preference shall forever be allowed. . . . .

It will be the duty of the commission to promote and extend and, as they find occasion, to improve the system of education already inaugurated by the military authorities. In doing this, they should regard as of first importance the extension of a system of primary education which shall be free to all, and which shall tend to fit the people for the duties of citizenship and for the ordinary avocations of a civilized community. This instruction should be given in the first instance in every part of the islands in the language of the people. In view of the great number of languages spoken by the different tribes, it is especially important to the prosperity of the islands that a common medium of communication may be established, and it is obviously desirable that this medium should be the English language. Especial attention should be at once given to affording full opportunity to all the people of the islands to acquire the use of the English language.

It may be well that the main changes which should be made in the system of taxation and in the body of the laws under which the people are governed, except such changes as have already been made by the military government, should be relegated to the civil government which is to be established under the auspices of the commission. It will, however, be the duty of the commission to inquire diligently as to whether there are any further changes which ought not to be delayed; and if so, they are authorized to make such changes, subject to your approval. In doing so, they are to bear in mind that taxes which tend to penalize or repress industry and enterprise are to be avoided; that provisions for taxation shoud be simple, so that they may be understood by the people; that they should affect the fewest practicable subjects of taxation which will serve for the general distribution of the burden.

The main body of the laws which regulate the rights and obligations of the people should be maintained with as little interference as possible. Changes made should be mainly in procedure; and in the criminal laws, to secure speedy and impartial trials, and at the same time effective administration and respect for individual rights. In dealing with the uncivilized tribes of the islands, the commission should adopt the same course followed by Congress in permitting the tribes of our North American Indians to maintain their tribal organization and government, and under which many of those tribes are now living in peace and contentment, surrounded by a civilization to which they are unable or unwilling to conform. Such tribal governments should, however, be subjected to wise and firm regulation, and, without undue or petty interference, constant and active effort should be exercised to prevent barbarous practices and introduce civilized customs.

Upon all officers and employees of the United States, both civil and military, should be impressed a sense of the duty to observe not merely the material but the personal and social rights of the people of the islands, and to treat them with the same courtesy and respect for their personal dignity which the people of the United States are accustomed to require from each other.

The articles of capitulation of the city of Manila on the thirteenth of August, 1898, concluded with these words:

"This city, its inhabitants, its churches and religious worship, its educational establishments, and its private property of all descriptions, are placed under the special safeguard of the faith and honor of the American Army."

I believe that this pledge has been faithfully kept. As high and sacred an obligation rests upon the government of the United States to give protection for property and life, civil and religious freedom, and wise, firm, and unselfish guidance in the paths of peace and prosperity to all the people of the Philippine Islands. I charge this commission to labor for the full performance of this obligation, which concerns the honor and conscience of their country, in the firm hope that through their labors all the inhabitants of the Philippine Islands may come to look back with gratitude to the day when God gave victory to American arms at Manila and set their land under the sovereignty and the protection of the people of the United States.

WILSON OUTLINES THE NEW FREEDOM

1913

On the fifth of November, 1912, the incredible came to pass: a scholar and a Democrat was elected President of the United States.

Three years earlier Woodrow Wilson had looked forward to a period of retirement which he could devote to study and writing. Suddenly a new field opened. Millions of Americans were becoming increasingly dissatisfied with the rule of the Republican party. The times, they believed, called for a change of course—for a public policy that would curb the power of big business and restore to the plain citizen the independence, both economic and political, which he had lost. Democrats, scenting victory, looked for new faces. In Wilson they saw a man who could turn the Republicans out of office in his own state of New Jersey. President of Princeton, a confirmed liberal, an eloquent speaker, he had led a bitter fight against class distinctions in the university which he headed; in a political campaign he could be presented as the opponent of privilege and the champion of the people. Party managers accepted him as the Democratic candidate for governor. The popular trend, and his own unsuspected abilities as a campaigner, swept him into office.

In two years Wilson pushed through reform measures so successfully that he became a national figure. After the leading contenders for the Democratic presidential nomination in 1912 had eliminated each other, he emerged as the candidate. Voters soon heard talk that reminded the oldsters of Lincoln.

"The reason that America was set up," Wilson declared, "was that she might be different from all the nations of the world in this: that the strong could not prevent the weak from entering the race. America stands for opportunity. America stands for a free field and no favor. America stands for a government responsive to the interests of all. And until America recovers those ideals in practice, she will not have the right to hold her head high again amidst the nations as she used to hold it."

Aided by a fatal split in the Republican party, Wilson won the election.

Now, on the fourth of March, 1913, he would take the oath of office as the first Democratic President in sixteen years. The ceremonies followed the traditional pattern—a parade along Pennsylvania Avenue with the President and President-elect riding in an open carriage, a vast audience in the plaza of the Capitol, the justices of the Supreme Court, members of Congress, and the diplomatic corps seated on the platform. The crowd roared its greeting as Taft and Wilson appeared—the one huge of frame and jovial of mien, the other spare and quick of movement, with his scholar's face giving plain evidence of the solemnity of the hour. Chief Justice White, venerable ex-Confederate soldier, administered the oath, and the new President, in a voice strong and clear but devoid of rhetorical effort, read an inaugural address notable for brevity, depth of feeling, and felicity of expression.

Wilson's First Inaugural Address

March 4, 1913

My Fellow-Citizens: There has been a change of government. It began two years ago, when the House of Representatives became Democratic by a decisive majority. It has now been completed. The Senate about to assemble will also be Democratic. The offices of President and Vice-President have been put into the hands of Democrats. What does the change mean? That is the question that is uppermost in our minds today. That is the question I am going to try to answer, in order, if I may, to interpret the occasion.

It means much more than the mere success of a party. The success of a party means little except when the nation is using that party for a large and definite purpose. No one can mistake the purpose for which the nation now seeks to use the Democratic party. It seeks to use it to interpret a change in its own plans and point of view. Some old things with which we had grown familiar, and which had begun to creep into the very habit of our thought and of our lives, have altered their aspect as we have latterly looked critically upon them, with fresh, awakened eyes; have dropped their disguises and shown themselves alien and sinister. Some new things, as we look frankly upon them, willing to comprehend their real character, have come to assume the aspect of things long believed in and familiar—stuff of our own convictions. We have been refreshed by a new insight into our own life.

We see that in many things that life is very great. It is incomparably great in its material aspects, in its body of wealth, in the diversity and sweep of its energy, in the industries which have been conceived and built up by the genius of individual men and the limitless enterprise of groups of men. It is great, also, very great, in its moral force.

Nowhere else in the world have noble men and women exhibited in more striking forms the beauty and the energy of sympathy and helpfulness and counsel in their efforts to rectify wrong, alleviate suffering, and set the weak in the way of strength and hope. We have built up, moreover, a great system of government, which has stood through a long age as in many respects a model for those who seek to set liberty upon foundations that will endure against fortuitous change, against storm and accident. Our life contains every great thing, and contains it in rich abundance.

But the evil has come with the good, and much fine gold has been corroded. With riches has come inexcusable waste. We have squandered a great part of what we might have used, and have not stopped to conserve the exceeding bounty of nature without which our genius for enterprise would have been worthless and impotent—scorning to be careful, shamefully prodigal as well as admirably efficient.

We have been proud of our industrial achievements, but we have not hitherto stopped thoughtfully enough to count the human cost, the cost of lives snuffed out, of energies overtaxed and broken, the fearful physical and spiritual cost to the men and women and children upon whom the dead weight and burden of it all has fallen pitilessly the years through. The groans and agony of it all had not yet reached our ears—the solemn, moving undertone of our life, coming up out of the mines and factories and out of every home where the struggle had its intimate and familiar seat. With the great government went many deep secret things which we too long delayed to look into and scrutinize with candid, fearless eyes. The great government we loved has too often been made use of for private and selfish purposes, and those who used it had forgotten the people.

At last a vision has been vouchsafed us of our life as a whole. We see the bad with the good, the debased and decadent with the sound and vital. With this vision we approach new affairs. Our duty is to cleanse, to reconsider, to restore, to correct the evil without impairing the good, to purify and humanize every process of our common life without weakening or sentimentalizing it.

There has been something crude and heartless and unfeeling in our haste to succeed and be great. Our thought has been, "Let every man look out for himself, let every generation look out for

itself," while we reared giant machinery which made it impossible that any but those who stood at the levers of control should have a chance to look out for themselves. We had not forgotten our morals. We remembered well enough that we had set up a policy which was meant to serve the humblest as well as the most powerful, with an eye single to the standards of justice and fair play, and remembered it with pride. But we were very heedless and in a hurry to be great.

We have come now to the sober second thought. The scales of

heedlessness have fallen from our eyes. We have made up our minds to square every process of our national life again with the standards we so proudly set up at the beginning and have always carried at our hearts. Our work is a work of restoration.

We have itemized with some degree of particularity the things that ought to be altered and here are some of the chief items: A tariff which cuts us off from our proper part in the commerce of the world, violates the just principles of taxation, and makes the government a facile instrument in the hands of private interests; a banking and currency system based upon the necessity of the government to sell its bonds fifty years ago and perfectly adapted to concentrating cash and restricting credits; an industrial system which, take it on all its sides, financial as well as administrative, holds capital in leading strings, restricts the liberties and limits the opportunities of labor, and exploits without renewing or conserving the natural resources of the country; a body of agricultural activities never yet given the efficiency of great business undertakings or served as it should be through the instrumentality of science taken directly to the farm, or afforded the facilities of credit best suited to its practical needs; water-courses undeveloped, waste places unreclaimed, forests untended, fast disappearing without plan or prospect of renewal, unregarded waste heaps at every mine. We have studied as perhaps no other nation has the most effective means of production, but we have not studied cost or economy as we should, either as organizers of industry, as statesmen, or as individuals.

Nor have we studied and perfected the means by which government may be put at the service of humanity—in safeguarding the health of the nation, the health of its men and its women and its children, as well as their rights in the struggle for existence.

This is no sentimental duty. The firm basis of government is justice, not pity. These are matters of justice. There can be no equality or opportunity—the first essential of justice in the body politic—if men and women and children be not shielded in their lives, their very vitality, from the consequences of great industrial and social processes which they cannot alter, control, or singly cope with. Society must see to it that it does not itself crush or weaken or damage its own constituent parts. The first duty of law is to keep sound the society it serves. Sanitary laws, pure-food laws, and laws determining conditions of labor which individuals are powerless to determine for themselves are intimate parts of the very business of justice and legal efficiency.

These are some of the things we ought to do, and not leave the others undone, the old-fashioned, never-to-be-neglected, fundamental safeguarding of property and of individual right. This is the high enterprise of the new day: To lift everything that concerns our life as a nation to the light that shines from the hearthfire of every man's conscience and vision of the right. It is inconceivable that we should do this as partisans; it is inconceivable we should do it in ignorance of the facts as they are, or in blind haste. We shall restore, not destroy. We shall deal with our economic system as it is and as it may be modified, not as it might be if we had a clean sheet of paper to write upon; and step by step we shall make it what it should be, in the spirit of those who question their own wisdom and seek counsel and knowledge, not shallow self-satisfaction or the excitement of excursions whither they cannot tell. Justice, and only justice, shall always be our motto.

And yet it will be no cool process of mere science. The nation has been deeply stirred, stirred by a solemn passion, stirred by the knowledge of wrong, of ideals lost, of government too often debauched and made an instrument of evil. The feelings with which we face this new age of right and opportunity sweep across our heartstrings like some air out of God's own presence, where justice and mercy are reconciled and the judge and the brother are one. We know our task to be no mere task of politics, but a task which shall search us through and through, whether we be able to understand our time and the need of our people, whether we be indeed their spokesmen and interpreters, whether we have the pure heart to comprehend and the rectified will to choose our high course of action.

This is not a day of triumph; it is a day of dedication. Here muster, not the forces of party, but the forces of humanity. Men's hearts wait upon us; men's lives hang in the balance; men's hopes call upon us to say what we will do. Who shall live up to the great trust? Who dares fail to try? I summon all honest men, all patriotic, all forward-looking men, to my side. God helping me, I will not fail them, if they will but counsel and sustain me!

WILSON: PEACE WITHOUT VICTORY

1917

As the year 1916 came to its end, Woodrow Wilson found the responsibilities of his office almost unendurable. With the indecisive Battle of the Somme, the First World War, now in its third year, had reached a stalemate. Both Allied and Central Powers gave signs of turning to extreme measures in an effort to break the deadlock —Great Britain and her allies by applying heavy economic and propagandist pressures to the United States in an effort to bring her into the conflict on their side, Germany by resorting to the unrestricted submarine warfare that she had agreed to refrain from. Wilson was determined that the United States should remain neutral —he had just been reelected on the strength of the claim that he had kept the country out of war—but tensions were mounting so rapidly that a neutral position could not be maintained much longer.

The President saw that the only hope of keeping the United States out of the world conflict lay in bringing about an early peace. For some time Germany had indicated that she might be willing to negotiate. He had no assurances from Great Britain and France, but perhaps their attitude was not as inflexible as it seemed to be. The effort, in any event, was worth making. On December 18, 1916, Wilson sent a note to all the nations at war, asking them to state their war aims and suggesting that he would be willing to take the lead in bringing the fighting to an end.

His innate fairness led him to assert, in the note, "that the objects which the statesmen of the belligerents on both sides have in mind in this war are virtually the same, as stated in general terms to their own people and to the world." This statement—a simple matter of fact—aroused deep resentment in the Allied Nations and on the part of millions of Americans who had been shocked by Germany's violation of Belgian neutrality, and by her ruthless sinking of the *Lusitania* and other merchant ships. From all sides critics denounced the President.

Dismayed by the immediate reaction to his note, harassed by anxiety, still worn by the strenuous campaign of the summer and fall, Wilson welcomed the transitory relief that the Christmas season held out to him. On the afternoon of the day before Christmas, a pleasant Sunday, he and Mrs. Wilson, with friends and relatives, took part in a community gathering on the steps of the Treasury Building and joined in singing carols. Christmas in the White House resembled Christmas in millions of homes over the country—a tree surrounded by gifts for grandchildren and other young relatives, a bountiful dinner, and in the afternoon, games and talk. Three days later the President celebrated his sixtieth birthday.

Then came the return to the world and its almost intolerable cares. The German reply to his note had arrived on December 27. The Central Powers, the note made clear, were no longer interested in mediation. Three days later a note from the Allies shattered whatever hopes of peace the President may still have held. Germany's position, the Allies contended, lacked both "sincerity" and "import," and was intended only to deceive neutral opinion and prepare the way for a new series of crimes against international law.

His good offices spurned, the President decided to appeal to a court in which he had never lost confidence—the court composed of the people of the world. He could not believe that the masses wanted the war to continue. To them he would take his case, proposing his own terms for the cessation of hostilities and holding out the promise of a "League for Peace" which would assure tranquillity and order for all time. He began to cover scraps of paper with shorthand notes before the end of the Christmas season; as the new year opened, he shaped his ideas into a coherent whole. On January 22, 1917, he appeared unexpectedly before the Senate to plead, in his own clear voice, for "peace without victory."

Wilson's Address to the Senate

January 22, 1917

Gentlemen of the Senate: On the eighteenth of December last I addressed an identic note to the governments of the nations now at war, rquesting them to state, more definitely than they had yet been stated by either group of belligerents, the terms upon which they would deem it possible to make peace. I spoke on behalf of humanity and of the rights of all neutral nations like our own, many of whose most vital interests the war puts in constant jeopardy. The Central Powers united in a reply which stated merely that they were ready to meet their antagonists in conference to discuss terms of peace. The Entente Powers have replied much more definitely and have stated, in general terms, indeed, but with sufficient definiteness to imply details, the arrangements, guarantees, and acts of reparation which they deem to be the indispensable conditions of a satisfactory settlement.

We are that much nearer a definite discussion of the peace which shall end the present war. We are that much nearer the discussion of the international concert which must thereafter hold the world at peace. In every discussion of the peace that must end this war, it is taken for granted that that peace must be followed by some definite concert of power which will make it virtually impossible that any such catastrophe should ever overwhelm us again. Every lover of mankind, every sane and thoughtful man must take that for granted.

I have sought this opportunity to address you because I thought that I owed it to you, as the counsel associated with me in the final determination of our international obligations, to disclose to you without reserve the thought and purpose that have been taking form in my mind in regard to the duty of our government in the days to come when it will be necessary to lay afresh, and upon a new plan, the foundations of peace among the nations.

It is inconceivable that the people of the United States should play no part in that great enterprise. To take part in such a service will be the opportunity for which they have sought to prepare themselves by the very principles and purposes of their polity and the approved practices of their government ever since the days when they set up a new nation in the high and honorable hope that it might, in all that it was and did, show mankind the way to liberty. They cannot in honor withhold the service to which they are now about to be challenged. They do not wish to withhold it. But they owe it to themselves and to the other nations of the world to state the conditions under which they will feel free to render it.

That service is nothing less than this, to add their authority and their power to the authority and force of other nations to guarantee peace and justice throughout the world. Such a settlement cannot now be long postponed. It is right that before it comes, this government should frankly formulate the conditions upon which it would feel justified in asking our people to approve its formal and solemn adherence to a League for Peace. I am here to attempt to state those conditions.

The present war must first be ended; but we owe it to candor, and to a just regard for the opinion of mankind, to say that, so far as our participation in guarantees of future peace is concerned, it makes a great deal of difference in what way and upon what terms it is ended. The treaties and agreements which bring it to an end must embody terms which will create a peace that is worth guaranteeing and preserving, a peace that will win the approval of mankind, not merely a peace that will serve the several interests and immediate aims of the nations engaged. We shall have no voice in determining what those terms shall be, but we shall, I feel sure, have a voice in determining whether they shall be made lasting or not by the guarantees of a universal covenant; and our judgment upon what is fundamental and essential as a condition precedent to permanency should be spoken now, not afterward when it may be too late.

No covenant of co-operative peace that does not include the peoples of the New World can suffice to keep the future safe against war; and yet there is only one sort of peace that the peoples of America could join in guaranteeing. The elements of that peace must be elements that engage the confidence and satisfy the principles of the American governments, elements consistent with their political faith and with the practical convictions which the peoples of America have once for all embraced and undertaken to defend.

I do not mean to say that any American government would throw any obstacle in the way of any terms of peace the governments now at war might agree upon, or seek to upset them when made, whatever they might be. I only take it for granted that mere terms of peace between the belligerents will not satisfy even the belligerents themselves. Mere agreements may not make peace secure. It will be absolutely necessary that a force be created as a guarantor of the permanency of the settlement so much greater than the force of any nation now engaged or any alliance hitherto formed or projected that no nation, no probable combination of nations, could face or withstand it. If the peace presently to be made is to endure, it must be a peace made secure by the organized major force of mankind.

The terms of the immediate peace agreed upon will determine whether it is a peace for which such a guarantee can be secured. The question upon which the whole future peace and policy of the world depends is this: Is the present war a struggle for a just and secure peace, or only for a new balance of power? If it be only a struggle for a new balance of power, who will guarantee, who can guarantee the stable equilibrium of the new arrangement? Only a tranquil Europe can be a stable Europe. There must be, not a balance of power, but a community of power; not organized rivalries, but an organized common peace.

Fortunately we have received very explicit assurances on this point. The statesmen of both of the groups of nations now arrayed against one another have said, in terms that could not be misinterpreted, that it was no part of the purpose they had in mind to crush their antagonists. But the implications of these assurances may not be equally clear to all—may not be the same on both sides of the water. I think it will be serviceable if I attempt to set forth what we understand them to be.

They imply, first of all, that it must be a peace without victory. It is not pleasant to say this. I beg that I may be permitted to put my own interpretation upon it and that it may be understood that no other interpretation was in my thought. I am seeking only to face realities and to face them without soft concealments. Victory would mean peace forced upon the loser, a victor's terms imposed upon the vanquished. It would be accepted in humiliation, under duress, at an intolerable sacrifice, and would leave a sting, a resentment, a bitter memory upon which terms of peace

would rest, not permanently, but only as upon quicksand. Only a peace between equals can last: only a peace the very principle of which is equality and a common participation in common benefit. The right state of mind, the right feeling between nations, is as necessary for a lasting peace as is the just settlement of vexed questions of territory, or of racial and national allegiance.

The equality of nations upon which peace must be founded if it is to last must be an equality of rights; the guarantees exchanged must neither recognize nor imply a difference between big nations and small, between those that are powerful and those that are weak. Right must be based upon the common strength, not upon the individual strength, of the nations upon whose concert peace will depend. Equality of territory or of resources there of course cannot be; nor any other sort of equality not gained in the ordinary peaceful and legitimate development of the peoples themselves. But no one asks or expects anything more than an equality of rights. Mankind is looking now for freedom of life, not for equipoises of power.

And there is a deeper thing involved than even equality of right among organized nations. No peace can last, or ought to last, which does not recognize and accept the principle that governments derive all their just powers from the consent of the governed, and that no right anywhere exists to hand peoples about from sovereignty to sovereignty as if they were property. I take it for granted, for instance, if I may venture upon a single example, that statesmen everywhere are agreed that there should be a united, independent, and autonomous Poland; and that henceforth inviolable security of life, of worship, and of industrial and social development should be guaranteed to all peoples who have lived hitherto under the power of governments devoted to a faith and purpose hostile to their own.

I speak of this, not because of any desire to exalt an abstract political principle which has always been held very dear by those who have sought to build up liberty in America, but for the same reason that I have spoken of the other conditions of peace which seem to me clearly indispensable—because I wish frankly to uncover realities. Any peace which does not recognize and accept this principle will inevitably be upset. It will not rest upon the affections or the convictions of mankind. The ferment of spirit of whole populations will fight subtly and constantly against it, and all the world will sympathize. The world can be at peace only if its life is stable, and there can be no stability where the will is in rebellion, where there is not tranquillity of spirit and a sense of justice, of freedom, and of right.

So far as practicable, moveover, every great people now struggling toward a full development of its resources and of its powers should be assured a direct outlet to the great highways of the sea. Where this cannot be done by the cession of territory, it can no doubt be done by the neutralization of direct rights of way under the general guarantee which will assure the peace itself. With a right comity of arrangement, no nation need be shut away from free access to the open paths of the world's commerce.

And the paths of the sea must alike in law and in fact be free. The freedom of the seas is the *sine qua non* of peace, equality, and co-operation. No doubt a somewhat radical reconsideration of many of the rules of international practice hitherto thought to be established may be necessary in order to make the seas indeed free and common in practically all circumstances for the use of mankind; but the motive for such changes is convincing and compelling. There can be no trust or intimacy between the peoples of the world without them. The free, constant, unthreatened intercourse of nations is an essential part of the process of peace and of development. It need not be difficult either to define or to secure the freedom of the seas if the governments of the world sincerely desire to come to an agreement concerning it.

It is a problem closely connected with the limitation of naval armaments and the co-operation of the navies of the world in keeping the seas at once free and safe. And the question of limiting naval armaments opens the wider and perhaps more difficult question of the limitation of armies and of all programs of military preparation. Difficult and delicate as these questions are, they must be faced with the utmost candor and decided in a spirit of real accommodation if peace is to come with healing in its wings, and come to stay.

Peace cannot be had without concession and sacrifice. There can be no sense of safety and equality among the nations if great preponderating armaments are henceforth to continue here and there to be built up and maintained. The statesmen of the world must plan for peace, and nations must adjust and accommodate their policy to it as they have planned for war and made ready for pitiless contest and rivalry. The question of armaments, whether on land or sea, is the most immediately and intensely practical question connected with the future fortunes of nations and of mankind.

I have spoken upon these great matters without reserve and with the utmost explicitness because it has seemed to me to be necessary if the world's yearning desire for peace was anywhere to find free voice and utterance. Perhaps I am the only person in high authority amongst all the peoples of the world who is at liberty to speak and hold nothing back. I am speaking as an individual, and yet I am speaking also, of course, as the responsible head of a great government, and I feel confident that I have said what the people of the United States would wish me to say.

May I not add that I hope and believe that I am in effect speaking for liberals and friends of humanity in every nation and of every program of liberty? I would fain believe that I am speaking for the silent mass of mankind everywhere who have as yet had no place or opportunity to speak their real hearts out concerning the death and ruin they see to have come already upon the persons and the homes they hold most dear.

And in holding out the expectation that the people and government of the United States will join the other civilized nations of the world in guaranteeing the permanence of peace upon such terms as I have named, I speak with the greater boldness and confidence because it is clear to every man who can think that there is in this promise no breach in either our traditions or our policy as a nation, but a fulfillment, rather, of all that we have professed or striven for.

I am proposing, as it were, that the nations should with one accord adopt the doctrine of President Monroe as the doctrine of the world: That no nation should seek to extend its polity over any other nation or people, but that every people should be left free to determine its own polity, its own way of development, unhindered, unthreatened, unafraid, the little along with the great and powerful.

I am proposing that all nations henceforth avoid entangling alliances which would draw them into competitions of power; catch them in a net of intrigue and selfish rivalry, and disturb their own affairs with influences intruded from without. There is no entangling alliance in a concert of power. When all unite to act in the same sense and with the same purpose, all act in the common interest and are free to live their own lives under a common protection.

I am proposing government by the consent of the governed; that freedom of the seas which in international conference after conference representatives of the United States have urged with the eloquence of those who are the convinced disciples of liberty; and that moderation of armaments which makes of armies and navies a power for order merely, not an instrument of aggression or of selfish violence.

These are American principles, American policies. We could stand for no others. And they are also the principles and policies of forward-looking men and women everywhere, of every modern nation, of every enlightened community. They are the principles of mankind and must prevail.

A RELUCTANT PRESIDENT ASKS FOR WAR

1917

Late in March, 1917, Woodrow Wilson summoned Congress to meet on April 2 "to receive a communication by the Executive on grave questions of national policy which should be taken immediately under consideration."

The President had determined to ask Congress for a declaration of war against Germany. Yet to the very end, all the while he was preparing his war message and directing such advance measures as could be taken, he hoped that somehow the resort to arms might be avoided. On the night of April 1, a trusted friend, calling at the White House by request, found him seated at his typewriter, haggard for lack of sleep. Although it was after midnight, the President summarized the situation as he saw it. He had tried to avoid, by every means at his command, this last expedient; but at every turn Germany had blocked his measures by committing, as if deliberately, some new outrage.

Then he talked about what war would mean to the people of the United States. His visitor, Frank I. Cobb of the *New York World*, remembered his words:

"Once lead this people into war, and they'll forget there ever was such a thing as tolerance. To fight you must be brutal and ruthless, and the spirit of ruthless brutality will enter into the very fibre of our national life, infecting Congress, the courts, the policeman on the beat, the man on the street. . . . . If there is any alternative, for God's sake, let's take it!"

Cobb answered that he saw none.

On April 2, Congress convened at noon. Long before that hour a crowd gathered around the White House, and large numbers of people moved along the streets. Many carried little American flags. The President tried to quiet his nerves with a round of golf, and then had luncheon with his family. The hands of the clock dragged interminably—three, four, five—until finally word came that Congress had completed its organization and would receive the President at eight-thirty.

At eight-twenty Wilson left the White House, with a cavalry squadron supplementing the usual police escort. Rain gave fresh fragrance to the soft spring air, and added brilliance to the lighted dome of the Capitol. In the House of Representatives the justices of the Supreme Court sat before the Speaker's desk; members of the Cabinet were placed at one side, with the diplomatic corps behind them. A few minutes after the members of the House and Senate had taken their seats, the Speaker announced:

"The President of the United States."

What followed is best described in the words of Ray Stannard Baker, Wilson's biographer:

"The Supreme Court justices arose, followed by the entire gathering. The applause that followed was the greatest that Wilson had ever received in that historic room.

"The President walked directly to the rostrum and faced the audience. Men remarked his distinguished bearing, his gravity, the deep lines of purpose in his face.

"He shifted the small sheets of his address, waiting somewhat impatiently until the applause died away. An intense stillness fell upon the room.

"The President rested his arm on the high green-covered desk and began to read, at first in a voice that was husky with feeling. Occasionally he looked up: it was the only gesture he made. In recounting the stark elements of the crisis that confronted the nation, he avoided every oratorical emphasis, lest he arouse unwarranted emotion. The record itself was enough. . . ."

When Wilson finished there were seconds of silence, then a tumult of cheers and handclapping. He left the room quickly. Two days later the Senate passed a joint resolution declaring that "the state of war between the United States and the Imperial German Government which has been thrust upon the United States is hereby formally declared." The House took final action on April 6. That same day the President gave the resolution his approval.[1]

---

[1] These paragraphs follow closely Ray Stannard Baker, *Woodrow Wilson, Life and Letters* (New York: Doubleday & Company, 1927), VI, pp. 505–10. Quotations are by permission of the publisher.

Wilson's Message to Congress

April 2, 1917

I have called the Congress into extraordinary session because there are serious, very serious, choices of policy to be made, and made immediately, which it was neither right nor constitutionally permissible that I should assume the responsibility of making.

On the third of February last, I officially laid before you the extraordinary announcement of the Imperial German Government that on and after the first day of February it was its purpose to put aside all restraints of law or of humanity and use its submarines to sink every vessel that sought to approach either the ports of Great Britain and Ireland, or the western coasts of Europe, or any of the ports controlled by the enemies of Germany within the Mediterranean.

That had seemed to be the object of the German submarine warfare earlier in the war; but since April of last year the Imperial Government had somewhat restrained the commanders of its undersea craft in conformity with its promise then given to us that passenger boats should not be sunk and that due warning would be given to all other vessels which its submarines might seek to destroy, when no resistance was offered or escape attempted, and care taken that their crews were given at least a fair chance to save their lives in their open boats. The precautions taken were meager and haphazard enough, as was proved in distressing instance after instance in the progress of the cruel and unmanly business, but a certain degree of restraint was observed.

The new policy has swept every restriction aside. Vessels of every kind, whatever their flag, their character, their cargo, their destination, their errand, have been ruthlessly sent to the bottom without warning and without thought of help or mercy for those on board—the vessels of friendly neutrals along with those of belligerents. Even hospital ships and ships carrying relief to the sorely bereaved and stricken people of Belgium, though the latter were provided with safe conduct through the proscribed areas by the German Government itself and were distinguished by unmistakable marks of identity, have been sunk with the same reckless lack of compassion or of principle.

I was for a little while unable to believe that such things would in fact be done by any government that had hitherto subscribed to the humane practices of civilized nations. International law had its origin in the attempt to set up some law which would be respected and observed upon the seas, where no nation had right of dominion and where lay the free highways of the world. By painful stage after stage has that law been built up, with meager enough results, indeed, after all was accomplished that could be accomplished, but always with a clear view, at least, of what the heart and conscience of mankind demanded.

This minimum of right the German Government has swept aside under the plea of retaliation and necessity and because it had no weapons which it could use at sea except those which it is impossible to employ as it is employing them without throwing to the winds all scruples of humanity or of respect for the understandings that were supposed to underlie the intercourse of the world. I am not now thinking of the loss of property involved, immense and serious as that is, but only of the wanton and wholesale destruction of the lives of noncombatants, men, women, and children, engaged in pursuits which have always, even in the darkest periods of modern history, been deemed innocent and legitimate. Property can be paid for; the lives of peaceful and innocent people cannot be. The present German submarine warfare against commerce is a warfare against mankind.

It is a war against all nations. American ships have been sunk, American lives taken, in ways which it has stirred us very deeply to learn of, but the ships and people of other neutral and friendly nations have been sunk and overwhelmed in the waters in the same way. There has been no discrimination. The challenge is to all mankind. Each nation must decide for itself how it will meet it. The choice we make for ourselves must be made with a moderation of counsel and a temperateness of judgment befitting our character and our motives as a nation. We must put excited feeling away. Our motive will not be revenge or the victorious assertion of the physical might of the nation, but only the vindication of right, of human right, of which we are only a single champion.

When I addressed the Congress on the twenty-sixth of February last, I thought that it would suffice to assert our neutral rights with arms, our right to use the seas against unlawful interference, our right to keep our people safe against unlawful violence. But armed neutrality, it now appears, is impracticable. Because submarines are in effect outlaws when used as the German submarines have been used against merchant shipping, it is impossible to defend ships against their attacks as the law of nations has assumed that merchantmen would defend themselves against privateers or cruisers—visible craft giving chase upon the open sea. It is common prudence in such circumstances, grim necessity indeed, to endeavor to destroy them before they have shown their own intention. They must be dealt with upon sight, if dealt with at all.

The German Government denies the right of neutrals to use arms at all within the areas of the sea which it has proscribed, even in the defense of rights which no modern publicist has ever before questioned their right to defend. The intimation is conveyed that the armed guards which we have placed on our merchant ships will be treated as beyond the pale of law and subject to be dealt with as pirates would be. Armed neutrality is ineffectual enough at best; in such circumstances, and in the face of such pretensions, it is worse than ineffectual: it is likely only to produce what it was meant to prevent; it is practically certain to draw us into the war without either the rights or the effectiveness of belligerents. There is one choice we cannot make, we are incapable of making: we will not choose the path of submission and suffer the most sacred rights of our nation and our people to be ignored or violated. The wrongs against which we now array ourselves are no common wrong; they cut to the very roots of human life.

With a profound sense of the solemn and even tragical character of the step I am taking, and of the grave responsibilities which it involves, but in unhesitating obedience to what I deem my constitutional duty, I advise that the Congress declare the recent course of the Imperial German Government to be in fact nothing less than war against the government and people of the United States; that it formally accept the status of belligerent which has thus been thrust upon it; and that it take immediate steps not only to put the country in a more thorough state of defense, but also to exert all its power and employ all its resources to bring the government of the German Empire to terms and end the war.

What this will involve is clear. It will involve the utmost practicable co-operation in counsel and action with the governments now at war with Germany; and, as incident to that, the extension to those governments of the most liberal financial credits, in order that our resources may so far as possible be added to theirs. It will involve the organization and mobilization of all the material resources

of the country to supply the materials of war and serve the incidental needs of the nation in the most abundant and yet the most economical and efficient way possible.

It will involve the immediate full equipment of the navy in all respects, but particularly in supplying it with the best means of dealing with the enemy's submarines. It will involve the immediate addition to the armed forces of the United States, already provided for by law in case of war, at least five hundred thousand men, who should, in my opinion, be chosen upon the principle of universal liability to service, and also the authorization of subsequent additional increments of equal force so soon as they may be needed and can be handled in training. It will involve also, of course, the granting of adequate credits to the government, sustained, I hope, so far as they can equitably be sustained by the present generation, by well-conceived taxation. . . . .

While we do these things, these deeply momentous things, let us be very clear, and make very clear to all the world, what our motives and our objects are. My own thought has not been driven from its habitual and normal course by the unhappy events of the last two months, and I do not believe that the thought of the nation has been altered or clouded by them. I have exactly the same things in mind now that I had in mind when I addressed the Senate on the twenty-second of January last; the same that I had in mind when I addressed the Congress on the third of February and on the twenty-sixth of February. Our object now, as then, is to vindicate the principles of peace and justice in the life of the world as against selfish and autocratic power and to set up amongst the really free and self-governed peoples of the world such a concert of purpose and of action as will henceforth insure the observance of those principles.

Neutrality is no longer feasible or desirable where the peace of the world is involved and the freedom of its peoples; and the menace to that peace and freedom lies in the existence of autocratic governments backed by organized force which is controlled wholly by their will, not by the will of their people. We have seen the last of neutrality in such circumstances. We are at the beginning of an age in which it will be insisted that the same standards of conduct and of responsibility for wrong done shall be observed among nations and their governments that are observed among the individual citizens of civilized states.

We have no quarrel with the German people. We have no feeling toward them but one of sympathy and friendship. It was not upon their impulse that their government acted in entering this war. It was not with their previous knowledge or approval. It was a war determined upon as wars used to be determined upon in the old, unhappy days when peoples were nowhere consulted by their rulers, and wars were provoked and waged in the interest of dynasties or little groups of ambitious men who were accustomed to use their fellow-men as pawns and tools.

Self-governed nations do not fill their neighbor states with spies or set the course of intrigue to bring about some critical posture of affairs which will give them an opportunity to strike and make conquest. Such designs can be successfully worked out only under cover and where no one has the right to ask questions. Cunningly contrived plans of deception or aggression, carried, it may be, from generation to generation, can be worked out and kept from the light only within the privacy of courts or behind the carefully guarded confidences of a narrow and privileged class. They are happily impossible where public opinion commands and insists upon full information concerning all the nation's affairs.

A steadfast concert for peace can never be maintained except by a partnership of democratic nations. No autocratic government could be trusted to keep faith within it or observe its covenants. It must be a league of honor, a partnership of opinion. Intrigue would eat its vitals away; the plottings of inner circles who could plan what they would and render account to no one would be a corruption seated at its very heart. Only free peoples can hold their purpose and their honor steady to a common end and prefer the interests of mankind to any narrow interest of their own.

Does not every American feel that assurance has been added to our hope for the future peace of the world by the wonderful and heartening things that have been happening within the last few weeks in Russia? Russia was known by those who knew it best to have been always in fact democratic at heart, in all the vital habits of her thought, in all the intimate relationships of her people that spoke their natural instinct, their habitual attitude toward life. The autocracy that crowned the summit of her political structure, long as it had stood and terrible as was the reality of its power, was not in fact Russian in origin, character, or purpose; and now it has been shaken off, and the great, generous Russian people have been added in all their naïve majesty and might to the forces that are fighting for freedom in the world, for justice, and for peace. Here is a fit partner for a league of honor.

One of the things that has served to convince us that the Prussian autocracy was not and could never be our friend is that from the very outset of the present war it has filled our unsuspecting communities and even our offices of government with spies and set criminal intrigues everywhere afoot against our national unity of counsel, our peace within and without, our industries and our commerce. Indeed it is now evident that its spies were here even before the war began; and it is unhappily not a matter of conjecture but a fact proved in our courts of justice that the intrigues which have more than once come perilously near to disturbing the peace and dislocating the industries of the country have been carried on at the instigation, with the support, and even under the personal direction of official agents of the Imperial Government accredited to the government of the United States.

Even in checking these things and trying to extirpate them we have sought to put the most generous interpretation possible upon them because we know that their source lay, not in any hostile feeling or purpose of the German people toward us (who were, no doubt, as ignorant of them as we ourselves were), but only in the selfish designs of a government that did what it pleased and told its people nothing. But they have played their part in serving to convince us at last that that government entertains no real friendship for us and means to act against our peace and security at its convenience. That it means to stir up enemies against us at our very doors, the intercepted note to the German Minister at Mexico City is eloquent evidence.

We are accepting this challenge of hostile purpose because we know that in such a government, following such methods, we can never have a friend; and that in the presence of its organized power, always lying in wait to accomplish we know not what purpose, there can be no assured security for the democratic governments of the world. We are now about to accept gauge of battle with this natural foe to liberty, and shall, if necessary, spend the whole force of the nation to check and nullify its pretensions and its power.

We are glad, now that we see the facts with no veil of false pretense about them, to fight thus for the ultimate peace of the world and for the liberation of its peoples, the German peoples included: for the rights of nations great and small and the privilege of men everywhere to choose their way of life and of obedience. The world must be made safe for democracy. Its peace must be planted upon the tested foundations of political liberty. We have no selfish ends to serve. We desire no conquest, no dominion. We seek no indemnities for ourselves, no material compensation for the sacrifices we shall freely make. We are but one of the champions of the rights of mankind. We shall be satisfied when those rights have been made as secure as the faith and the freedom of nations can make them.

Just because we fight without rancor and without selfish object, seeking nothing for ourselves but what we shall wish to share with all free peoples, we shall, I feel confident, conduct our operations as belligerents without passion and ourselves observe with proud punctilio the principles of right and of fair play we profess to be fighting for.

I have said nothing of the governments allied with the Imperial Government of Germany because they have not made war upon us or challenged us to defend our right and our honor. The Austro-Hungarian Government has, indeed, avowed its unqualified endorsement and acceptance of the reckless and lawless submarine warfare adopted now without disguise by the Imperial German Government, and it has therefore not been possible for this government to receive Count Tarnowski, the ambassador recently accredited to this government by the Imperial and Royal Government of Austria-Hungary; but that government has not actually engaged in warfare against citizens of the United States on the seas, and I take the liberty, for the present at least, of postponing a discussion of our relations with the authorities at Vienna. We enter this war only where we are clearly forced into it because there are no other means of defending our rights.

It will be all the easier for us to conduct ourselves as belligerents in a high spirit of right and fairness because we act without animus, not in enmity toward a people or with the desire to bring any injury or disadvantage upon them, but only in armed opposition to an irresponsible government which has thrown aside all considerations of humanity and of right and is running amuck. We are, let me say again, the sincere friends of the German people, and shall desire nothing so much as the early re-establishment of intimate relations of mutual advantage between us—however hard it may be for them, for the time being, to believe that this is spoken from our hearts.

We have borne with their present government through all these bitter months because of that friendship—exercising a patience and forbearance which would otherwise have been impossible. We shall, happily, still have an opportunity to prove that friendship in our daily attitude and actions toward the millions of men and women of German birth and native sympathy who live amongst us and share our life, and we shall be proud to prove it toward all who are in fact loyal to their neighbors and to the government in the hour of test. They are, most of them, as true and loyal Americans as if they had never known any other fealty or allegiance. They will be prompt to stand with us in rebuking and restraining the few who may be of a different mind and purpose. If there should be disloyalty, it will be dealt with with a firm hand of stern repression; but, if it lifts its head at all, it will lift it only here and there and without countenance except from a lawless and malignant few.

It is a distressing and oppressive duty, Gentlemen of the Congress, which I have performed in thus addressing you. There are, it may be, many months of fiery trial and sacrifice ahead of us. It is a fearful thing to lead this great peaceful people into war, into the most terrible and disastrous of all wars, civilization itself seeming to be in the balance. But the right is more precious than peace, and we shall fight for the things which we have always carried nearest our hearts—for democracy, for the right of those who submit to authority to have a voice in their own governments, for the rights and liberties of small nations, for a universal dominion of right by such a concert of free peoples as shall bring peace and safety to all nations and make the world itself at last free. To such a task we can dedicate our lives and our fortunes, everything that we are and everything that we have, with the pride of those who know that the day has come when America is privileged to spend her blood and her might for the principles that gave her birth and happiness and the peace which she has treasured. God helping her, she can do no other.

MR. JUSTICE HOLMES DISSENTS

1919

When Wilson talked with Frank I. Cobb in the early morning hours of the day when he would ask Congress to declare war against Germany, the President had doubted whether the Constitution would survive the conflict. "Free speech and the right of assembly would go," he had said. "A nation couldn't put its strength into a war and keep its head level."

The Constitution turned out to be tougher than Wilson in his pessimistic mood had realized, but traditional rights were quickly called in question. The Espionage Act, passed in 1917, placed definite limits on the right of free speech. Under that act, one Schenck, general secretary of the Socialist party, and an associate were convicted and sentenced to imprisonment for publishing a pamphlet opposing the draft and circulating it among men who had been called for military service. The United States Supreme Court, in reviewing the case, gave Oliver Wendell Holmes the occasion for one of his most celebrated opinions.

"We admit," the Justice said, "that in many places and in ordinary times the defendants in saying all that was said in the circular would have been within their constitutional rights. But the character of every act depends upon the circumstances in which it is done. . . . . The most stringent protection of free speech would not protect a man in falsely shouting fire in a theatre and causing a panic. . . . . The question in every case is whether the words used are used in such circumstances and are of such a nature as to create a clear and present danger that they will bring about the substantive evils that Congress has a right to prevent. It is a question of proximity and degree. When a nation is at war many things that might be said in time of peace are such a hindrance to its effort that their utterance will not be endured so long as men fight and that no court could regard them as protected by any constitutional right."

Soon after the Schenck case the Supreme Court reviewed *Abrams et al.* v. *United States*, which also involved the right of free speech. In the summer of 1918 Abrams and four other Russian aliens had printed and distributed two leaflets denouncing the United States and urging workers to call a general strike. The five were indicted under the Espionage Act for printing and publishing "disloyal, scurrilous and abusive language about the form of government of the United States," for inciting "curtailment of production of things and products . . . . necessary and essential to the prosecution of the war," and for similar actions that the congressional act made unlawful. At the trial, the defendants were found guilty, and sentenced to twenty years' imprisonment.

The Supreme Court heard the arguments in the Abrams case in a setting redolent of history. In this room, formerly the Senate

Chamber, the voices of Calhoun, Webster, and Clay had resounded; here Roger Brooke Taney had presided over the court in his last years. Marble columns, dark mahogany, and rich red draperies suited the gravity of the nine justices as they listened attentively to the arguments of counsel.

The Court annouced its decision on November 10, 1919. Mr. Justice Clarke read the opinion of the majority: the judgment of the lower court was affirmed, and the conviction of Abrams and his four associates stood. Then Mr. Justice Holmes, a familiar figure because of his great shock of white hair and flowing mustache, leaned forward to read, for himself and Mr. Justice Brandeis, a dissent destined to become more famous than the opinion of the court—a dissent which, in the words of Francis Biddle, Holmes's biographer, "had added to our national heritage a concept of freedom to speak that Americans will cherish as long as they cherish that freedom."

Holmes's Dissent in the Case of the Russian Aliens

November 10, 1919

This indictment is founded wholly upon the publication of two leaflets which I shall describe in a moment. The first count charges a conspiracy, pending the war with Germany, to publish abusive language about the form of government of the United States, laying the preparation and publishing of the first leaflet as overt acts. The second count charges a conspiracy, pending the war, to publish language intended to bring the form of government into contempt, laying the preparation and publishing of the two leaflets as overt acts. The third count alleges a conspiracy to encourage resistance to the United States in the same war and to attempt to effectuate the purpose by publishing the same leaflets. The fourth count lays a conspiracy to incite curtailment of production of things necessary to the prosecution of the war and to attempt to accomplish it by publishing the second leaflet to which I have referred.

The first of these leaflets says that the President's cowardly silence about the intervention in Russia reveals the hypocrisy of the plutocratic gang in Washington. It intimates that "German militarism combined with allied capitalism to crush the Russian revolution," goes on that the tyrants of the world fight each other until they see a common enemy—working-class enlightenment, when they combine to crush it; and that now militarism and capitalism combined, though not openly, to crush the Russian revolution. It says that there is only one enemy of the workers of the world and that is capitalism; that it is a crime for workers of America, etc., to fight the workers' republic of Russia, and ends: "Awake! Awake, you Workers of the World! Revolutionists." A note adds: "It is absurd to call us pro-German. We hate and despise German militarism more than do you hypocritical tyrants. We have more reasons for denouncing German militarism than has the coward of the White House."

The other leaflet, headed "Workers—Wake Up," with abusive language says that America together with the Allies will march for Russia to help the Czechoslovaks in their struggle against the Bolsheviki, and that this time the hypocrites shall not fool the Russian emigrants and friends of Russia in America. It tells the Russian emigrants that they now must spit in the face of the false military propaganda by which their sympathy and help to the prosecution of the war have been called forth, and says that with the money they have lent or are going to lend "they will make bullets not only for the Germans but also for the Workers Soviets of Russia"; and further, "Workers in the ammunition factories, you are producing bullets, bayonets, cannon, to murder not only the Germans, but also your dearest, best, who are in Russia and are fighting for freedom."

It then appeals to the same Russian emigrants at some length not to consent to the "inquisitionary expedition to Russia," and says that the destruction of the Russian revolution is "the politics of the march to Russia." The leaflet winds up by saying: "Workers, our reply to this barbaric intervention has to be a general strike!"; and after a few words on the spirit of revolution, exhortations not to be afraid, and some usual tall talk, ends: "Woe unto those who will be in the way of progress. Let solidarity live! The Rebels."

No argument seems to me necessary to show that these pronunciamentos in no way attack the form of government of the United States, or that they do not support either of the first two counts. What little I have to say about the third count may be postponed until I have considered the fourth.

With regard to that, it seems too plain to be denied that the suggestion to workers in the ammunition factories that they are producing bullets to murder their dearest, and the further advocacy of a general strike, both in the second leaflet, do urge curtailment of production of things necessary to the prosecution of the war within the meaning of the Act of May 16, 1918, c. 75, 40 Stat. 553, amending ¶ 3 of the earlier Act of 1917. But to make the conduct criminal, that statute requires that it should be "with intent by such curtailment to cripple or hinder the United States in the prosecution of the war." It seems to me that no such intent is proved.

I am aware of course that the word "intent" as vaguely used in ordinary legal discussion means no more than knowledge at the time of the act that the consequences said to be intended will ensue. Even less than that will satisfy the general principle of civil and criminal liability. A man may have to pay damages, may be sent to prison, at common law might be hanged, if at the time of his act he knew facts from which common experience showed that the consequences would follow, whether he individually could foresee them or not. But, when words are used exactly, a deed is not done with intent to produce a consequence unless that consequence is the aim of the deed. It may be obvious, and obvious to the actor, that the consequence will follow, and he may be liable for it even if he regrets it, but he does not do the act with intent to produce it unless the aim to produce it is the proximate motive of the specific act, although there may be some deeper motive behind.

It seems to me that this statute must be taken to use its words in a strict and accurate sense. They would be absurd in any other. A patriot might think that we were wasting money on aeroplanes, or making more cannon of a certain kind than we needed, and might advocate curtailment with success; yet even if it turned out that the curtailment hindered and was thought by other minds to have been obviously likely to hinder the United States in the prosecution of the war, no one would hold such conduct a crime. I admit that my illustration does not answer all that might be said, but it is enough to show what I think and to let me pass to a more important aspect of the case. I refer to the First Amendment to the Constitution that Congress shall make no law abridging the freedom of speech.

I have never seen any reason to doubt that the questions of law that alone were before this court in the cases of *Schenck*, *Frohwerk*, and *Debs*, 249 U. S. 47, 204, 211, were rightly decided. I do not doubt for a moment that by the same reasoning that would justify punishing persuasion to murder, the United States constitutionally may punish speech that produces or is intended to produce a clear and imminent danger that it will bring about forthwith certain substantive evils that the United States constitutionally may seek to prevent. The power undoubtedly is greater in time of war than in time of peace because war opens dangers that do not exist at other times.

But as against dangers peculiar to war, as against others, the principle of the right to free speech is always the same. It is only the present danger of immediate evil or an intent to bring it about that warrants Congress in setting a limit to the expression of opinion where private rights are not concerned. Congress certainly cannot forbid all effort to change the mind of the country.

Now nobody can suppose that the surreptitious publishing of a silly leaflet by an unknown man, without more, would present any immediate danger that its opinions would hinder the success of the government arms, or have any appreciable tendency to do so. Publishing those opinions for the very purpose of obstructing, however, might indicate a greater danger and at any rate would have the quality of an attempt. So I assume that the second leaflet if published for the purposes alleged in the fourth count might be punishable. But it seems pretty clear to me that nothing less than that would bring these papers within the scope of this law.

An actual intent in the sense that I have explained is necessary to constitute an attempt, where a further act of the same individual is required to complete the substantive crime, for reasons given in *Swift & Co.* v. *United States*, 196 U. S. 375, 396. It is necessary where the success of the attempt depends upon others because if that intent is not present, the actor's aim may be accomplished without bringing about the evils sought to be checked. An intent to prevent interference with the revolution in Russia might have been satisfied without any hindrance to carrying on the war in which we were engaged.

I do not see how anyone can find the intent required by the statute in any of the defendants' words. The second leaflet is the only one that affords even a foundation for the charge, and there, without invoking the hatred of German militarism expressed in the former one, it is evident from the beginning to the end that the only object of the paper is to help Russia and stop American intervention there against the popular government—not to impede the United States in the war that it was carrying on. To say that two phrases taken literally might import a suggestion of conduct that would have interference with the war as an indirect and probably undesired effect seems to me by no means enough to show an attempt to produce that effect.

I return for a moment to the third count. That charges an intent to provoke resistance to the United States in its war with Germany. Taking the clause in the statute that deals with that in connection with the other elaborate provisions of the act, I think that resistance to the United States means some forcible act of opposition to some proceeding of the United States in pursuance of the war. I think the intent must be the specific intent that I have described; and for the reasons that I have given, I think that no such intent was proved or existed in fact. I also think that there is no hint at resistance to the United States as I construe the phrase.

In this case sentences of twenty years' imprisonment have been imposed for the publishing of two leaflets that I believe the defendants had as much right to publish as the government has to publish the Constitution of the United States now vainly invoked by them. Even if I am technically wrong and enough can be squeezed from these poor and puny anonymities to turn the color of legal litmus paper—I will add, even if what I think the necessary intent were shown—the most nominal punishment seems to me all that possibly could be inflicted, unless the defendants are to be made to suffer not for what the indictment alleges but for the creed that they avow—a creed that I believe to be the creed of ignorance and immaturity when honestly held, as I see no reason to doubt that it was held here, but which, although made the subject of examination at the trial, no one has a right even to consider in dealing with the charges before the court.

Persecution for the expression of opinions seems to me perfectly logical. If you have no doubt of your premises or your power and want a certain result with all your heart, you naturally express your wishes in law and sweep away all opposition. To allow opposition by speech seems to indicate that you think the speech impotent, as when a man says that he has squared the circle, or that you do not care wholeheartedly for the result, or that you doubt either your power or your premises. But when men have realized that time has upset many fighting faiths, they may come to believe even more than they believe the very foundations of their own conduct that the ultimate good desired is better reached by free trade in ideas—that the best test of truth is the power of the thought to get itself accepted in the competition of the market, and that truth is the only ground upon which their wishes safely can be carried out.

That at any rate is the theory of our Constitution. It is an experiment, as all life is an experiment. Every year if not every day we have to wager our salvation upon some prophecy based upon imperfect knowledge. While that experiment is part of our system I think that we should be eternally vigilant against attempts to check the expression of opinions that we loathe and believe to be fraught with death, unless they so imminently threaten immediate interference with the lawful and pressing purposes of the law that an immediate check is required to save the country.

I wholly disagree with the argument of the government that the First Amendment left the common law as to seditious libel in force. History seems to me against the notion. I had conceived that the United States through many years had shown its repentance for the Sedition Act of 1798, by repaying fines that it imposed. Only the emergency that makes it immediately dangerous to leave the correction of evil counsels to time warrants making any exception to the sweeping command, "Congress shall make no law . . . . abridging the freedom of speech." Of course I am speaking only of expressions of opinion and exhortations, which were all that were uttered here, but I regret that I cannot put into more expressive words my belief that in their conviction upon this indictment the defendants were deprived of their rights under the Constitution of the United States.

MR. JUSTICE BRANDEIS concurs with the foregoing opinion.

A COURT DEFENDS FREEDOM OF READING

1933

James Joyce had more than a young writer's normal difficulty in finding a publisher. *Dubliners,* his first volume of prose, was rejected twenty-two times, and when the book at last came out (in 1914) a reader, offended by the author's use of words not ordinarily committed to paper, bought and burned the entire edition. Only an obscure publisher in London was venturesome enough to put into print Joyce's second book, *Portrait of the Artist as a Young Man.* When the author, himself a Dubliner, went to Paris in the summer of 1920, weighted with the manuscript of *Ulysses,* he had little hope of success. The *Little Review,* in which the book had been appearing serially in the United States, had been suppressed, and there seemed to be small likelihood that anyone in any country would run the double risk of financial failure and trouble with the authorities. Nevertheless, Joyce found a proprietor of a Paris bookshop, Sylvia Beach, who refused to be intimidated. In due time *Ulysses,* set in English on a press at Dijon, was published. The author received the first printed copy on February 2, 1922, his fortieth birthday.

Copies of the book, shipped to England and the United States, were promptly confiscated by the customs authorities on the ground that it was obscene. For a decade the people of the two great English-speaking nations could read what was reputed to be a masterpiece only if they were fortunate enough to come across a smuggled copy. Finally an American publisher, Bennett Cerf, decided to test the legality of the ban against the importation of *Ulysses* into the United States. In the United States District Court for the Southern District of New York, Judge John M. Woolsey rendered an opinion that has become a landmark in the history of the struggle for free expression.

The Opinion of Judge Woolsey

December 6, 1933

Woolsey, J. I. . . . It seems to me that a procedure of this kind is highly appropriate in libels for the confiscation of books such as this. It is an especially advantageous procedure in the instant case because on account of the length of *Ulysses* and the difficulty of reading it, a jury trial would have been an extremely unsatisfactory, if not an almost impossible, method of dealing with it.

II. I have read *Ulysses* once in its entirety and I have read those passages of which the government particularly complains several times. In fact, for many weeks, my spare time has been devoted to the consideration of the decision which my duty would require me to make in this matter.

Ulysses is not an easy book to read or to understand. But there has been much written about it, and in order properly to approach the consideration of it, it is advisable to read a number of other books which have now become its satellites. The study of *Ulysses* is, therefore, a heavy task.

III. The reputation of *Ulysses* in the literary world, however, warranted my taking such time as was necessary to enable me to satisfy myself as to the intent with which the book was written, for, of course, in any case where a book is claimed to be obscene it must first be determined, whether the intent with which it was written was what is called, according to the usual phrase, pornographic—that is, written for the purpose of exploiting obscenity.

If the conclusion is that the book is pornographic that is the end of the inquiry and forfeiture must follow.

But in *Ulysses*, in spite of its unusual frankness, I do not detect anywhere the leer of the sensualist. I hold, therefore, that it is not pornographic.

IV. In writing *Ulysses*, Joyce sought to make a serious experiment in a new, if not wholly novel, literary genre. He takes persons of the lower middle class living in Dublin in 1904 and seeks not only to describe what they did on a certain day early in June of that year as they went about the city bent on their usual occupations, but also to tell what many of them thought about the while.

Joyce has attempted—it seems to me, with astonishing success—to show how the screen of consciousness with its ever shifting kaleidoscopic impressions carries, as it were on a plastic palimpsest, not only what is in the focus of each man's observation of the actual things about him, but also in a penumbral zone residua of past impressions, some recent and some drawn up by association from the domain of the subconscious. He shows how each of these impressions affects the life and behavior of the character which he is describing.

What he seeks to get is not unlike the result of a double or, if that is possible, a multiple exposure on a cinema film which would give a clear foreground with a background visible but somewhat blurred and out of focus in varying degrees.

To convey by words an effect which obviously lends itself more appropriately to a graphic technique, accounts, it seems to me, for much of the obscurity which meets a reader of *Ulysses*. And it also explains another aspect of the book, which I have further to consider, namely, Joyce's sincerity and his honest effort to show exactly how the minds of his characters operate.

If Joyce did not attempt to be honest in developing the technique which he has adopted in *Ulysses*, the result would be psychologically misleading and thus unfaithful to his chosen technique. Such an attitude would be artistically inexcusable.

It is because Joyce has been loyal to his technique and has not funked its necessary implications, but has honestly attempted to tell fully what his characters think about, that he has been the subject of so many attacks and that his purpose has been so often misunderstood and misrepresented. For his attempt sincerely and honestly to realize his objective has required him incidentally to use certain words which are generally considered dirty words, and has led at times to what many think is a too poignant preoccupation with sex in the thoughts of his characters.

The words which are criticized as dirty are old Saxon words known to almost all men and, I venture, to many women, and are such words as would be naturally and habitually used, I believe, by the types of folk whose life, physical and mental, Joyce is seeking to describe. In respect of the recurrent emergence of the theme of sex in the minds of his characters, it must always be remembered that his locale was Celtic and his season spring.

Whether or not one enjoys such a technique as Joyce uses is a matter of taste on which disagreement or argument is futile, but to

rather strong draught to ask some sensitive, though normal, persons to take. But my considered opinion, after long reflection, is that whilst in many places the effect of *Ulysses* on the reader undoubtedly is somewhat emetic, nowhere does it tend to be an aphrodisiac.

Ulysses may, therefore, be admitted into the United States.

ROOSEVELT CONDEMNS THE DICTATORS

1937

Chicagoans expected no more than the graceful dedication of a major public improvement. The city had just completed the bridge across the Chicago River that joined the two sections of the Outer Drive—the magnificent stretch of roadway that sweeps along the shore of Lake Michigan from the southern part of Chicago almost to its northernmost limits. Franklin D. Roosevelt, triumphantly re-elected in 1936, was at the height of his popularity, and the people of the city in which he had first been nominated turned out in force to welcome him. Thousands lined the streets and cheered lustily as he rode in an open car from the railroad station to the south end of the bridge for the dedication ceremonies.

But the President's mind was occupied with events that threatened the peace of the world rather than with a local improvement, no matter how important. The intervention of Germany and Italy in the Spanish Civil War, and the more recent attack of Japan on China, disturbed him deeply. The United States, disillusioned by the aftermath of World War I, had passed a series of Neutrality Acts designed to keep the nation out of future wars and was thoroughly committed to a policy of nonintervention. Roosevelt, however, had become convinced that aggressive dictatorship anywhere in the world threatened American security. He believed it to be his duty, moreover, to bring public opinion to face this fact.

In choosing Chicago as a setting, the President exhibited courage that approached foolhardiness. The city was the metropolis of the Middle West, and the Middle West was the stronghold of isolationism. Yet he devoted only two sentences to the bridge which he had come to dedicate, and then, his face set, his voice grave, turned to the subject closest to his heart. The thousands who had come to witness just another ceremony, though one lifted out of the ordinary by the presence of the President, listened in sober silence, broken only occasionally by applause, as they realized that they were hearing the announcement of a major and far-reaching change in the foreign policy of their country.

Speech at Chicago

October 5, 1937

I am glad to come once again to Chicago and especially to have the opportunity of taking part in the dedication of this important project of civic betterment.

On my trip across the continent and back I have been shown many evidences of the result of common-sense co-operation between municipalities and the federal government, and I have been greeted by tens of thousands of Americans who have told me in every book and word that their material and spiritual well-being has made great strides forward in the past few years.

And yet, as I have seen with my own eyes the prosperous farms, the thriving factories, and the busy railroads, as I have seen the happiness and security and peace which covers our wide land, almost inevitably I have been compelled to contrast our peace with very different scenes being enacted in other parts of the world.

It is because the people of the United States under modern conditions must, for the sake of their own future, give thought to the rest of the world, that I, as the responsible executive head of the nation, have chosen this great inland city and this gala occasion to speak to you on a subject of definite national importance.

The political situation in the world, which of late has been growing progressively worse, is such as to cause grave concern and anxiety to all the peoples and nations who wish to live in peace and amity with their neighbors.

Some fifteen years ago the hopes of mankind for a continuing era of international peace were raised to great heights when more than sixty nations solemnly pledged themselves not to resort to arms in furtherance of their national aims and policies. The high aspirations expressed in the Briand-Kellogg Peace Pact, and the hopes for peace thus raised, have of late given way to a haunting fear of calamity. The present reign of terror and international lawlessness began a few years ago.

It began through unjustified interference in the internal affairs of other nations or the invasion of alien territory in violation of treaties; and has now reached a stage where the very foundations of civilization are seriously threatened. The landmarks and traditions which have marked the progress of civilization toward a condition of law, order, and justice are being wiped away.

Without a declaration of war, and without warning or justification of any kind, civilians, including vast numbers of women and children, are being ruthlessly murdered with bombs from the air. In times of so-called peace, ships are being attacked and sunk by submarines without cause or notice. Nations are fomenting and taking sides in civil warfare in nations that have never done them any harm. Nations claiming freedom for themselves deny it to others.

Innocent peoples, innocent nations, are being cruelly sacrificed to a greed for power and supremacy which is devoid of all sense of justice and humane considerations.

To paraphrase a recent author, "perhaps we foresee a time when men, exultant in the technique of homicide, will rage so hotly over the world that every precious thing will be in danger, every book and picture and harmony, every treasure garnered through two millenniums, the small, the delicate, the defenseless–all will be lost or wrecked or utterly destroyed."

If those things come to pass in other parts of the world, let no one imagine that America will escape, that America may expect mercy, that this Western Hemisphere will not be attacked, and that it will continue tranquilly and peacefully to carry on the ethics and the arts of civilization.

If those days come, "there will be no safety by arms, no help from authority, no answer in science. The storm will rage till every flower of culture is trampled and all human beings are leveled in a vast chaos."

If those days are not to come to pass–if we are to have a world in which we can breathe freely and live in amity without fear–the peace-loving nations must make a concerted effort to uphold laws and principles on which alone peace can rest secure.

The peace-loving nations must make a concerted effort in opposition to those violations of treaties and those ignorings of humane instincts which today are creating a state of international anarchy and instability from which there is no escape through mere isolation or neutrality.

Those who cherish their freedom and recognize and respect the equal right of their neighbors to be free and live in peace must work together for the triumph of law and moral principles in order that peace, justice, and confidence may prevail in the world. There must be a return to a belief in the pledged word, in the value of a signed treaty. There must be recognition of the fact that national morality is as vital as private morality.

A bishop wrote me the other day: "It seems to me that something greatly needs to be said in behalf of ordinary humanity against the present practice of carrying the horrors of war to helpless civilians, especially women and children. It may be that such a protest might be regarded by many, who claim to be realists, as futile, but may it not be that the heart of mankind is so filled with horror at the present needless suffering that that force should be mobilized in sufficient volume to lessen such cruelty in the days ahead. Even though it may take twenty years, which God forbid, for civilization to make effective its corporate protest against this barbarism, surely strong voices may hasten the day."

There is a solidarity and interdependence about the modern world, both technically and morally, which makes it impossible for any nation completely to isolate itself from economic and political upheavals in the rest of the world, especially when such upheavals appear to be spreading and not declining. There can be no stability or peace either within nations or between nations except under laws and moral standards adhered to by all. International anarchy destroys every foundation for peace. It jeopardizes either the immediate or the future security of every nation, large or small. It is, therefore, a matter of vital interest and concern to the people of the United States that the sanctity of international treaties and the maintenance of international morality be restored.

The overwhelming majority of the peoples and nations of the world today want to live in peace. They seek the removal of barriers against trade. They want to exert themselves in industry, in agriculture, and in business that they may increase their wealth through the production of wealth-producing goods rather than striving to produce military planes and bombs and machine guns and cannon for the destruction of human lives and useful property.

In those nations of the world which seem to be piling armament on armament for purposes of aggression, and those other nations which fear acts of aggression against them and their security, a very high proportion of their national income is being spent directly for armaments. It runs from thirty to as high as fifty per cent. We are fortunate. The proportion that we in the United States spend is far less—eleven or twelve per cent.

How happy we are that the circumstances of the moment permit us to put our money into bridges and boulevards, dams and reforestation, the conservation of our soil, and many other kinds of useful works, rather than into huge standing armies and vast supplies of implements of war.

I am compelled and you are compelled, nevertheless, to look ahead. The peace, the freedom, and the security of ninety per cent of the population of the world is being jeopardized by the remaining ten per cent who are threatening a breakdown of all international order and law. Surely the ninety per cent who want to live in peace under law and in accordance with moral standards that have received almost universal acceptance through the centuries can and must find some way to make their will prevail.

The situation is definitely of universal concern. The questions involved relate not merely to violations of specific provisions of particular treaties; they are questions of war and of peace, of international law and especially of principles of humanity. It is true that they involve definite violations of agreements, and especially of the Covenant of the League of Nations, the Briand-Kellogg Pact, and the Nine Power Treaty. But they also involve problems of world economy, world security, and world humanity.

It is true that the moral consciousness of the world must recognize the importance of removing injustices and well-founded grievances; but at the same time it must be aroused to the cardinal necessity of honoring sanctity of treaties, of respecting the rights and liberties of others, and of putting an end to acts of international aggression.

It seems to be unfortunately true that the epidemic of world lawlessness is spreading.

When an epidemic of physical disease starts to spread, the community approves and joins in a quarantine of the patients in order to protect the health of the community against the spread of the disease.

It is my determination to pursue a policy of peace. It is my determination to adopt every practicable measure to avoid involvement in war. It ought to be inconceivable that in this modern era, and in the face of experience, any nation could be so foolish and ruthless as to run the risk of plunging the whole world into war by invading and violating, in contravention of solemn treaties, the territory of other nations that have done them no real harm and are too weak to protect themselves adequately. Yet the peace of the world and the welfare and security of every nation, including our own, is today being threatened by that very thing.

No nation which refuses to exercise forbearance and to respect the freedom and rights of others can long remain strong and retain the confidence and respect of other nations. No nation ever loses its dignity or its good standing by conciliating its differences, and by exercising great patience with, and consideration for, the rights of other nations.

War is a contagion, whether it be declared or undeclared. It can engulf states and peoples remote from the original scene of hostilities. We are determined to keep out of war, yet we cannot insure ourselves against the disastrous effects of war and the dangers of involvement. We are adopting such measures as will minimize our risk of involvement, but we cannot have complete protection in a world of disorder in which confidence and security have broken down.

If civilization is to survive, the principles of the Prince of Peace must be restored. Trust between nations must be revived.

Most important of all, the will for peace on the part of peace-loving nations must express itself to the end that nations that may be tempted to violate their agreements and the rights of others will desist from such a course. There must be positive endeavors to preserve peace.

America hates war. America hopes for peace. Therefore, America actively engages in the search for peace.

CHIEF JUSTICE HUGHES WIPES OUT A COLOR LINE

1938

Lloyd Gaines wanted to enter the law school of the University of Missouri. A resident of St. Louis, twenty-five years of age, and the holder of an A.B. degree from Lincoln University, he possessed all the requisite qualifications, yet his application for admission was rejected. Lloyd Gaines was a Negro, and under the constitution and law of Missouri, no Negro could attend the state university.

In Lincoln University, Gaines was informed, the state provided higher education for Negroes. Since Lincoln University had no law school, he could choose between the law schools of four adjacent states—Kansas, Nebraska, Iowa, and Illinois—and Missouri would pay his tuition. Gaines refused to exercise this privilege, contending that he had the same right as a white youth to attend his own state university. The trial court held against him, and the Supreme Court of Missouri affirmed the decision.

To justify the policy of discrimination, Missouri's highest court cited not only the law and the state constitution, but quoted its own opinion in an earlier case involving separate educational facilities for Negro and white children: "It will be said the classification now in question is one based on color, and so it is; but the color carries with it natural race peculiarities which furnish the reason for the classification. There are differences in races, and between individuals of the same race, not created by human laws, some of which can never be eradicated. These differences create different social relations rcognized by all well-organized governments."

The United States Supreme Court, in an opinion by Charles Evans Hughes, Chief Justice, held that Missouri had no right to deny Negroes the opportunities it offered to whites.

Opinion in the Case of the Negro Law Student, Lloyd Gaines

December 12, 1938

Hughes, C. E. . . . . The state court stresses the advantages that are afforded by the law schools of the adjacent states–Kansas, Nebraska, Iowa, and Illinois–which admit nonresident Negroes. The court considered that these were schools of high standing where one desiring to practice law in Missouri can get "as sound, comprehensive, valuable legal education" as in the University of Missouri; that the system of education in the former is the same as that in the latter and is designed to give the students a basis for the practice of law in any state where the Anglo-American system of law obtains; that the law school of the University of Missouri does not specialize in Missouri law and that the course of study and the casebooks used in the five schools are substantially identical.

Petitioner insists that for one intending to practice in Missouri, there are special advantages in attending a law school there, both in relation to the opportunities for the particular study of Missouri law and for the observation of the local courts, and also in view of the prestige of the Missouri law school among the citizens of the state, his prospective clients. Proceeding with its examination of relative advantages, the state court found that the difference in distances to be traveled afforded no substantial ground of complaint and that there was an adequate appropriation to meet the full tuition fees which petitioner would have to pay.

We think that these matters are beside the point. The basic consideration is not as to what sort of opportunities other states provide, or whether they are as good as those in Missouri, but as to what opportunities Missouri itself furnishes to white students and denies to Negroes solely upon the ground of color. The admissibility of laws separating the races in the enjoyment of privileges afforded by the state rests wholly upon the equality of the privileges which the laws give to the separated groups within the state. The question here is not of a duty of the state to supply legal training, or of the quality of the training which it does supply, but of its duty when it provides such training to furnish it to the residents of the state upon the basis of an equality of right.

By the operation of the laws of Missouri a privilege has been created for white law students which is denied to Negroes by reason of their race. The white resident is afforded legal education within the state; the Negro resident having the same qualifications is refused it there and must go outside the state to obtain it. That is a denial of the equality of legal right to the enjoyment of the privilege which the state has set up, and the provision for the payment of tuition fees in another state does not remove the discrimination.

The equal protection of the laws is "a pledge of the protection of equal laws." *Yick Wo* v. *Hopkins*, 118 U.S. 356, 369. Manifestly, the obligation of the state to give the protection of equal laws can be performed only where its laws operate, that is, within its own jurisdiction. It is there that the equality of legal right must be maintained. That obligation is imposed by the Constitution upon the states severally as governmental entities—each responsible for its own laws establishing the rights and duties of persons within its borders. It is an obligation the burden of which cannot be cast by one state upon another, and no state can be excused from performance by what another state may do or fail to do. That separate responsibility of each state within its own sphere is of the essence of statehood maintained under our dual system.

It seems to be implicit in respondents' argument that if other states did not provide courses for legal education, it would nevertheless be the constitutional duty of Missouri when it supplied such courses for white students to make equivalent provision for Negroes. But that plain duty would exist because it rested upon the state independently of the action of other states. We find it impossible to conclude that what otherwise would be an unconstitutional discrimination, with respect to the legal right to the enjoyment of opportunities within the state, can be justified by requiring resort to opportunities elsewhere. That resort may mitigate the inconvenience of the discrimination but cannot serve to validate it.

Nor can we regard the fact that there is but a limited demand in Missouri for the legal education of Negroes as excusing the discrimination in favor of whites. We had occasion to consider a cognate question in the case of *McCabe* v. *Atchison, T. & S. F. Ry. Co., supra*. There the argument was advanced, in relation to the provision by a carrier of sleeping cars, dining and chair cars, that the limited demand by Negroes justified the state in permitting the furnishing of such accommodations exclusively for white persons.

We found that argument to be without merit. It made, we said, the constitutional right "depend upon the number of persons who may be discriminated against, whereas the essence of the constitutional right is that it is a personal one. Whether or not particular facilities shall be provided may doubtless be conditioned upon there being a reasonable demand therefor, but, if facilities are provided, substantial equality of treatment of persons traveling under like conditions cannot be refused. It is the individual who is entitled to the equal protection of the laws, and if he is denied by a common carrier, acting in the matter under the authority of a state law, a facility or convenience in the course of his journey which under substantially the same circumstances is furnished to another traveler, he may properly complain that his constitutional privilege has been invaded." *Id.*, pp. 161, 162.

Here, petitioner's right was a personal one. It was as an individual that he was entitled to the equal protection of the laws, and the state was bound to furnish him within its borders facilities for legal education substantially equal to those which the state there afforded for persons of the white race, whether or not other Negroes sought the same opportunity.

It is urged, however, that the provision for tuition outside the state is a temporary one–that it is intended to operate merely pending the establishment of a law department for Negroes at Lincoln University. While in that sense the discrimination may be termed temporary, it may nevertheless continue for an indefinite period by reason of the discretion given to the curators of Lincoln University and the alternative of arranging for tuition in other states, as permitted by the state law as construed by the state court, so long as the curators find it unnecessary and impracticable to provide facilities for the legal instruction of Negroes within the state. In that view, we cannot regard the discrimination as excused by what is called its temporary character.

We do not find that the decision of the state court turns on any procedural question. The action was for mandamus, but it does not appear that the remedy would have been deemed inappropriate if the asserted federal right had been sustained. In that situation the remedy by mandamus was found to be a proper one in *University of Maryland* v. *Murray*, *supra.*

In the instant case, the state court did note that petitioner had not applied to the management of Lincoln University for legal training. But, as we have said, the state court did not rule that it would have been the duty of the curators to grant such an application, but on the contrary took the view, as we understand it, that the curators were entitled under the state law to refuse such an application and in its stead to provide for petitioner's tuition in an adjacent state.

That conclusion presented the federal question as to the constitutional adequacy of such a provision while equal opportunity for legal training within the state was not furnished, and this federal question the state court entertained and passed upon. We must conclude that in so doing the court denied the federal right which petitioner set up and the question as to the correctness of that decision is before us. We are of the opinion that the ruling was error, and that petitioner was entitled to be admitted to the law school of the state university in the absence of other and proper provision for his legal training within the state.

The judgment of the Supreme Court of Missouri is reversed and the cause is remanded for further proceedings not inconsistent with this opinion.

ROOSEVELT DEFINES FOUR FREEDOMS

1941

When Roosevelt, in his speech at Chicago in 1937, warned his countrymen of the threat posed by the dictator nations, the people, by and large, greeted his words with indifference. But under the pressure of grim events, public opinion began to change. Munich, Hitler's seizure of Czechoslovakia, Mussolini's rape of Albania, the German assault on Poland, and the outbreak of World War II convinced millions of Americans that their own security depended on the defeat of Germany and Italy. Millions more were converted by the fall of Denmark, Norway, Belgium, Holland, and France in the spring of 1940, and by the heroic withdrawal of the British from Dunkirk. The general public, in consequence, approved the President's transfer of fifty destroyers to hard-pressed Britain and the other measures that he took to sustain the Allied cause.

Early in 1941, with the prestige of an unprecedented third-term election to give weight to his words, Roosevelt decided that the time had come to marshal the moral weight of the United States in support of the opponents of totalitarianism. For the occasion he chose his message to the Seventy-seventh Congress on the State of the Union.

The scene was one which has been witnessed time after time in the history of the Republic, yet has never lost its impressiveness. In the chamber of the House of Representatives sat the members of both House and Senate, the Cabinet, the Supreme Court, and the diplomatic corps. Visitors, among them the Crown Princess Martha of Norway, filled the gallery. The assemblage included several men who had been present on the night when Woodrow Wilson had asked Congress to declare war on Germany. They knew that Roosevelt would not go that far on this occasion, but they could not escape the sobering reflection that history would almost certainly repeat itself in the months to come.

The President, heavily guarded, entered the chamber at 2:03 P.M. Leaning on the rostrum for support, he opened his black-leather notebook and began to read. As he progressed, his voice took on depth and strength and emotion. Now and then the audience applauded, but the handclapping was subdued, as befitted the gravity of the occasion.

When he finished, Roosevelt handed Vice-President Garner and Speaker Rayburn presentation copies of his address, shook their hands, and made his way slowly, on the arms of attendants, down the ramp and out of the chamber.

Message to Congress

January 6, 1941

I address you, the Members of the Seventy-seventh Congress, at a moment unprecedented in the history of the Union. I use the word "unprecedented" because at no previous time has American security been as seriously threatened from without as it is today.

Since the permanent formation of our government under the

Constitution, in 1789, most of the periods of crisis in our history have related to our domestic affairs. Fortunately, only one of these—the four-year War Between the States—ever threatened our national unity. Today, thank God, one hundred and thirty million Americans, in forty-eight states, have forgotten points of the compass in our national unity.

It is true that prior to 1914 the United States often had been disturbed by events in other continents. We had even engaged in two wars with European nations and in a number of undeclared wars in the West Indies, in the Mediterranean, and in the Pacific for the maintenance of American rights and for the principles of peaceful commerce. But in no case had a serious threat been raised against our national safety or our continued independence.

What I seek to convey is the historic truth that the United States as a nation has at all times maintained clear, definite opposition to any attempt to lock us in behind an ancient Chinese wall while the procession of civilization went past. Today, thinking of our children and of their children, we oppose enforced isolation for ourselves or for any other part of the Americas.

That determination of ours, extending over all these years, was proved, for example, during the quarter-century of wars following the French Revolution.

While the Napoleonic struggles did threaten interests of the United States because of the French foothold in the West Indies and in Louisiana, and while we engaged in the War of 1812 to vindicate our right to peaceful trade, it is nevertheless clear that neither France nor Great Britain, nor any other nation, was aiming at domination of the whole world.

In like fashion, from 1815 to 1914—ninety-nine years—no single war in Europe or in Asia constituted a real threat against our future or against the future of any other American nation.

Except in the Maximilian interlude in Mexico, no foreign power sought to establish itself in this hemisphere; and the strength of the British fleet in the Atlantic has been a friendly strength. It is still a friendly strength.

Even when the World War broke out in 1914, it seemed to contain only small threat of danger to our own American future. But, as time went on, the American people began to visualize what the downfall of democratic nations might mean to our own democracy.

We need not overemphasize imperfections in the Peace of Versailles. We need not harp on failure of the democracies to deal with problems of world reconstruction. We should remember that the Peace of 1919 was far less unjust than the kind of "pacification" which began even before Munich, and which is being carried on under the new order of tyranny that seeks to spread over every continent today. The American people have unalterably set their faces against that tyranny.

Every realist knows that the democratic way of life is at this moment being directly assailed in every part of the world—assailed either by arms, or by secret spreading of poisonous propaganda by those who seek to destroy unity and promote discord in nations that are still at peace.

During sixteen long months this assault has blotted out the whole pattern of democratic life in an appalling number of independent nations, great and small. The assailants are still on the march, threatening other nations, great and small.

Therefore, as your President, performing my constitutional duty to "give to the Congress information of the state of the Union," I find it, unhappily, necessary to report that the future and the safety of our country and of our democracy are overwhelmingly involved in events far beyond our borders.

Armed defense of democratic existence is now being gallantly waged in four continents. If that defense fails, all the population and all the resources of Europe, Asia, Africa, and Australasia will be dominated by the conquerors. Let us remember that the total of those populations and their resources in those four continents greatly exceeds the sum total of the population and the resources of the whole of the western hemisphere—many times over.

In times like these it is immature—and incidentally, untrue—for anybody to brag that an unprepared America, single-handed, and with one hand tied behind its back, can hold off the whole world.

No realistic American can expect from a dictator's peace international generosity, or return of true independence, or world disarmament, or freedom of expression, or freedom of religion—or even good business.

Such a peace would bring no security for us or for our neighbors.

"Those, who would give up essential liberty to purchase a little temporary safety, deserve neither liberty nor safety."

As a nation, we may take pride in the fact that we are soft-hearted; but we cannot afford to be softheaded.

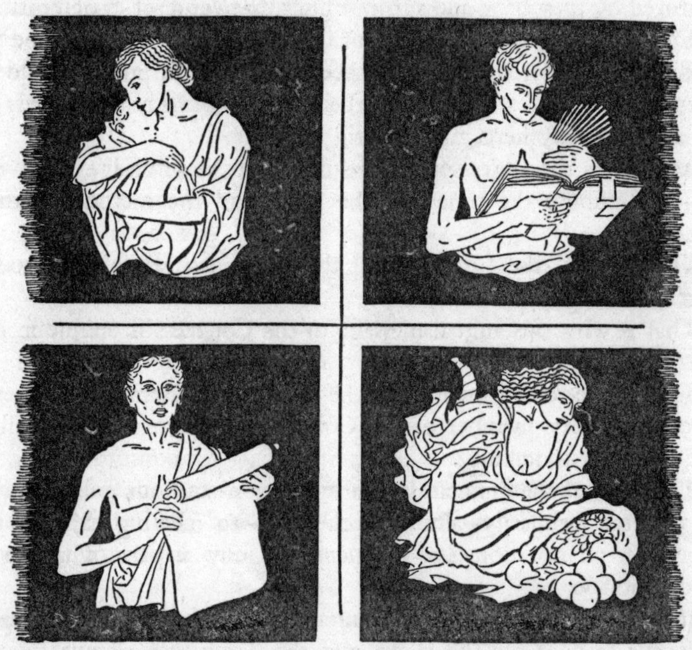

We must always be wary of those who with sounding brass and a tinkling cymbal preach the "ism" of appeasement.

We must especially beware of that small group of selfish men who would clip the wings of the American eagle in order to feather their own nests.

I have recently pointed out how quickly the tempo of modern warfare could bring into our very midst the physical attack which we must eventually expect if the dictator nations win this war.

There is much loose talk of our immunity from immediate and direct invasion from across the seas. Obviously, as long as the British Navy retains its power, no such danger exists. Even if there were no British Navy, it is not probable that any enemy would be stupid enough to attack us by landing troops in the United States from across thousands of miles of ocean until it had acquired strategic bases from which to operate.

But we learn much from the lessons of the past years in Europe –particularly the lesson of Norway, whose essential seaports were captured by treachery and surprise built up over a series of years.

The first phase of the invasion of this hemisphere would not be the landing of regular troops. The necessary strategic points would be occupied by secret agents and their dupes–and great numbers of them are already here, and in Latin America.

As long as the aggressor nations maintain the offensive, they–not we–will choose the time and the place and the method of their attack.

That is why the future of all the American republics is today in serious danger.

That is why this annual message to the Congress is unique in our history.

That is why every member of the executive branch of the government and every member of the Congress faces great responsibility and great accountability.

The need of the moment is that our actions and our policy should be devoted primarily–almost exclusively–to meeting this foreign peril. For all our domestic problems are now a part of the great emergency.

Just as our national policy in internal affairs has been based upon a decent respect for the rights and the dignity of all our fellowmen within our gates, so our national policy in foreign affairs has been based on a decent respect for the rights and dignity of all nations, large and small. And the justice of morality must and will win in the end.

Our national policy is this:

First, by an impressive expression of the public will and without regard to partisanship, we are committed to all-inclusive national defense.

Second, by an impressive expression of the public will and without regard to partisanship, we are committed to full support of all those resolute peoples, everywhere, who are resisting aggression and are thereby keeping war away from our hemisphere. By this support, we express our determination that the democratic cause shall prevail; and we strengthen the defense and the security of our own nation.

Third, by an impressive expression of the public will and without regard to partisanship, we are committed to the proposition that principles of morality and considerations for our own security will never permit us to acquiesce in a peace dictated by aggressors and sponsored by appeasers. We know that enduring peace cannot be bought at the cost of other people's freedom.

In the recent national election there was no substantial difference between the two great parties in respect to that national policy. No issue was fought out on this line before the American electorate. Today it is abundantly evident that American citizens everywhere are demanding and supporting speedy and complete action in recognition of obvious danger.

Therefore, the immediate need is a swift and driving increase in our armament production.

Leaders of industry and labor have responded to our summons. Goals of speed have been set. In some cases these goals are being reached ahead of time; in some cases we are on schedule; in other cases there are slight but not serious delays; and in some cases–and I am sorry to say very important cases–we are all concerned by the slowness of the accomplishment of our plans.

The army and navy, however, have made substantial progress during the past year. Actual experience is improving and speeding up our methods of production with every passing day. And today's best is not good enough for tomorrow.

I am not satisfied with the progress thus far made. The men in charge of the program represent the best in training, in ability, and in patriotism. They are not satisfied with the progress thus far made. None of us will be satisfied until the job is done.

No matter whether the original goal was set too high or too low, our objective is quicker and better results.

To give you two illustrations: We are behind schedule in turning out finished airplanes; we are working day and night to solve the innumerable problems and to catch up. We are ahead of schedule in building warships, but we are working to get even further ahead of that schedule.

To change a whole nation from a basis of peacetime production of implements of peace to a basis of wartime production of implements of war is no small task. And the greatest difficulty comes at the beginning of the program when new tools, new plant facilities, new assembly lines, and new shipways must first be constructed before the actual matériel begins to flow steadily and speedily from them.

The Congress, of course, must rightly keep itself informed at all times of the progress of the program. However, there is certain information, as the Congress itself will readily recognize, which, in the interests of our own security and those of the nations that we are supporting, must of needs be kept in confidence.

New circumstances are constantly begetting new needs for our safety. I shall ask this Congress for greatly increased new appropriations and authorizations to carry on what we have begun.

I also ask this Congress for authority and for funds sufficient to manufacture additional munitions and war supplies of many kinds, to be turned over to those nations which are now in actual war with aggressor nations.

Our most useful and immediate role is to act as an arsenal for them as well as for ourselves. They do not need manpower, but they do need billions of dollars worth of the weapons of defense.

The time is near when they will not be able to pay for them all in ready cash. We cannot, and we will not, tell them that they must surrender, merely because of inability to pay for the weapons which we know they must have.

I do not recommend that we make them a loan of dollars with which to pay for these weapons—a loan to be repaid in dollars.

I recommend that we make it possible for those nations to continue to obtain war materials in the United States, fitting their orders into our own program. Nearly all their matériel would, if the time ever came, be useful for our own defense.

Taking counsel of expert military and naval authorities, considering what is best for our own security, we are free to decide how much should be kept here and how much should be sent abroad to our friends who, by their determined and heroic resistance, are giving us time in which to make ready our own defense.

For what we send abroad, we shall be repaid within a reasonable time following the close of hostilities, in similar materials, or, at our option, in other goods of many kinds, which they can produce and which we need.

Let us say to the democracies: "We Americans are vitally concerned in your defense of freedom. We are putting forth our energies, our resources, and our organizing powers to give you the strength to regain and maintain a free world. We shall send you, in ever increasing numbers, ships, planes, tanks, guns. This is our purpose and our pledge."

In fulfillment of this purpose we will not be intimidated by the threats of dictators that they will regard as a breach of international law, or as an act of war, our aid to the democracies which dare to resist their aggression. Such aid is not an act of war, even if a dictator should unilaterally proclaim it so to be.

When the dictators, if the dictators, are ready to make war upon us, they will not wait for an act of war on our part. They did not wait for Norway or Belgium or the Netherlands to commit an act of war.

Their only interest is in a new one-way international law, which lacks mutuality in its observance, and, therefore, becomes an instrument of oppression.

The happiness of future generations of Americans may well depend upon how effective and how immediate we can make our aid felt. No one can tell the exact character of the emergency situations that we may be called upon to meet. The nation's hands must not be tied when the nation's life is in danger.

We must all prepare to make the sacrifices that the emergency—almost as serious as war itself—demands. Whatever stands in the way of speed and efficiency in defense preparations must give way to the national need.

A free nation has the right to expect full co-operation from all groups. A free nation has the right to look to the leaders of business, of labor, and of agriculture to take the lead in stimulating effort, not among other groups but within their own groups.

The best way of dealing with the few slackers or trouble-makers in our midst is, first, to shame them by patriotic example, and, if that fails, to use the sovereignty of government to save government.

As men do not live by bread alone, they do not fight by armaments alone. Those who man our defenses, and those behind them who build our defenses, must have the stamina and the courage which come from unshakable belief in the manner of life which they are defending. The mighty action that we are calling for cannot be based on a disregard of all things worth fighting for.

The nation takes great satisfaction and much strength from the things which have been done to make its people conscious of their individual stake in the preservation of democratic life in America. Those things have toughened the fiber of our people, have renewed their faith and strengthened their devotion to the institutions we make ready to protect.

Certainly this is no time for any of us to stop thinking about the social and economic problems which are the root cause of the social revolution which is today a supreme factor in the world.

For there is nothing mysterious about the foundations of a healthy and strong democracy. The basic things expected by our people of their political and economic systems are simple. They are:

Equality of opportunity for youth and for others.

Jobs for those who can work.

Security for those who need it.

The ending of special privilege for the few.

The preservation of civil liberties for all.

The enjoyment of the fruits of scientific progress in a wider and constantly rising standard of living.

These are the simple, basic things that must never be lost sight of in the turmoil and unbelievable complexity of our modern world. The inner and abiding strength of our economic and political systems is dependent upon the degree to which they fulfill these expectations.

Many subjects connected with our social economy call for immediate improvement.

As examples:

We should bring more citizens under the coverage of old-age pensions and unemployment insurance.

We should widen the opportunities for adequate medical care.

We should plan a better system by which persons deserving or needing gainful employment may obtain it.

I have called for personal sacrifice. I am assured of the willingness of almost all Americans to respond to that call.

A part of the sacrifice means the payment of more money in taxes. In my budget message I shall recommend that a greater portion of this great defense program be paid for from taxation than we are paying today. No person should try, or be allowed, to get rich out of this program; and the principle of tax payments in accordance with ability to pay should be constantly before our eyes to guide our legislation.

If the Congress maintains these principles, the voters, putting patriotism ahead of pocketbooks, will give you their applause.

In the future days, which we seek to make secure, we look forward to a world founded upon four essential human freedoms.

The first is freedom of speech and expression–everywhere in the world.

The second is freedom of every person to worship God in his own way–everywhere in the world.

The third is freedom from want–which, translated into world terms, means economic understandings which will secure to every nation a healthy peacetime life for its inhabitants–everywhere in the world.

The fourth is freedom from fear–which, translated into world terms, means a world-wide reduction of armaments to such a point and in such a thorough fashion that no nation will be in a position to commit an act of physical aggression against any neighbor–anywhere in the world.

That is no vision of a distant millennium. It is a definite basis for a kind of world attainable in our own time and generation. That kind of world is the very antithesis of the so-called new order of tyranny which the dictators seek to create with the crash of a bomb.

To that new order we oppose the greater conception–the moral order. A good society is able to face schemes of world domination and foreign revolutions alike without fear.

Since the beginnings of our American history, we have been engaged in change–in a perpetual peaceful revolution–a revolution which goes on steadily, quietly adjusting itself to changing conditions–without the concentration camp or the quicklime in the ditch. The world order which we seek is the co-operation of free countries, working together in a friendly, civilized society.

This nation has placed its destiny in the hands and heads and hearts of its millions of free men and women; and its faith in freedom under the guidance of God. Freedom means the supremacy of human rights everywhere. Our support goes to those who struggle to gain those rights or keep them. Our strength is our unity of purpose.

To that high concept there can be no end save victory.

ROOSEVELT AND CHURCHILL PLAN A SANER WORLD

1941

The sun was well up in the sky when the *Prince of Wales*, carrying Winston Churchill, made the rendezvous in Placentia Bay near the southeast tip of Newfoundland. The American cruiser *Augusta*, with Franklin D. Roosevelt aboard, already lay at anchor. After an exchange of naval courtesies, the British Prime Minister boarded the *Augusta*, where the President gave him the warmest of welcomes. The two men and their staffs then settled down to the succession of conferences that were to take up the next several days.

That was August 9, 1941. On the tenth, a Sunday, Roosevelt with his staff officers and several hundred sailors and marines went on board the *Prince of Wales* for divine service. Churchill has described the occasion eloquently. "This service was felt by us all to be a deeply moving expression of the unity of faith of our two peoples, and none who took part in it will forget the spectacle presented that sunlit morning on the crowded quarterdeck—the symbolism of the Union Jack and the Stars and Stripes draped side by side on the pulpit; the American and British chaplains sharing in the reading of the prayers; the highest naval, military, and air officers of Britain and the United States grouped in one body behind the President and me; the close-packed ranks of British and American sailors, completely intermingled, sharing the same books and joining fervently together in the prayers and hymns familiar to both. . . . . It was a great hour to live."

In the summer of 1941 the world situation seemed to call for a meeting between Roosevelt and Churchill. Great Britain had been at war for almost two years, and despite cruel losses, had proved her determination to fight through to victory. The United States, still formally neutral, was already heavily involved on the side of her future ally. She had sent Britain the fifty destroyers, she was supplying huge quantities of war matériel to the Allies, she was arming herself with all possible speed. Now new developments were causing concern and posing problems. In the West, Hitler's invasion of Russia was well launched; in the Far East Japan had recently moved into Indochina. It was a time for conference and closer co-operation.

During their first day at Placentia, Roosevelt told Churchill that he thought they should draw up a joint declaration of principles for the guidance of the two nations and for the information of the entire world. Churchill agreed, and on the following day produced a draft. Roosevelt added two paragraphs—the sixth and seventh of the final document—while the eighth was inserted at the instance of the British War Cabinet. After some verbal amendments, the text reached its final form on August 12. Two days later it was published to the world.

The Atlantic Charter

August 12, 1941

Joint Declaration by the President and the Prime Minister

The President of the United States of America and the Prime Minister, Mr. Churchill, representing His Majesty's Government in the United Kingdom, being met together, deem it right to make known certain common principles in the national policies of their respective countries on which they base their hopes for a better future for the world.

First, their countries seek no aggrandizement, territorial or other.

Second, they desire to see no territorial changes that do not accord with the freely expressed wishes of the peoples concerned.

Third, they respect the rights of all peoples to choose the form of government under which they will live; and they wish to see sovereign rights and self-government restored to those who have been forcibly deprived of them.

Fourth, they will endeavor, with due respect for their existing obligations, to further the enjoyment by all states, great or small, victor or vanquished, of access, on equal terms, to the trade and to the raw materials of the world which are needed for their economic prosperity.

Fifth, they desire to bring about the fullest collaboration between all nations in the economic field, with the object of securing for all improved labor standards, economic advancement, and social security.

Sixth, after the final destruction of the Nazi tyranny they hope to see established a peace which will afford to all nations the means of dwelling in safety within their own boundaries, and which will afford assurance that all the men in all the lands may live out their lives in freedom from fear and want.

Seventh, such a peace should enable all men to traverse the high seas and oceans without hindrance.

Eighth, they believe that all the nations of the world, for realistic as well as spiritual reasons, must come to the abandonment of the use of force. Since no future peace can be maintained if land, sea, or air armaments continue to be employed by nations which threaten, or may threaten, aggression outside of their frontiers, they believe, pending the establishment of a wider and permanent system of general security, that the disarmament of such nations is essential. They will likewise aid and encourage all other practicable measures which will lighten for peace-loving peoples the crushing burden of armaments.

FRANKLIN D. ROOSEVELT   WINSTON S. CHURCHILL

ROOSEVELT ACCEPTS THE CHALLENGE OF JAPAN

1941

Throughout most of the United States, Sunday, the seventh of December, 1941, was a dull, gray day. Millions of families spent the afternoon indoors, enjoying a leisurely holiday. Suddenly a flash broke into radio programs: Japanese planes, in overwhelming force, were attacking the American naval base at Pearl Harbor in the Hawaiian Islands.

Consternation at the success of the attack, which brought heavy casualties and disastrous damage to the Pacific fleet, was mingled with relief. Months of indecision had ended. There would be no more arguments over the role that the United States should play in the conflict then in progress. She was herself a participant, and now it would be a fight to the finish.

On Monday, December 8, President Roosevelt went to the Capitol to ask for a declaration of war against Japan. In the crowded hall of the House of Representatives, Speaker Rayburn and Vice-President Wallace stood beneath a huge American flag. As the President entered, applause broke out, then rocketed through the chamber until the Speaker brought it to an end with a smashing blow that broke his gavel.

Gripping the reading clerk's stand with one strong hand, Roosevelt opened his loose-leaf notebook, looked at the audience in silence, and then read the brief message he had prepared—a simple recounting of the events of the preceding day. "I ask," he concluded, "that the Congress declare that since the unprovoked and dastardly attack by Japan on Sunday, December seventh, a state of war has existed between the United States and the Japanese Empire."

As soon as the President left the House, members called for a vote. At 1:00 P.M., less than an hour after Roosevelt had started to read his message, the Senate passed a resolution declaring war. Thirty-two minutes later the House took action. In both Senate and House the vote was unanimous. The President's signature, affixed at 4:10, completed the formal declaration.

On the following evening Roosevelt turned to his favored medium of communication, the radio, to inform the people of the country of what had happened and impress upon them the significance of the struggle into which the nation had been plunged. His broadcast, rather than the brief war message of the preceding day, is the counterpart of Wilson's address asking for a declaration of war against Germany.

Broadcast to the Nation

December 9, 1941

My Fellow-Americans: The sudden criminal attacks perpetrated by the Japanese in the Pacific provide the climax of a decade of international immorality.

Powerful and resourceful gangsters have banded together to make war upon the whole human race. Their challenge has now been flung at the United States of America. The Japanese have treacherously violated the long-standing peace between us. Many American soldiers and sailors have been killed by enemy action. American ships have been sunk; American airplanes have been destroyed.

The Congress and the people of the United States have accepted that challenge.

Together with other free peoples, we are now fighting to maintain our right to live among our world neighbors in freedom and in common decency, without fear of assault.

I have prepared the full record of our past relations with Japan, and it will be submitted to the Congress. It begins with the visit of Commodore Perry to Japan eighty-eight years ago. It ends with the visit of two Japanese emissaries to the Secretary of State last Sunday, an hour after Japanese forces had loosed their bombs and machine guns against our flag, our forces, and our citizens.

I can say with utmost confidence that no Americans today or a thousand years hence need feel anything but pride in our patience and in our efforts through all the years toward achieving a peace in the Pacific which would be fair and honorable to every nation, large or small. And no honest person, today or a thousand years hence, will be able to suppress a sense of indignation and horror at the treachery committed by the military dictators of Japan under the very shadow of the flag of peace borne by their special envoys in our midst.

The course that Japan has followed for the past ten years in

Asia has paralleled the course of Hitler and Mussolini in Europe and in Africa. Today, it has become far more than a parallel. It is collaboration, actual collaboration, so well calculated that all the continents of the world, and all the oceans, are now considered by the Axis strategists as one gigantic battlefield.

In 1931, ten years ago, Japan invaded Manchukuo—without warning.

In 1935, Italy invaded Ethiopia—without warning.

In 1938, Hitler occupied Austria—without warning.

In 1939, Hitler invaded Czechoslovakia—without warning.

Later in 1939, Hitler invaded Poland—without warning.

In 1940, Hitler invaded Norway, Denmark, the Netherlands, Belgium, and Luxembourg—without warning.

In 1940, Italy attacked France and later Greece—without warning.

And in this year, 1941, the Axis Powers attacked Yugoslavia and Greece and they dominated the Balkans—without warning.

In 1941 also, Hitler invaded Russia—without warning.

And now Japan has attacked Malaya and Thailand—and the United States—without warning.

It is all of one pattern.

We are now in this war. We are all in it—all the way. Every single man, woman, and child is a partner in the most tremendous undertaking of our American history. We must share together the bad news and the good news, the defeats and the victories—the changing fortunes of war.

So far, the news has all been bad. We have suffered a serious setback in Hawaii. Our forces in the Philippines, which include the brave people of that commonwealth, are taking punishment, but are defending themselves vigorously. The reports from Guam and Wake and Midway islands are still confused, but we must be prepared for the announcement that all these three outposts have been seized.

The casualty lists of these first few days will undoubtedly be large. I deeply feel the anxiety of all the families of the men in our armed forces and the relatives of people in cities which have been bombed. I can only give them my solemn promise that they will get news just as quickly as possible.

This government will put its trust in the stamina of the American people and will give the facts to the public just as soon as two conditions have been fulfilled: first, that the information has been definitely and officially confirmed; and, second, that the release of the information at the time it is received will not prove valuable to the enemy directly or indirectly. . . .

Of necessity, there will be delays in officially confirming or denying reports of operations, but we will not hide facts from the country if we know the facts and if the enemy will not be aided by their disclosure.

To all newspapers and radio stations—all those who reach the eyes and ears of the American people—I say this: You have a most grave responsibility to the nation now and for the duration of this war.

If you feel that your government is not disclosing enough of the truth, you have every right to say so. But—in the absence of all the facts, as revealed by official sources—you have no right in the ethics of patriotism to deal out unconfirmed reports in such a way as to make people believe that they are gospel truth.

Every citizen, in every walk of life, shares this same responsibility. The lives of our soldiers and sailors—the whole future of this nation—depend upon the manner in which each and every one of us fulfills his obligation to our country.

Now a word about the recent past—and the future. A year and a half has elapsed since the fall of France, when the whole world first realized the mechanized might which the Axis nations had been building for so many years. America has used that year and a half to great advantage. Knowing that the attack might reach us in all too short a time, we immediately began greatly to increase our industrial strength and our capacity to meet the demands of modern warfare.

Precious months were gained by sending vast quantities of our war matériel to the nations of the world still able to resist Axis aggression. Our policy rested on the fundamental truth that the defense of any country resisting Hitler or Japan was in the long run the defense of our own country. That policy has been justified. It has given us time, invaluable time, to build our American assembly lines of production.

Assembly lines are now in operation. Others are being rushed to completion. A steady stream of tanks and planes, of guns, ships, and shells and equipment—that is what these eighteen months have given us.

But it is all only a beginning of what still has to be done. We must be set to face a long war against crafty and powerful bandits. The attack at Pearl Harbor can be repeated at any one of many points, points on both oceans and along both our coast lines and against all the rest of the hemisphere.

It will not only be a long war, it will be a hard war. That is the basis on which we now lay all our plans. That is the yardstick by which we measure what we shall need and demand: money, materials, doubled and quadrupled production—ever increasing. The production must be not only for our own army and navy and air forces. It must reinforce the other armies and navies and air forces fighting the Nazis and the war lords of Japan throughout the Americas and throughout the world. . . . .

Over the hard road of the past months we have at times met obstacles and difficulties, divisions and disputes, indifference and callousness. That is now all past—and, I am sure, forgotten.

The fact is that the country now has an organization in Washington built around men and women who are recognized experts in their own fields. I think the country knows that the people who are actually responsible in each and every one of these many fields are pulling together with a teamwork that has never before been excelled.

On the road ahead there lies hard work—gruelling work—day and night, every hour and every minute.

I was about to add that ahead there lies sacrifice for all of us. But it is not correct to use that word. The United States does not consider it a sacrifice to do all one can, to give one's best to our nation, when the nation is fighting for its existence and its future life.

It is not a sacrifice for any man, old or young, to be in the army or the navy of the United States. Rather is it a privilege.

It is not a sacrifice for the industrialist or the wage earner, the farmer or the shopkeeper, the trainman or the doctor, to pay more taxes, to buy more bonds, to forego extra profits, to work longer or harder at the task for which he is best fitted. Rather, it is a privilege.

It is not a sacrifice to do without many things to which we are accustomed if the national defense calls for doing without them. . . . .

And I am sure that the people in every part of the nation are prepared in their individual living to win this war. I am sure that they will cheerfully help to pay a large part of its financial cost while it goes on. I am sure they will cheerfully give up those material things that they are asked to give up.

And I am sure that they will retain all those great spiritual things without which we cannot win through.

I repeat that the United States can accept no result save victory, final and complete. Not only must the shame of Japanese treachery be wiped out, but the sources of international brutality, wherever they exist, must be absolutely and finally broken.

In my message to the Congress yesterday I said that we "will make very certain that this form of treachery shall never endanger us again." In order to achieve that certainty, we must begin the great task that is before us by abandoning once and for all the illusion that we can ever again isolate ourselves from the rest of humanity.

In these past few years–and, most violently, in the past few days–we have learned a terrible lesson.

It is our obligation to our dead–it is our sacred obligation to their children and to our children–that we must never forget what we have learned.

And what we have learned is this:

There is no such thing as security for any nation–or any individual–in a world ruled by the principles of gangsterism.

There is no such thing as impregnable defense against powerful aggressors who sneak up in the dark and strike without warning.

We have learned that our ocean-girt hemisphere is not immune from severe attack–that we cannot measure our safety in terms of miles on any map any more.

We may acknowledge that our enemies have performed a brilliant feat of deception, perfectly timed and executed with great skill. It was a thoroughly dishonorable deed, but we must face the fact that modern warfare as conducted in the Nazi manner is a dirty business. We don't like it–we didn't want to get in it–but we are in it and we're going to fight it with everything we've got. . . . .

The true goal we seek is far above and beyond the ugly field of battle. When we resort to force, as now we must, we are determined that this force shall be directed toward ultimate good as well as against immediate evil. We Americans are not destroyers—we are builders.

We are now in the midst of a war, not for conquest, not for vengeance, but for a world in which this nation, and all that this nation represents, will be safe for our children. We expect to eliminate the danger from Japan, but it would serve us ill if we accomplished that and found that the rest of the world was dominated by Hitler and Mussolini.

So, we are going to win the war and we are going to win the peace that follows.

And in the difficult hours of this day—and through dark days that may be yet to come—we will know that the vast majority of the members of the human race are on our side. Many of them are fighting with us. All of them are praying for us. For, in representing our cause, we represent theirs as well—our hope and their hope for liberty under God.

MARSHALL PROPOSES AID TO EUROPE

1947

No one had any reason to suppose that the commencement exercises of 1947 would differ in any notable feature from the three hundred and more similar occasions that had marked the end of each academic year at the nation's oldest university. In fact, no one knew until the fourth of June that George Catlett Marshall, Secretary of State, would be present at Harvard University to receive an honorary degree. Weeks earlier he had been tendered one, but had demurred. Suddenly, on the eve of commencement he had telephoned the president of the university to ask whether he might, after all, receive the honor that had been offered to him, and whether he might also have the privilege of making a short address at some time during the exercises.

So it was that on the morning of June 5, 1947, the Secretary of State, wearing a plain business suit instead of the traditional cap and gown, marched in the Harvard academic procession along with more than two thousand others upon whom degrees would be conferred. As he moved to the front of the platform before Memorial Church in the Harvard Yard, the proud parents and alumni who made up the audience welcomed him with applause, and applauded him again after President Conant conferred the degree of Doctor of Laws.

Except for Marshall's request that he be granted the privilege of making a brief address, that would have been all. But that afternoon Harvard alumni gathered in an open-air theater in the middle of the Yard, and there the Secretary of State, reading without flourish, outlined the unprecedented program of foreign aid that bears his name. His auditors heard only a few words before they realized that they were witnessing an historic occasion, and few of those who were present have forgotten the impressiveness of his manner as he added this extemporaneous sentence to his text: "I cannot overstate the importance to this country of facing up to the opportunity that confronts us."

Address at Harvard University

June 5, 1947

I need not tell you, gentlemen, that the world situation is very serious. That must be apparent to all intelligent people. I think one difficulty is that the problem is one of such enormous complexity that the very mass of facts presented to the public by press and radio make it exceedingly difficult for the man in the street to reach a clear appraisement of the situation. Furthermore, the people of this country are distant from the troubled areas of the earth, and it is hard for them to comprehend the plight and consequent reactions of the long-suffering peoples, and the effect of those reactions on their governments in connection with our efforts to promote peace in the world.

In considering the requirements for the rehabilitation of Europe, the physical loss of life, the visible destruction of cities, factories, mines, and railroads was correctly estimated; but it has become obvious during recent months that this visible destruction was probably less serious than the dislocation of the entire fabric of European economy. For the past ten years conditions have been highly abnormal.

The feverish preparation for war and the more feverish maintenance of the war effort engulfed all aspects of national economies. Machinery has fallen into disrepair or is entirely obsolete. Under the arbitrary and destructive Nazi rule, virtually every possible enterprise was geared into the German war machine. Long-standing commercial ties, private institutions, banks, insurance companies, and shipping companies disappeared through loss of capital, absorption through nationalization, or by simple destruction.

In many countries confidence in the local currency has been severely shaken. The breakdown of the business structure of Europe during the war was complete. Recovery has been seriously retarded by the fact that two years after the close of hostilities a peace settlement with Germany and Austria has not been agreed upon. But even given a more prompt solution of these difficult problems, the rehabilitation of the economic structure of Europe quite evidently will require a much longer time and greater effort than had been foreseen.

There is a phase of this matter which is both interesting and serious. The farmer has always produced the foodstuffs to exchange with the city dweller for the other necessities of life. This division of labor is the basis of modern civilization. At the present time it is threatened with breakdown. The town and city industries are not producing adequate goods to exchange with the food-producing farmer. Raw material and fuel are in short supply. Machinery is lacking or worn out.

The farmer or the peasant cannot find the goods for sale which he desires to purchase. So the sale of his farm produce for money which he cannot use seems to him an unprofitable transaction. He, therefore, has withdrawn many fields from crop cultivation and is using them for grazing. He feeds more grain to stock and finds for himself and his family an ample supply of food, however short he may be on clothing and the other ordinary gadgets of civilization. Meanwhile, people in the cities are short of food and fuel. So the governments are forced to use their foreign money and credits to procure these necessities abroad. This process exhausts funds which are urgently needed for reconstruction. Thus a very serious situation is rapidly developing which bodes no good for the world. The modern system of the division of labor upon which the exchange of products is based is in danger of breaking down.

The truth of the matter is that Europe's requirements for the next three or four years of foreign food and other essential products —principally from America—are so much greater than her present ability to pay that she must have substantial additional help, or face economic, social, and political deterioration of a very grave character.

The remedy lies in breaking the vicious circle and restoring the confidence of the European people in the economic future of their own countries, and of Europe as a whole. The manufacturer and the farmer throughout wide areas must be able and willing to exchange their products for currencies, the continuing value of which is not open to question.

Aside from the demoralizing effect on the world at large and the possibilities of disturbances arising as a result of the desperation of the people concerned, the consequences to the economy of the United States should be apparent to all. It is logical that the United States should do whatever it is able to do to assist in the return of normal economic health in the world, without which there can be no political stability and no assured peace.

Our policy is directed not against any country or doctrine but against hunger, poverty, desperation, and chaos. Its purpose should be the revival of a working economy in the world so as to permit the emergence of political and social conditions in which free institutions can exist. Such assistance, I am convinced, must not be on a piecemeal basis as various crises develop. Any assistance that this government may render in the future should provide a cure rather than a mere palliative.

Any government that is willing to assist in the task of recovery will find full co-operation, I am sure, on the part of the United States Government. Any government which maneuvers to block the recovery of other countries cannot expect help from us. Furthermore, governments, political parties, or groups which seek to perpetuate human misery in order to profit therefrom politically or otherwise will encounter the opposition of the United States.

It is already evident that, before the United States Government can proceed much further in its efforts to alleviate the situation and help start the European world on its way to recovery, there must be some agreement among the countries of Europe as to the requirements of the situation and the part those countries themselves will take in order to give proper effect to whatever action might be undertaken by this government. It would be neither fitting nor efficacious for this government to undertake to draw up unilaterally a program designed to place Europe on its feet economically. This is the business of the Europeans. The initiative, I think, must come from Europe. The role of this country should consist of friendly aid in the drafting of a European program, and of later support of such a program so far as it may be practical for us to do so. The program should be a joint one, agreed to by a number, if not all, European nations.

An essential part of any successful action on the part of the United States is an understanding on the part of the people of America of the character of the problem and the remedies to be applied. Political passion and prejudice should have no part. With foresight, and a willingness on the part of our people to face up to the vast responsibility which history has clearly placed upon our country, the difficulties I have outlined can and will be overcome.

EISENHOWER CHARTS A CHANGE OF COURSE

1953

Mild, sunny weather smiled on the host that turned out to attend the first inauguration of a Republican President in twenty years. At 12:32 P.M. Dwight D. Eisenhower stood before one hundred thousand of his fellow-countrymen, raised his right hand, and took the oath of office from Chief Justice Vinson. As he repeated the words, his left hand lay on two open Bibles—one his own, the other the one used at the first inauguration of George Washington.

The oath concluded, the President read a prayer.

"My friends, before I begin the expression of those thoughts that I deem appropriate to this moment, would you permit me the privilege of uttering a little private prayer of my own. And I ask that you bow your heads.

"Almighty God, as we stand here at this moment, my future associates in the executive branch of government join me in beseeching that Thou will make full and complete our dedication to the service of the people in this throng, and their fellow-citizens everywhere.

"Give us, we pray, the power to discern clearly right from wrong, and allow all our words and actions to be governed thereby, and by the laws of this land. Especially we pray that our concern shall be for all the people regardless of station, race, or calling.

"May co-operation be permitted and be the mutual aim of those who, under the concepts of our Constitution, hold to differing political faiths; so that all may work for the good of our beloved country and Thy glory. Amen."

The subdued murmur that ran through the crowd at the conclusion of the prayer ended suddenly as the President took up the sheets of his inaugural address and began to read.

Eisenhower's Inaugural Address

January 20, 1953

My Fellow-Citizens: The world and we have passed the midway point of a century of continuing challenge. We sense with all our faculties that forces of good and evil are massed and armed and opposed as rarely before in history.

This fact defines the meaning of this day. We are summoned by this honored and historic ceremony to witness more than the act of one citizen swearing his oath of service, in the presence of God. We are called as a people to give testimony in the sight of the world, to our faith that the future shall belong to the free.

Since this century's beginning, a time of tempest has seemed to come upon the continents of the earth. Masses of Asia have awakened to strike off shackles of the past. Great nations of Europe have fought their bloodiest wars. Thrones have toppled and their vast empires have disappeared. New nations have been born.

For our own country, it has been a time of recurring trial. We have grown in power and in responsibility. We have passed through the anxieties of depression and of war to a summit unmatched in man's history. Seeking to secure peace in the world, we have had to fight through the forests of the Argonne to the shores of Iwo Jima, and to the cold mountains of Korea.

In the swift rush of great events, we find ourselves groping to know the full sense and meaning of these times in which we live. In our quest of understanding, we beseech God's guidance. We summon all our knowledge of the past and we scan all signs of the future. We bring all our wit and all our will to meet the question:

How far have we come in man's long pilgrimage from darkness toward the light? Are we nearing the light—a day of freedom and of peace for all mankind? Or are the shadows of another night closing in upon us?

Great as are the preoccupations absorbing us at home, concerned as we are with matters that deeply affect our livelihood today and our vision of the future, each of these domestic problems is dwarfed by, and often even created by, this question that involves all humankind.

This trial comes at a moment when man's power to achieve good or to inflict evil surpasses the brightest hopes and the sharpest fears of all ages. We can turn rivers in their courses, level mountains to the plains. Oceans and land and sky are avenues for our colossal commerce. Disease diminishes and life lengthens.

Yet the promise of this life is imperiled by the very genius that has made it possible. Nations amass wealth. Labor sweats to create —and turns out devices to level not only mountains but also cities. Science seems ready to confer upon us, as its final gift, the power to erase human life from this planet.

At such a time in history, we who are free must proclaim anew our faith.

This faith is the abiding creed of our fathers. It is our faith in the deathless dignity of man, governed by eternal moral and natural laws.

This faith defines our full view of life. It establishes, beyond debate, those gifts of the Creator that are man's inalienable rights, and that make all men equal in His sight.

In the light of this equality, we know that the virtues most cherished by free people—love of truth, pride of work, devotion to country—all are treasures equally precious in the lives of the most humble and of the most exalted.

The men who mine coal and fire furnaces, and balance ledgers, and turn lathes, and pick cotton, and heal the sick, and plant corn—all serve as proudly and as profitably for America as the statesmen who draft treaties and the legislators who enact laws.

This faith rules our whole way of life. It decrees that we, the people, elect leaders not to rule but to serve. It asserts that we have the right to choice of our own work and to the reward of our own toil.

It inspires the initiative that makes our productivity the wonder of the world. And it warns that any man who seeks to deny equality among all his brothers betrays the spirit of the free and invites the mockery of the tyrant.

It is because we, all of us, hold to these principles that the political changes accomplished this day do not imply turbulence, upheaval, or disorder. Rather this change expresses a purpose of strengthening our dedication and devotion to the precepts of our founding documents, a conscious renewal of faith in our country and in the watchfulness of a divine providence.

The enemies of this faith know no god but force, no devotion but its use. They tutor men in treason. They feed upon the hunger of others. Whatever defies them, they torture, especially the truth.

Here, then, is joined no argument between slightly different philosophies. This conflict strikes directly at the faith of our fathers and the lives of our sons. No principle or treasure that we hold, from the spiritual knowledge of our free schools and churches to the creative magic of free labor and capital, nothing lies safely beyond the reach of this struggle. Freedom is pitted against slavery; lightness against the dark.

The faith we hold belongs not to us alone but to the free of all the world. This common bond binds the grower of rice in Burma and the planter of wheat in Iowa, the shepherd in southern Italy and the mountaineer in the Andes. It confers a common dignity upon the French soldier who dies in Indochina, the British soldier killed in Malaya, the American life given in Korea.

We know, beyond this, that we are linked to all free peoples not merely by a noble idea but by a simple need. No free people can for long cling to any privilege or enjoy any safety in economic solitude.

For all our own material might, even we need markets in the world for the surpluses of our farms and our factories. Equally, we need for these same farms and factories vital materials and products of distant lands. This basic law of interdependence, so manifest in the commerce of peace, applies with thousandfold intensity in the event of war.

So we are persuaded by necessity and by belief that the strength of all free peoples lies in unity, their danger in discord.

To produce this unity, to meet the challenge of our time, destiny has laid upon our country the responsibility of the free world's leadership.

So it is proper that we assure our friends once again that, in the discharge of this responsibility, we Americans know and we observe the difference between world leadership and imperialism; between firmness and truculence; between a thoughtfully calculated goal and spasmodic reaction to the stimulus of emergencies.

We wish our friends the world over to know this above all: we face the threat—not with dread and confusion—but with confidence and conviction.

We feel this moral strength because we know that we are not helpless prisoners of history. We are free men. We shall remain free, never to be proven guilty of the one capital offense against freedom, a lack of stanch faith.

In pleading our just cause before the bar of history and in pressing our labor for world peace, we shall be guided by certain fixed principles.

These principles are:

I. Abhorring war as a chosen way to balk the purposes of those who threaten us, we hold it to be the first task of statesmanship to develop the strength that will deter the forces of aggression and promote the conditions of peace. For, as it must be the supreme purpose of all free men, so it must be the dedication of their leaders, to save humanity from preying upon itself.

In the light of this principle, we stand ready to engage with any and all others in joint effort to remove the causes of mutual fear and distrust among nations, so as to make possible drastic reduction of armaments.

The sole requisites for undertaking such effort are that–in their purpose–they be aimed logically and honestly toward secure peace for all; and that–in their result–they provide methods by which every participating nation will prove good faith in carrying out its pledge.

II. Realizing that common sense and common decency alike dictate the futility of appeasement, we shall never try to placate an aggressor by the false and wicked bargain of trading honor for security. Americans, indeed, all free men, remember that in the final choice a soldier's pack is not so heavy a burden as a prisoner's chains.

III. Knowing that only a United States that is strong and immensely productive can help defend freedom in our world, we view our nation's strength and security as a trust, upon which rests the hope of free men everywhere. It is the firm duty of each of our free citizens and of every free citizen everywhere to place the cause of his country before the comfort, the convenience of himself.

IV. Honoring the identity and the special heritage of each nation in the world, we shall never use our strength to try to impress upon another people our own cherished political and economic institutions.

V. Assessing realistically the needs and capacities of proven friends of freedom, we shall strive to help them to achieve their own security and well-being. Likewise, we shall count upon them to assume, within the limits of their resources, their full and just burdens in the common defense of freedom.

VI. Recognizing economic health as an indispensable basis of military strength and the free world's peace, we shall strive to foster everywhere, and to practice ourselves, policies that encourage productivity and profitable trade. For the impoverishment of any single people in the world means danger to the well-being of all other peoples.

VII. Appreciating that economic need, military security, and political wisdom combine to suggest regional groupings of free peoples, we hope, within the framework of the United Nations, to help strengthen such special bonds the world over. The nature of these ties must vary with the different problems of different areas.

In the Western Hemisphere, we enthusiastically join with all our neighbors in the work of perfecting a community of fraternal trust and common purpose.

In Europe, we ask that enlightened and inspired leaders of the Western nations strive with renewed vigor to make the unity of their peoples a reality. Only as free Europe unitedly marshals its strength can it effectively safeguard, even with our help, its spiritual and cultural heritage.

VIII. Conceiving the defense of freedom, like freedom itself, to be one and indivisible, we hold all continents and peoples in equal regard and honor. We reject any insinuation that one race or another, one people or another, is in any sense inferior or expendable.

IX. Respecting the United Nations as the living sign of all peoples' hope for peace, we shall strive to make it not merely an eloquent symbol but an effective force. And in our quest for an honorable peace, we shall neither compromise, nor tire, nor ever cease.

By these rules of conduct, we hope to be known to all peoples. By their observance, an earth of peace may become not a vision but a fact.

This hope—this supreme aspiration—must rule the way we live.

We must be ready to dare all for our country. For history does not long entrust the care of freedom to the weak or the timid. We must acquire proficiency in defense and display stamina in purpose.

We must be willing, individually and as a nation, to accept whatever sacrifices may be required of us. A people that values its privileges above its principles soon loses both.

These basic precepts are not lofty abstractions, far removed from matters of daily living. They are laws of spiritual strength that generate and define our material strength.

Patriotism means equipped forces and a prepared citizenry. Moral stamina means more energy and more productivity, on the farm and in the factory. Love of liberty means the guarding of every resource that makes freedom possible—from the sanctity of our families and the wealth of our soil to the genius of our scientists.

And so each citizen plays an indispensable role. The productivity of our heads, our hands, and our hearts is the source of all the strength we can command, for both the enrichment of our lives and the winning of the peace.

No person, no home, no community can be beyond the reach of this call. We are summoned to act in wisdom and in conscience, to work with industry, to teach with persuasion, to preach with conviction, to weigh our every deed with care and with compassion. For this truth must be clear before us: whatever America hopes to bring to pass in the world must first come to pass in the heart of America.

The peace we seek, then, is nothing less than the practice and fulfillment of our whole faith among ourselves and in our dealings with others. This signifies more than the stilling of guns, easing the sorrow of war. More than escape from death, it is a way of life. More than a haven for the weary, it is a hope for the brave.

This is the hope that beckons us onward in this century of trial. This is the work that awaits us all, to be done with bravery, with charity, and with prayer to Almighty God.

My citizens—I thank you.

Appendix

For the reader interested in an exact transcript of the document, and in the complete text of those that have been shortened, the following sources are recommended.

The Mayflower Compact

BEN: PERLEY POORE, ed., *The Federal and State Constitutions, Colonial Charters, and Other Organic Laws of the United States* (Washington, 1877), Part I, p. 931.

The Fundamental Orders of Connecticut

BEN: PERLEY POORE, ed., *The Federal and State Constitutions, Colonial Charters, and Other Organic Laws of the United States* (Washington, 1877), Part I, pp. 249–51.

Roger Williams: Letter to the Townsmen of Providence

Publications of the Narragansett Club (Providence, 1874), VI, p. 278.

The Concessions and Agreements of West Jersey
AARON LEAMING and JACOB SPICER, eds., *The Grants, Concessions, and Original Constitutions of the Province of New Jersey* (Somerville, N. J., 1881), pp. 382–411.

The Zenger Case: Andrew Hamilton's Argument
LIVINGSTON RUTHERFORD, *John Peter Zenger, His Press, His Trial and a Bibliography of Zenger Imprints* (New York, 1904), pp. 74–125.

Otis' Speech against Writs of Assistance
CHARLES FRANCIS ADAMS, ed., *The Works of John Adams* (Boston, 1850), II, pp. 523–25.

Resolutions of the Stamp Act Congress
"Journal of the Stamp Act Congress," in *Niles Weekly Register*, II, pp. 337–42.

Declarations and Resolves of the First Continental Congress
WORTHINGTON C. FORD, ed., *Journals of the Continental Congress, 1774–1789* (Washington, 1904), I, pp. 63–73.

The Declaration of Independence
FRANCIS NEWTON THORPE, ed., *The Federal and State Constitutions, Colonial Charters, and Other Organic Laws of the States, Territories, and Colonies* (Washington, 1909), I, pp. 3–7.

The Articles of Confederation
FRANCIS NEWTON THORPE, ed., *The Federal and States Constitutions, Colonial Charters, and Other Organic Laws of the States, Territories, and Colonies* (Washington, 1909), I, pp. 9–17.

The Virginia Statute for Religious Freedom
WILLIAM W. HENING, ed., *The Statutes at Large; Being a Collection of All the Laws of Virginia* (Richmond, 1823), XII, pp. 84–86.

Lincoln's Second Inaugural Address
ROY P. BASLER, ed., *The Collected Works of Abraham Lincoln* (New Brunswick, N. J., 1953), VIII, pp. 332–33.

Lee's Farewell to the Army of Northern Virginia
ROBERT E. LEE, JR., *Letters and Recollections of Robert E. Lee* (New York, 1904), pp. 153–54.

Opinion in the Milligan Case
SAMUEL KLAUS, ed., *The Milligan Case* (New York, 1929), pp. 225–42.

Johnson's Annual Message to Congress, December 3, 1866
JAMES D. RICHARDSON, *A Compilation of the Messages and Papers of the Presidents, 1789–1897* (Washington, 1899), VI, pp. 445–59.

Altgeld's Protest to Cleveland
HARRY BARNARD, "*Eagle Forgotten*": *The Life of John Peter Altgeld* (Indianapolis and New York, 1938), pp. 304–06.

Instructions to the Philippine Commission
U. S. Senate Journal, 56th Congress, Second Session (Washington, 1901), pp. 11–12.

Wilson's First Inaugural Address
RAY STANNARD BAKER and WILLIAM E. DODD, eds., *The Public Papers of Woodrow Wilson* (New York and London, 1926), II, 1–6.

Wilson's Address to the Senate, January 22, 1917
RAY STANNARD BAKER and WILLIAM E. DODD, eds., *The Public Papers of Woodrow Wilson* (New York and London, 1926), IV, pp. 407–14.

Wilson's Message to Congress, April 2, 1917
RAY STANNARD BAKER and WILLIAM E. DODD, eds., *The Public Papers of Woodrow Wilson* (New York and London, 1926), V, pp. 6–16.

Holmes's Dissent in the Case of the Russian Aliens
250 United States Reports (1920), 624.

Woolsey's Opinion in the Case of the Book *Ulysses*
JAMES JOYCE, *Ulysses* (American Edition, New York, 1934), pp. ix–xiv.

Roosevelt's Speech at Chicago, October 5, 1937
SAMUEL I. ROSENMAN, ed., *The Public Papers and Addresses of Franklin D. Roosevelt* (New York, 1941), VI, pp. 406–11.

Opinion in the Case of the Negro Law Student, Lloyd Gaines
305 United States Reports (1939), 337.

Roosevelt's Message to Congress, January 6, 1941
SAMUEL I. ROSENMAN, ed., *The Public Papers and Addresses of Franklin D. Roosevelt* (New York, 1941), IX, pp. 663–72.

The Atlantic Charter
WINSTON S. CHURCHILL, *The Second World War*, Vol. III: *The Grand Alliance* (Boston, 1950), pp. 443–44.

Roosevelt's Broadcast to the Nation, December 9, 1941
New York Times, December 10, 1941.

Marshall's Address at Harvard University, June 5, 1947
New York Times, June 6, 1947.

Eisenhower's Inaugural Address
New York Times, January 21, 1953.

Most of the documents in this book can be found, although not always in complete and definitive form, in Henry Steele Commager, *Documents of American History*, and William MacDonald, *Documentary Source Book of American History*. Both books have gone through several editions.

Index